STRIKE

SARAH E. BOND

Strike

LABOR, UNIONS, AND RESISTANCE
IN THE ROMAN EMPIRE

Yale
UNIVERSITY PRESS
NEW HAVEN & LONDON

Copyright © 2025 by Sarah E. Bond. All rights reserved. This book may
not be reproduced, in whole or in part, including illustrations, in any
form (beyond that copying permitted by Sections 107 and 108 of the U.S.
Copyright Law and except by reviewers for the public press),
without written permission from the publishers.

Yale University Press books may be purchased in quantity for
educational, business, or promotional use. For information, please e-mail
sales.press@yale.edu (U.S. office) or sales@yaleup.co.uk (U.K. office).

Set in Scala type by Integrated Publishing Solutions.
Printed in the United States of America.

Library of Congress Control Number: 2024938874
ISBN 978-0-300-27314-4 (hardcover : alk. paper)

A catalogue record for this book is available from the British Library.

Authorized Representative in the EU: Easy Access System Europe,
Mustamäe tee 50, 10621 Tallinn, Estonia, gpsr.requests@easproject.com.

10 9 8 7 6 5 4 3 2

Dedicated to the two I have labored for the most,
Sascha and Wilkes

CONTENTS

Acknowledgments ix
Maps xii

Introduction: Striking from the Record 1

1 The Plebs, Secession, and Military Strikes 21

2 We Are Spartacus: Labor and Resistance in the Late Republic 44

3 Freedom of Assembly during the Fall of the Republic 72

4 Anxiety and Associations in the Early Roman Empire 88

5 Strikes, Riots, and Associations in the Roman Imperial Period 110

6 Castes, Law, and Compulsory Labor in Late Antiquity 132

7 Athletic Factions and Popular Rebellion 156

Conclusion: Uniting Ancient and Modern Laborers 181

Notes 189
Bibliography 219
Index 241

ACKNOWLEDGMENTS

IN 2021, I BEGAN TO REVISIT MY PREVIOUS writing on the rebellion of mint workers under Aurelian and Roman anti-corruption tactics in late antiquity. I had published a chapter on them for an edited volume in 2018 called *Anticorruption in History: From Antiquity to the Modern Era*, published with Oxford University Press and edited by Ronald Kroeze, André Vitória, and Guy Geltner. Guy Geltner gave me permission to modify the chapter for this book and provided helpful feedback. At the time, I had begun to think more deeply about the capabilities, experiences, and tactics of both formal and informal Roman associations, hoping to write a new type of Roman history that underscored how collectivity could provide identity, community, and empowerment. My husband, Tom, as well as Candida Moss eventually encouraged me to reach out to Jennifer Banks, the senior executive editor at Yale University Press. She connected me with Heather Gold, the editor who covered classics and ancient history at the press. As it turned out, she too was a new mother who had similarly had her first child during the pandemic. With support from Heather, Candida, Tom, and Nyasha Junior, I began waking up in the early morning to write. Suddenly, retelling familiar Roman histories with an eye toward associations, labor, and collective action felt achievable. Demonstrating that unification was a tactic to overcome adversity and marginalization felt like an important message.

Along the way, I reached back out to mentors I have long relied on for aid and support. Richard J. A. Talbert, my PhD advisor at the University of North Carolina at Chapel Hill, read through chapter drafts and cautioned me not to be too anachronistic in labeling ancient associations as labor unions. Elizabeth Meyer, my undergraduate advisor at the University of Virginia, also read chapters and provided her ever-insightful, meticulous feedback. I received important critiques, aid, and bibliography from Noel Lenski, Jinyu Liu, Andrew Riggsby, Brent Shaw, Tony Keddie, Steve Tuck, Jordan Rosenblum, Sinclair Bell, Brenda Longfellow, and Candida Moss as well. Halfway through writing the book, Alicia and Greg Aldrete came on board to help me try to strike a tone more accessible to the public and to edit the manuscript. I felt overwhelmed because, just as I had begun to gain headway into the research and then writing of the book, I found out I was pregnant again. Alicia dealt with dozens (if not hundreds) of emails to help me check footnotes, clarify my prose, and prepare the manuscript for submission. As with my first book, I could not have written this one without Alicia's and Greg's help.

With a few months left until the book was due, my editor, Heather, found out she was pregnant as well. Having an editor who not only believed in me and my writing, but who was going through the same physical and mental issues I was, inspired me to keep going through some rough trimesters. On the day I was induced, I was writing the conclusion to the manuscript. Heather understood and gave me space to turn in the draft when I could, in the weeks after we brought our second child home. The three reviewers she sent the manuscript out to provided helpful and important feedback on how to improve my argument and pointed out many errors I am grateful they caught. Michael Kulikowski and Mark Humphries provided unparalleled support, encouragement, and advice at this time, as did my academic brother, Lee Brice. Another academic brother, Gabriel Moss, created the maps for this book and provided sage advice about spatial elements of the manuscript. Our department administrator in the history department at the University of Iowa, Patricia Goodwin, was incredibly helpful in getting the illustrations and maps approved. My history department chair at Iowa, Colin Gordon, was supportive and inspirational, as was Gregory Hays.

Arum Park, Ellen Muehlberger, and Philipp Stelzel provided moral support on days I felt too nauseous or tired to write. Walter Scheidel read a draft of the book and provided important reactions and critiques, as did Zachary Herz. I was also continually inspired by the social justice journalism and activism of my current and former Hyperallergic colleagues, particularly Hrag Vartanian and Seph Rodney. My husband helped me to rewrite large swaths of my overly academic prose in hopes that this book could explain Roman history in new ways, both to a more general public and to undergraduates looking to understand Roman labor history "from below," through the lens of the association. Along the way, the memory of Garrett Fagan and his incomparable work to change Roman social histories sat in the back of my mind, as did the memory of my father, who died over a year before the pandemic began. He was a veteran, a southerner from West Virginia, and a voracious reader who always encouraged me to speak to and about regular people.

Books may only have one name on the cover, but in reality, they involve hundreds of hours of invisible, donated labor from friends, family, reviewers, and colleagues. I am indebted to each of them for their help and terrified I will let them down. All mistakes and errors are my own and are in no way a reflection on those who helped me along the way. This book is and was an experiment in how we might more effectively rewrite well-known narratives about the past in ways that might inform and enlighten those in the present. As a whole, it is meant to be a testament to the power and influence we can realize when we come together. It is also a warning about the ways in which this power may sometimes be viewed as a threat by those who hold the most social and economic might in a community. I am eternally grateful to everyone who helped me to balance becoming a parent with continuing to research the ancient world. This book is dedicated to our beloved Wilkes and Sascha, but it is also for everyone laboring for something or someone they believe in.

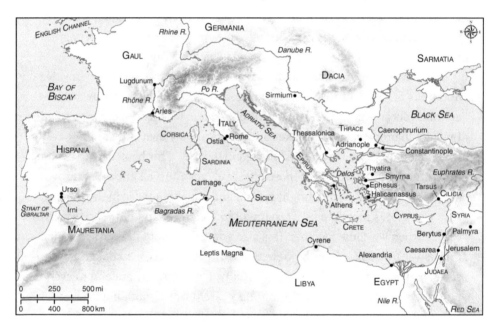

Fig. 1. Map of the pivotal locations mentioned in the Roman Mediterranean. (Map created by Gabriel Moss.)

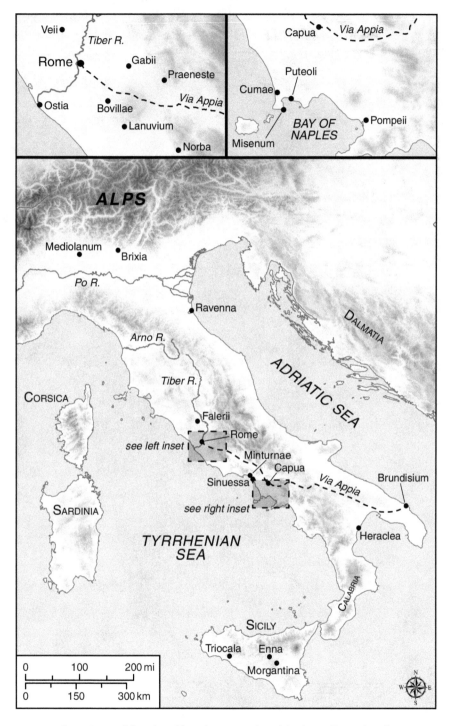

Fig. 2. Map of the pivotal locations mentioned in the Italic peninsula.
(Map created by Gabriel Moss.)

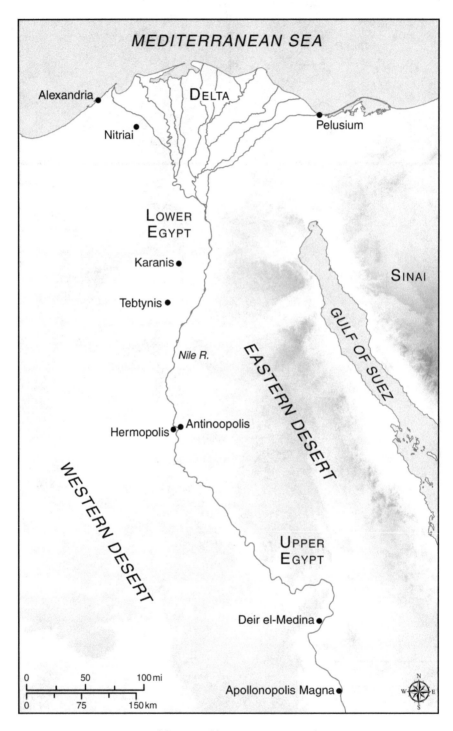

Fig. 3. Map of the pivotal locations mentioned in Egypt.
(Map created by Gabriel Moss.)

STRIKE

Introduction: Striking from the Record

IN APRIL OF 1768, FRUSTRATED BRITISH SAILORS working in the busy Port of Sunderland in northern Britain lowered, or "struck," the topsails of the merchant ships docked there. The sailors were in pursuit of higher wages and, by striking the sails, they prevented the vessels from leaving the port. With the trade hub brought to a standstill, shipowners faced the prospect of their dwindling economic might. Across many areas of the British labor force, workers were dissatisfied, restless, and looking for a way to acquire higher pay for their work.[1] The shipowners quickly consented to a pay raise for the sailors who, in turn, restored the sails. By May, another group of sailors, this time along London's Thames River, followed the lead of the Sunderland sailors. Petitioning Parliament and the lord mayor for their own pay raise, the sailors struck the sails of the ships along the bustling Thames. This second striking of the sails delivered the term "strike" into modern usage as a reference to labor-related protests. But while the usage was new, the action was not. Workers had been withholding their labor as a form of protest and as a collective negotiation method for thousands of years.

Over three thousand years earlier, in 1157 or 1155 BCE, necropolis workers and artisans in the Egyptian town of Deir el-Medina were growing tired of late wage payments and declining rations. Twenty-nine years of foreign military exploits by the pharaoh Ramses III had taken their toll on the home front. The tomb-builders and craftspeople laid down their tools, walked off the job, and gathered for a sit-in outside various temples. They withheld their skills during various successive labor strikes as they bargained for better working conditions, eventually extracting timely payments of emmer and other staples from the pharaoh. The actions of the Deir el-Medina workers can (and have been) variously described as a work stoppage, a turnout, a temporary secession, a withdrawal, a walkout, a *grève*, a strike, and many other terms in other contexts and languages. Regardless of the terminology, the history of collectives of workers strategically withholding their labor extends back to antiquity.

While we may not often hear the artisans of Deir el-Medina compared to the sailors of Sunderland, they—and the Roman workers focused on in this book—had plenty in common. Critical examinations of more recent labor strikes scarcely look past the Industrial Revolution for comparisons. And yet, in antiquity and today, the revoking of labor, goods, or services in protest has been a means of achieving a fiscal or environmental shift in working conditions.[2] These shared strategies and tactics lie at the heart of this book, as I examine how workers organized themselves, formally and informally, to navigate labor conflicts. In the process, we may trace more common threads of collective action among all workers, from ancient Egypt to Rome to eighteenth-century England to today.

The labor upheavals in Britain during the eighteenth century did more than just gift us the modern term "strike." Those sailors provided us with one of many data points in the broader history of workers. Their actions bring the social and economic impacts of labor organization into focus and allow us to parse how laborers wielded their power—particularly in the face of governmental authority. For these sailors were not alone in their complaints. At the same time that they were striking the sails of merchant ships, British journeyman groups made up of artisans and craftsmen began to mobilize across the country, often meeting in pubs, and organizing into "friendly societies" (a sort of union precursor) for monthly meetings.[3] Like many ancient associations, these societies charged dues, provided burial and sickness insurance, created camaraderie through leisure events, and consolidated political advocacy among their members. Despite the benefits these societies provided to workers, many business owners and the British government itself failed to see them as friendly.

Because these groups could disrupt both commerce and civic order, the British government increasingly tried to use legislation to cap the workers' growing power and limit the use of strikes for higher wages. Frequently, the government enacted anti-conspiracy laws to prosecute and ban such actions by certain trade groups.[4] Hatters, shoemakers, tailors, and weavers—among many others—could be tried as "conspirators" against their employers or prosecuted as members of illegal secret societies. New laws and legal precedents seemingly provided the government with the legal tools to curtail future economic disruptions. These laws, which redefined oaths, clandestine meetings, and collective action as conspiracies, became a crucial tactic for the government as it sought to combat the rise of trade unionism into the early nineteenth century. American courts, companies, and political constituencies were paying attention, and similar laws were soon in place across the Atlantic.[5] This was not the first time that labor collectives had been cast as conspirators. Across another ocean of time, Roman elites had recast private groups such as the worshippers of Bacchus and even provincial fire brigades as possible threats to the civic order to prevent social or economic disruptions.

The historically long practice of governments using legislation to limit people's ability to congregate is commonly known as anti-assembly legislation. For reasons realistic or invented, defensive or opportunistic, a government labels certain collectives as conspiratorial, seditious, or perhaps criminal. Once branded as a threat, these groups find themselves subject to new legislation designed to hem in or prevent their actions. As early as 186 BCE, elite Roman senators and magistrates in the middle Republic took issue with the religious cults dedicated to Bacchus, the Greek god of wine and vegetation. Labeling the worshipers a drunken threat to public order and a foreign threat to Roman religion, the elites used their rhetorical skills and legal powers to craft new laws largely banning the assembly of Bacchic worshippers without special permission.

But religious cults were not the only target for such Roman laws. In 64 BCE, during the political tumult of the late Republic and in the midst of a rising tide of populism, the Roman Senate again began to use similar language and present legal justifications to halt the meetings of ambiguously defined collectives called *collegia* (associations). Roman elites began to fear popular action and the political sway built through *collegia*, which dangerously empowered the citizenry. Laws prohibiting assemblies in the Roman Mediterranean sprung up ostensibly to stop these groups from threatening the so-called civic interests of the Republic. Such legislation against formal and informal collectives and their actions is evident from the late Roman

Republic well into the period we call late antiquity (200–800 CE). The people these laws targeted, and the elite politicians who tried to stymie their collective power, are the main characters of this book.

Ancient peoples created their own collectives for a range of religious, social, and occupational purposes. These groups included persons engaged in shared crafts and business pursuits. The Roman world was already filled with thousands of collectives across the Mediterranean and beyond. Formal membership in a collective was not required to participate in labor conflicts. There were, however, some benefits to joining formal groups. They could often organize and mobilize members more quickly. They also could rally associates to back the election of magistrates who would, in turn, support them economically and socially in their businesses. Graffiti at Pompeii show artisan collectives such as goldsmiths haranguing the people to vote for a man named Gaius Cuspius Pansa for a position as a market overseer called an aedile.[6] Just like today, having politicians in your corner who might support your workshop, or even look the other way in the forum, if need be, was important to trade collectives. Some of these groups had charters, dues, and swanky clubhouses, while others were less official and lacking the funds and written regulations of the more well-known associations. These ancient associations—whether a collective of enslaved and freed tent-makers in Rome or a group of purple-dye sellers gathering at Thessalonica in Roman Macedonia—often (but not always) shared a common trade, profession, or industry.[7]

Roman collectives mattered to the people who joined them. That much is clear in the historical record purely in terms of the frequency with which they are mentioned on epitaphs and in letters, monuments, statues, and graffiti. A more granular reading of each of these groups—the particulars of their membership, the structures of their governance, their services, meeting spaces, and social impact—is harder to pin down. Perhaps as little as 4 percent of the writings from the ancient world have survived through to our contemporary moment. When we begin the work of reconstructing ancient history, we must acknowledge that we are working with largely fragmented and biased sources from antiquity. And, as many modern scholars studying Roman associations have noted, most *collegia* and their ilk were ignored by contemporary aristocratic literati even in their own day. Writers such as Livy or Tacitus tended to provide upper-class audiences with elite accounts of Roman history. In turn, these sources were then relied upon to tell the story of Rome we know today. As a result, ancient historians hoping to recover the daily lives of regular Romans and their associations from the Iberian peninsula to Syria have had to use different types of written sources. Inscriptions, papyri, graffiti, archaeological remains, and non-narrative writings often help social historians to reconstruct the dynamic reality of these groups and their significance to many everyday Romans.

But how many of these groups were there? Digital projects have collected data for over 3200 Greek, Roman, and Hellenistic associations from 500 BCE to 300 CE; this is likely just a fraction of the ones that existed. Despite the often-fragmented evidence for the existence of these associations, to omit them from our analyses in the present would be, as archaeologist Francesca Diosono rightly argues, to leave out a fundamental element of the society, economy, and legacy of the Roman Mediterranean.[8] These small but essential social units were capable of providing financial and social support, local prestige, reputation, and networks of trust to thousands in a society that largely rejected the funding of state welfare programs and social safety nets. The silencing of their story by aristocratic writers leaves a devasting gap in our understanding of that society. These fragmentary sources help return the voice of collective action to a conversation about labor in the ancient world.

Recovering a History from Below for Ancient Collectives and Their Actions

All historical narratives leave things out. Historians—both today and in antiquity—make decisions about what to include and exclude in service to the story they are telling. And those choices often tell us a lot about the authors and their audiences. For many Roman authors writing in antiquity, associations, trade, the everyday lives of enslaved or freedpersons, and even small-scale civic disruptions such as strikes were not the sort of fodder they regularly deigned to record. The imperial historian and statesman Tacitus chose to gloss over details concerning Nero's building of a wooden amphitheater in 57 CE in Rome's Campus Martius. The historian defended this exclusion by noting that it suited the dignity of the Roman people to record only "illustrious matters" in the pages of his *Annals*—and to leave petty, quotidian matters, such as the amphitheater construction, to the city's daily register.[9] Tacitus's conviction was clear: to be worthy of being recorded in the annals of history, a thing or a person had to have a certain level of dignity.

Dignity and reputation were difficult things to come by in Roman antiquity. Social currency was not available to all, and Romans rarely granted such auspicious trappings to manual laborers and tradespeople.[10] Deprived of that elevated status, those workers were kept on the sidelines of the triumphal narrative created for Rome. On those rare occasions when ancient writers included mention of the less dignified classes, they often did so to demonstrate the character of an individual, rather than as a means of recording the lives of regular Romans. For instance, Tacitus's contemporary, the writer and biographer Suetonius, commented more extensively on the building of the same Neronian amphitheater in his biography of the emperor. In Suetonius's telling, Nero forced numerous senators and equestrians to fight as disreputable gladiators within the new arena. For Suetonius, the issues of financing the project, the organization of the construction workers, and the lives of the artisans who built the amphitheater were irrelevant. What did bear noting was the stigma Nero subjected the more elite Romans to by casting them as gladiators. In Roman law, such gladiators carried a stigma called *infamia* (infamy), which rendered them legally and socially marginalized. Suetonius uses this tale of the undignified to throw Nero's true nature into relief.[11] His mention of the amphitheater in Nero's biography was a way to demonstrate how the emperor degraded elites.

In an ancient Mediterranean world where history and biography were meant to be largely educational and to provide moral examples, daily life was all too often ignored unless it served a satirical, instructional, or moralistic purpose. This tendency of historians in antiquity to omit daily life makes it difficult to provide an account of the histories of ordinary people. What we today call a "history from below"—privileging those stories of regular folks over the lives of the elite—would have been an undignified, ignoble, and boring endeavor to Tacitus. But Tacitus is not writing this book. As many historians of the ancient world have done in the past century, we can revise our definitions of the discipline and, most importantly, of who deserves the dignity of inclusion. Today, we want to peer more closely into the daily lives of regular Romans. This book is an effort to recover the histories of ancient labor organization, mobilization, and resistance from below in the Roman Mediterranean from 509 BCE until 565 CE.

In this book, I tell the stories of Roman laborers, their associations, and their labor conflicts alongside the traditional, canonical story of Rome's emperors and political power players. In doing so, I am revising the all-too-familiar story of a village that became an empire and restoring to it some important context. In this telling, workers star alongside emperors. As we move through the book, we will track the volatile ways in which the state used its own tools of enforcement as a means of keeping certain collectives from assembling, growing, organizing, and challenging its own authority. These strategies will be familiar to many today: the use of police forces and soldiers to squelch popular movements, the operations of state surveillance, and the passing of anti-assembly legislation under the guise of patriotism. From the plebeians who withheld military service during the so-called Struggle of the Orders (c. 495–287 BCE) to the political advocacy of charioteer factions in late antiquity, we will see that where there was collective action from below, there would often be a civic or state reaction from above.

Historiography on Roman Strikes and the Roles of Associations

The work stoppage of the Egyptian necropolis workers in 1157 or 1155 BCE is today often viewed as the first instance of a rare event in antiquity: an ancient strike. If the withholding of labor in protest is mentioned, such actions are often cast as broadly uncharacteristic of ancient labor collectives—and particularly atypical of Roman workforces. The possible exception to this tendency was nineteenth-century Marxist analyses of the sociopolitical conflict between the plebeians and patricians of Rome during the Struggle of the Orders. At the beginning of *The Communist Manifesto* (issued in 1848), Friedrich Engels and Karl Marx cited this multi-century conflict between plebeians and patricians as a fundamental example of how all history was a history of class struggles.[12] Most historians today rightly recognize that the plebeians did not constitute a unified social class in the modern sense; however, Engels and Marx were correct that secession and the withholding of military service by many Roman plebeians were pivotal as leverage for their demands. In many ways, their tactics are analogous to the modern use of strikes to force negotiation.[13]

Most scholars have viewed strikes as seldom, if ever, occurring in antiquity and only genuinely taking off with the rise of modern capitalism. Influential early twentieth-century scholars of ancient economies such as Tenney Frank believed a lack of strikes was the result of Romans using enslaved labor and, later, the Roman dependence on compulsory, state-run occupational associations in the period known as late antiquity. Other scholars, such as famed historian and archaeologist Mikhail Ivanovich Rostovtzeff, noted the existence of strikes in antiquity but blamed a "low standard of industry" for their infrequency rather than Rome's use of enslaved laborers.[14] I argue, quite to the contrary, that enslaved laborers not only engaged in labor conflicts and small, everyday acts of rebellion, but at various points also took part in and drove strikes, well into the period of the late Roman Empire. Less commonly, but no less effectively, participants in state-run associations also used or threatened to use such tactics. If we look to the shipowners of Arles in the late second to early third century CE, or the mint workers under Aurelian in the late third century CE, we can see that these artisans, too, could resist Rome.

How, then, do we explain the relative dearth of evidence for regularized strikes in Roman antiquity? The bleak survival rates of texts and Roman literary biases may carry some blame. Part of the issue may also be the manner in which Roman crowds were described. Many ancient accounts of public violence over commercial matters cast groups broadly as a *turba* (crowd) or nameless multitude. Then as today, presenting mass movements in a city as an unruly and dangerous mob moralizes, but also revokes, the validity of popular causes. Whether deployed by Cicero in antiquity or by political pundits today, the rhetoric of uncontrolled "mob" violence helps marginalize a group and rob it of its ideologies, intents, and legitimacy. Cicero knew this when in 61 BCE he characterized the followers of the later triumvir Pompey who attended his political speeches as a miserable and starving mob.[15] And we might detect similar tactics at play in today's news media.

But the reach of such pejorative language can extend much further than singular instances of public, popular action. This speech can also obscure the underlying structures, hierarchies, and intents of social movements. In his assessment of the modern rhetoric surrounding crowds engaged in collective action, social psychologist John Drury argues, "The delegitimizing functions of such negative language and explanations are obvious. If the crowd is pathologized and criminalized, then its behaviour is not meaningful."[16] The largely scornful accounts of Roman crowds and their conduct only rarely mention the subunit of occupational associations, and only when it is to disparage the artisans who participated. These characterizations, in turn, may have fed the doubts of Frank and many other economic historians reading with the grain of Roman texts, and influenced their belief that collectives did not have the ability or economic interest to mobilize a strike or call for work stoppages in service to higher wages or better working conditions.

The earlier doubts about the economic aptitude or ability of ancient associations were later echoed by prominent Roman social historians, up through today.[17] Ancient writings' elisions and aversions concerning the economic capacity of associations have undoubtedly colored our contemporary approach to the subject matter. And while the absence of a cohesive narrative about organized labor in antiquity might be staring us in the face, historians have been understandably hesitant to fill that void. Historians harbor a deep-seated and reasonable nervousness about anachronism. We hesitate to cast the ancient world in contemporary terms for fear of appearing to puppeteer history. As a result, we might acknowledge the historical fact of labor riots or protests but fall short of ascribing the words "labor union" to their actors.

Yet metaphors and analogies can help us apprehend those actions and actors. Although most Roman associations did not function as modern labor unions that could advocate for wages, rights, or working conditions, some did; and that fact deserves to be more resolutely underscored and connected to the present. While the blanket label of "labor union" for all associations has rightly given most ancient historians pause, for fear of projecting the present onto the past, a growing contingent of scholars see the necessity of applying modern terms to the past, with nuance and care, if all criteria are met.[18] Underscoring some of the similarities between ancient and modern unions may also dispel lingering notions of the primitive nature of the Roman economy.

I will here admit to committing to a "strategic anachronism" by applying the term "labor union" to certain ancient Roman associations, particularly to the ancient artists of Dionysus and the athletic unions that appear most akin to labor unions today. This calculated analogy allows us to speak to the present and to capture both the continuities and functional differences of occupational groups who advocated for their members over the longue durée.[19] The merging of terminology can also encourage more engagement in comparative history. Orlando Patterson's cross-comparison of sixty-six different slaveholding societies further developed the global sociological concept of "social death" across time and space.[20] And while critics of Patterson and others engaged in comparative histories of servitude continue to reappraise and tweak his influential model, his comparative methods usefully put different historical time periods into conversation with each other.

Historical comparison often helps us understand the experience of alterity. Similarly, I argue in this book that coping mechanisms such as group formation might be best understood through this approach. Patterson's unprecedented efforts to understand the tactics of marginalization enacted by enslavers revealed that we cannot let excessive trepidation over the cardinal sin of historical anachronism keep us from engaging with the ancient world in all its complexity and connecting it with the present. Whether examining an association of Jews persecuted in Alexandria in the first century CE or the Brotherhood of Sleeping Car Porters in New York City in 1925, the united study of such groups can allow us to see the social and economic reasons that have caused marginalized humans to come together—and why those in power so often view these alliances as a threat. It is no accident that Black workers have the highest unionization rates in America today. Collectivization often increases equity and access to social and financial benefits in important ways. There are strong parallels to be (carefully) drawn between antiquity and the modern world in terms of this deeply human impulse to come together. These similarities can open necessary dialogues among labor historians from all times and places who seek to identify the historical and present advantages in the plural over the singular.

Defining the Ancient Association

In this book, I scrutinize the component parts of Roman labor and its organization into public and private associations over many successive centuries, examining the impact of hundreds of workers and the ways they came together between 509 BCE and 565 CE. Workers, professionals, and businesspeople belonged to numerous types of Mediterranean associations that went by many names: *collegia, sodalitates, hetaireiai, thiasoi, synodoi, corpora, koina,* and *synagogai,* among others. Other groups simply used collective nouns like "the bakers," from which we can infer various co-ops.[21] Not all of these collectives were alike. Each association was in many ways unique. But many of these known groups also shared commonalities in terms of function, membership, dues, services, and state regulation. Modern scholars classify many of these groups according to these variations in nomenclature and associative attributes, typically remarked on in existing inscriptions or papyri.[22] In this book, I take that typology a step further and label at least some of these groups as comparable to labor unions.

Named groups of laborers, artisans, merchants, and other commercial agents are often referred to in English as occupational guilds.[23] Although many scholars today associate guilds with monopolistic economic behaviors and price controls, the leading scholar on the medieval guild, Sheilagh Ogilvie, has shown that it was in fact a broad and extremely flexible concept: "A guild—in its most general form—is an association of people who share some common characteristic and pursue some common purpose."[24] In this study, I have chosen not to adopt the term "guild" for Roman artisan, merchant, or occupational associations, so as not to further complicate the terminology. As Ogilvie suggests, the guild was also an association with varying degrees of structure and formality. Like a Roman association, they were often a deeply meaningful part of daily life for many living in medieval Europe and cannot be spoken of as a homogenous type.

The choice to underscore the similarities between modern labor unions and Roman associations in this book is meant to be both provocative and unifying. The analogy challenges labor historians of the modern era to engage with Roman antiquity in more meaningful ways, rather than seeing labor organization, collective actions, economic networks, and unionizing behaviors such as wage bargaining or contract negotiations as solely progressive products of modern capitalism. The strategic anachronism is a challenge to the notion that labor unions were a modern or extraordinary product of the Industrial Revolution in Europe.[25] Historians of Europe and America focused on labor from the eighteenth to the twentieth centuries continue to portray the labor union as a modern invention created by workers from below in order to provide them with new methods for achieving economic empowerment. While medieval guilds are frequently identified as the progenitor of these modern labor unions, Roman associations get less credit for their economic capabilities, their advocacy for members, their political influence, or their ability to provoke strikes. This artificial origin story for the birth of the modern labor union supports a philosophy of exceptionalism that simply is not the full truth, and one that ancient Roman historians have, in the past three decades of important but less popularly recognized work, begun to erode.

The refusal to see ancient associations as akin to modern labor unions has a long history. The repudiation goes back to the European economists and social reformers of the late nineteenth century. In 1870, German economist Lujo Brentano argued instead for the connections between the modern labor union and the medieval guild; he represented the early modern associations of journeymen, which emerged as medieval guild protections were disintegrating, as the pivotal link between the two collectives.[26] For Brentano and many others, the preindustrial journeyman associations walked so that the labor unions could run. Interest in Roman *collegia* arose at about the same time, following classicist and epigrapher Theodor Mommsen's magisterial publication of Latin inscriptions in 1862, many of which revealed evidence for the myriad Roman associations not mentioned in the literary record. In the late nineteenth and early twentieth centuries, Belgian epigrapher Jean-Pierre Waltzing would argue in his extensive works that Roman associations were social in form and function.[27] Most scholars viewed ancient associations (as well as the Roman economy) through a simplistic, two-dimensional lens that cast social purposes such as feasting and burial as their raison d'être.

This view of Roman associations held sway into the mid-twentieth century. Ancient economist Moses Finley hated anachronisms and saw medieval guilds as more developed and economically capable than the earlier Roman *collegia*. He firmly stated, "Not only were there no Guildhalls in antiquity, there were no guilds, no matter how often the Roman *collegia* and their differently named Greek and Hellenistic counterparts are thus mistranslated."[28] Seconding Finley's disdain for perceived anachronism, Ramsay MacMullen would claim that *collegia* were social rather than economic entities—a view then blithely repeated by many scholars thereafter.[29] MacMullen's characterization of *collegia* as mere social clubs informed his assertion that he and other scholars could find "close to no" evidence of strikes in antiquity. For many, Roman associations were merely confraternities formed largely for feasting, burial insurance, community, and religious worship.

In the past two decades, analysis of the economic roles of Greco-Roman associations has greatly increased and made our understanding of their formation and impact much more dynamic.[30] A new generation of scholars studying these collectives and their dynamic characteristics has shown that a Roman association could serve both social and economic functions. Two things may, in fact, be true at once. Ancient associations could provide spaces for social interaction in pubs or clubhouses, opportunities for dining together at convivial meetings, and other means of fostering social relations. At the same time, they could also serve the economic and professional interests of their members, if need be, just as modern labor unions of teamsters, dockworkers, and welders do today. The false binary applied to the classification of the ancient versus the modern association—one for play or worship, the other for work—collapses as soon as one begins to read the charters of many Roman associations. These guiding documents frequently intermix concerns over credit and prices with stipulations about membership dues, monthly feasts, and burial policies. We ought not rob the people of antiquity of their complexity or their ability to create multidimensional associative bodies.

A desire for identity, purpose, and access to exclusive economic networks that provided stability and trust were the impetus for establishing many such groups for centuries within the ancient world, far outside of just Roman culture.[31] But there are also many differences between the past and the present to tease out. Unlike labor unions today, some associations in antiquity were imposed and overseen by the state as a means of control and a way to secure supply chains. These compulsory groups were usually called *corpora* and fell along a spectrum of intervention and regulation developed by the state in the late Roman Empire. Romans also had associations that formed organically, outside of state imposition. These were formed by workers, artisans, merchants, professionals like doctors and architects, and by wealthier businesspeople too.

To tell the story of these groups, their influence, and their actions in Roman history, we need to start with the mythical origins of these groups. This means the stories that Romans in the late Republic, seven hundred years after the alleged founding of Rome, told themselves about the nascence of occupational *collegia*, which many believed Rome's kings had formed many hundreds of years prior. These legends may not be historically accurate, but they are lore that reveal Roman attitudes and anxieties surrounding these groups. These stories also illustrate the Roman preference for a local tradition rooted in the ways of the ancestors over newfangled or foreign mores. Finally, reading about the later fabulations concerning the early years of Rome might give us one explanation for how later Romans understood when and why tradespeople were first placed into their own associations based on their professional skills.

Myths and Labor Organization in the Rome of the Early Kings

The city of Rome enjoys a number of legendary origin stories. Chief among these is that Romulus founded the city known in Latin as Roma along the banks of the Tiber River on April 21, 753 BCE.[32] Later tales of the seven early kings of Rome credit not Romulus, but rather the second king, Numa Pompilius (r. 716–674 BCE), with founding Rome's first occupational associations. These tales often suggest that it was Numa who organized the early Romans into groups based on their trade. The early imperial biographer Plutarch stated that Numa had distributed the populace into groups according to their artisan skills: "musicians, goldsmiths, carpenters, dyers, leather-workers, leather curriers, coppersmiths, and potters. The remaining arts, he gathered together into one corps out of all who belonged to this group. He also dictated associations and assemblies and rites of worship rendered to each association."[33]

Despite Plutarch's seeming confidence in the details of the regal period (c. 753–509 BCE), much remains murky about the timing and exact details of events involving these early kings—and how much is myth rather than historical fact. Romans later used the origin stories about this period to explain the ensuing labor taxonomies that structured and helped define the populace in the late Republic. And while the stories of the early kings are not always verifiable, and are often strategic memories of a valiant past, these fables do help us understand how later Romans in the Republic may have conceptualized Rome's beginnings and its social makeup. The stories surrounding Numa's creation of artisan associations also shed light on how elite Romans justified late Republican and early imperial legislation. Those laws used the perceived antiquity of a group going back to the age of Numa, as well as their public utility, as a litmus test for whether such workers were allowed to assemble in the period of the late first century BCE. In the conservative Roman mindset, there was often a respect for the ancient over the novel way of doing things.

In the past and still today, we tell ourselves stories—about the founding fathers of the United States, say, or about a multinational technology company that began in a humble garage in Palo Alto—in order to explain, romanticize, or parse a moment of crisis or innovation in which we are currently living. Romans living in the late Republic of the second and first centuries BCE turned to tales of Rome's early days to better understand the political tensions of their time. They also may have used them to help explain the demographic mix of peoples engaged in various professions, from farming to goldsmithing.[34] Successive generations of Romans remembered these origin stories, filtered unreliably through monuments and later written down in the histories of men like Lucius Calpurnius Piso in the late second century BCE, and then by Livy and Dionysius of Halicarnassus in the Augustan era (27 BCE–14 CE). Even ancient authors did not all agree upon the regal involvement in the creation of ancient *collegia* during the monarchy that controlled Rome from Romulus to Tarquinius Superbus (c. 753–509 BCE), Rome's last king.

The Numa myth took hold in Rome at a time of upheaval on almost every social and political front. This was also a period when, as Emilio Gabba has argued, the abolition of associations was frequently and hotly debated by politicians. In 49 BCE, Julius Caesar crossed the Rubicon with his troops and hastened the further crumbling of Republican conventions. Among many other sweeping changes and new laws thereafter, Caesar would move to draw up legislation in 47 or 46 BCE banning all but the most ancient or useful associations.[35] When he specified "ancient" in these laws, this presumably meant he allowed Numa's original associations or traditional Roman ones. Political leaders were wary of such groups. By around 46 BCE, there had been close to twenty years of upheavals, violence, and collective action by various associations, often in support of populist leaders. Most notorious among these would be the tavern keepers and their support for a man named Clodius, which will be discussed more in Chapter Three.

Associations were integral to the economic health of many ancient cities; however, there was an innate tension between the state and the private association. When Julius Caesar attempted to shore up loyalty for his new regime by dispelling divisive associations and passing a law disbanding all but the most ancient ones, he weaponized the myths of the early kings to justify which associations were ancient and thus legitimate. As we will see, his law was but one example in a long history of efforts to control clubs, associations, and collectives through legal means, manipulating history in the process.[36] Both local and imperial laws formed from the Augustan period onward would showcase imperial angst over associations. Fearing seditious intent, the state attempted to legislate them into submission. And as would be the case over seventeen hundred years later with Britain's sailors, the legal definitions of "sedition" and "conspiracy" lay with the government, rather than with private associations.

From the late Republic onward into the time of the early Principate (133 BCE–37 CE), the myth of the early kings' connection with the first Roman *collegia* only grew and became more self-serving to Roman emperors.[37] While the myth had variations to it, it always grounded only certain named associations as part of Rome's early history. Sometimes, it was not Numa who granted permission to establish these early trade groups. The historian Lucius Annaeus Florus, who lived and wrote during the reigns of Trajan and Hadrian in the second century CE, claimed that the establishment of associations for craftsmen should be attributed instead to the sixth king of Rome, Servius Tullius.[38] But whether it was Numa or Servius Tullius, what mattered was that there was a regal establishment of particular associations useful to the state. At best, it was a myth that allowed people to understand themselves and their background. At worst, the promotion of this myth may be seen as a political device that justified getting rid of all associations except those that were sufficiently old, Roman, and created by a monarch.

The archaeological record provides a more gradual story for the growth of Roman occupational associations than the legends in Rome's histories. Inscriptions and papyri indicate that in the middle to late Roman Republic, various associations took shape, based on trade, religious worship, drinking, and a host of other activities. These associations flourished in the city of Rome, in Italy, and throughout the provinces of Rome's empire, particularly in the East. Whatever the unifying factor for these social units, most associations had a religious aspect, such as a patron deity. But since each association had its own character and purpose, we cannot simply describe them in a uniform manner. We can, however, see how they often created communities for their members. In setting up their micro-prestige systems, associations often also copied the titles used for Roman state magistrates. Even if you could not be on the local civic council, you might, for instance, hold a position on the board of your local association of construction workers. Feasting was another significant activity for these groups. Associations sometimes held large dinners for their members. This banqueting element was as attractive to members as a private restaurant in a country club or a bar in an Elks Lodge might be today. Eating was an important part of community and identity in antiquity as today, and many more informal associations hung out in taverns and inns to discuss matters over hot food and fermented beverages.

For as much as they cared about the vivacious aspects of life, Romans also cared a great deal about the treatment of the dead. Burial insurance was another appealing reason to join an association. Many provided paying members assurances of a proper burial upon their deaths, often up to a certain distance. An inscription from Lanuvium, an Italian town just southeast of Rome, tells us about the founding of an association dedicated to the worship of the goddess Diana and Hadrian's lover, Antinous. It notes that the association would transport a person's body back for burial up to a maximum of twenty miles.[39] In these agreements, people could even stipulate the cleaning or placing of flowers on a tomb after their death. Roses and violets were popular. Because Rome had only minimal state services, akin to what we might think of as welfare programs, burial costs were the first thing taken from the deceased's legacy—that is, their personal wealth—upon death. Only extremely prestigious men or women received a state funeral paid for by the government. In a culture that greatly valued the observation of funerary rituals for the deceased, joining an association that people paid into guaranteed the proper treatment of their bodies after death and provided peace of mind.

By the middle of the first century BCE, the Mediterranean was teeming with these associations, formed for all kinds of businesses and pleasures. They were woven into the civic fabric and could establish broader networks of communication and exchange to aid in travel, as did the unions for athletes and entertainers.[40] All manner of private clubs, confraternities, involuntary associations, informal collectives, and formal unions had become commonplace in the ancient Mediterranean in both the West and the East. Associations were not an innovation limited to Rome and the western Mediterranean. They were characteristic of many societies in the Mediterranean, the Near East, India, China, and beyond in the ancient world. The Romans already knew that the Greeks used civic groups for political canvassing and what we might call lobbying. As one historian remarked about the myriad associations in Athens from the archaic period (c. 800–479 BCE) to the Hellenistic period (323–31 BCE), the complexity of the ancient Greek polis was due in part to an overlapping, living network of associations functioning within it.[41]

In Athens and far beyond it, ancient Greek associations influenced city formation, function, and identity. In the later fourth century BCE, Aristotle painted a rosy scenario for these groups in his *Nicomachean Ethics:* "But all associations are parts as it were of the association of the State."[42] The philosopher underscored a key aspect of occupational associations by noting their power to mitigate risk; he suggested that in the same the way travelers journeyed together to protect themselves and their possessions, sailors created associations to safeguard seafaring profits, and soldiers banded together in warfare. Historians of the ancient economy have more recently suggested that the trust networks created among many types of associations—for example, the Ptolemaic-era (305–30 BCE) religious associations in Hellenistic Egypt—could additionally function in an economically positive manner to reduce transaction costs and provide social capital to members.[43] Aristotle noted that associations often formed for religious reasons or for dining parties; still, social networks, ancient or modern, have a way of benefitting their members economically.[44] We might think here of alumni networks that hire young college graduates today as a way to grasp a social association that can and does influence economic choices made by employers. And where social and economic interests coincide, politics are not far behind.[45] For Aristotle, while private associations might have self-interests, they should ideally subordinate those aims to the civic good and political order maintained by the state. For their part, the associations did not always share this communal state-mindedness.

In Classical Athens (479–323 BCE), at about the same time that Rome was beginning its new Republic, membership in a political club was crucial for attaining political clout. Membership could confer authority on non-elites who needed to mobilize members for political support. One famous example of this concerns the fifth-century BCE Athenian naval general and statesman Themistocles. He came from a non-aristocratic background, and so joined an Athenian political club called a *hetaireia* to enhance his political standing. His more well-born political contemporary, Aristides, viewed membership in political clubs and reliance on one's fellow club members to gain power and exert influence in the polis as corrupt.[46] The use of such clubs was seen as a populist tactic. Greek literature of the time indicates that the civic landscape of Athens in the archaic period was already dotted with male-only political clubs, used especially to navigate the court system and attain certain state offices. The role and power of these private associations and their members, and the state's desire that the people adhere to its will, required a delicate balance. For the Greeks, as in Roman society, the two camps were not always in agreement.

Ancient laws provide us with one way to examine reactions to the formation of associations as well as state anxieties surrounding their unregulated growth. At the same time, we must keep in mind that—both in the past and in the present—there is a wide gap between proscriptive legislation and social reality. Just because a law bans a particular type of association does not mean that these groups did not exist or that the state had enough manpower to enforce such sweeping legislation. Just because a law prohibits jaywalking, this does not mean everyone is only using the crosswalks. But legislation from antiquity can tell us what lawmakers, Roman emperors, provincial governors, town councils, or any other entity that passed legislation aimed at governing voluntary associations hoped to accomplish.

Including Antiquity in Histories of Labor and Collective Action

Our contemporary moment has seen continued debate about many of the issues ancient Romans addressed. The issues of work, trade, and collective action have been part of an international dialogue in the years since the COVID-19 pandemic began. In the American Midwest, meatpacking plants forced migrant workers to work even when sick, and those classified as "essential workers" continued to provide groceries, medical care, and services we had long taken for granted. The pandemic also taught the world a great deal about the global supply chain, chiefly revealing its fragility. The need to secure supply chains by mitigating risk and creating resilience within the system is an ancient idea examined in the pages ahead.[47] In more recent history, dozens of unions were formed in the wake of the labor shake-up that followed the pandemic.

Perhaps the most remarked upon unionization efforts have been the Amazon workers who started a labor union at a warehouse in Staten Island, the wave of museum workers moving to unionize in arts institutions across the United States, and the Ukrainian mining unions working to support the Ukrainian economy in the midst of a Russian invasion. We are now experiencing a new, global labor movement—one that has accentuated the benefits of banding together to address rampant inequality in terms of wages and working conditions. Nothing like this massive new push toward labor unionization and regularized strikes existed in the ancient world on the scale we are now seeing. However, using Roman history to examine the ways in which regular Romans banded together in various forms can give us some empathy and insight into the ways that humans cope with marginalized identities, inequality, a lack of public prestige outlets for non-elites, and socioeconomic uncertainty. The voluntary and involuntary organization of labor into various types of informal collectives, formal associations, and unions supported many of the events, people, and places in Roman history. They influenced Rome's growth in ways we have not fully grasped in traditional histories from above that focus on emperors, elites, and the lives of the wealthy.

Lastly, this book provides a parallel to the modern world by examining Roman state anxieties over labor collectives, strikes, and challenges to state power. Just as is the case today, fear of economic disruptions drove elites and politicians to make choices that suppressed what we might call the freedom of assembly, comparable to modern union-busting legislation. Then and now, such legislation often employed the rhetoric of sedition or conspiracy to mask fears about how collective organization from below might challenge the economic, social, and political interests of the wealthy. From the involuntary associations of gladiatorial *familiae* that helped to start the Spartacan War from 73 to 71 BCE to the charioteer factions at the heart of the Nika revolt in Constantinople in January of 532 CE, peeling back the layers of Roman social history exposes a vast associative network at work within the Roman Mediterranean. While some preferred only to feast and to quietly bury their dead, other ancient groups engaged in labor conflicts such as strikes, secessions, and rebellion. These actions allowed their voices to be heard by those in power.

1
The Plebs, Secession, and Military Strikes

LEGEND HELD THAT ROMANS FOUNDED their republic in 509 BCE. Myths about this era were written down only later, but carried forth harrowing tales of the overthrow of a monarchy and the establishment of a republican government. But the creation of a republic did not create social harmony. Even after the last king of the regal period was allegedly forced into exile, there remained a civil divide within Rome's new state. The senators, called *patres* (fathers), who made up the Roman Senate and came from the early families of Rome, formed an elite social order called the patricians.[1] These patricians monopolized political and religious power, but there simply were not enough of them to fill the ranks of the Roman army. And, frankly, one gets the feeling that the patricians enjoyed being military officers and generals, but did not particularly like to do the day-to-day grunt work of a regular soldier. Patricians constantly called on the military service of the many male citizens outside their order, called the plebeians, instead. Over and over, these plebeians were asked to reenlist in the ranks of the army and fight in an increasing number of wars against local Italian tribes. The problem was that when these plebeians served as soldiers, they had to leave their shops, abandon their potter's wheel, depart from untilled farm fields, and again serve as citizen-soldiers in the Roman army.[2]

Regardless of whether plebeians were fighting for Rome, they were also still responsible for paying their debts. Unceasing military obligation and deepening credit balances owed to rapacious moneylenders caused widespread dissatisfaction, according to these tales. Exploitation of plebeians ultimately compelled them to join together and withhold their most valuable contribution: military service. Although the actions of the plebeians may have only taken place in the mythical imaginings of later historians who also lived through periods of popular commotion over debt and aristocratic power, these semi-mythical stories still have a worth. Tales of the early Republic and its army provide a framework for understanding imaginable types of popular resistance and collective action. We can certainly question the historicity of these secessions today. Still, it is patent that, in the minds of many Romans reading tales about the plebeians written down in the late Republic of the second and first centuries BCE, plebeian work stoppages and secessions were conceivable events. For those reading them, the stories were at the very least a plausible reaction by plebeians to the abuse of labor and power. The historical reimaginings of Rome's early days may also have proposed more peaceful reactions to displeasure with elites than had been evident in the days of the writers.

Today, we call the social, economic, and political clashes between plebeians and patricians the Struggle of the Orders. The likely fictional tales of Numa's early construction of trade associations served the ideological needs of Julius Caesar by justifying his ban on associations cast as not sufficiently ancient. Similarly, tales of the Struggle of the Orders may instead reflect the political rivalries and financial problems of the late Republic in the last two centuries BCE—rather than transmitting the historical reality of the fifth to third centuries BCE. As ancient historians today have pointed to, the late Republican competition between Roman politicians who supported traditional senatorial causes and interests, called the *optimates,* and those who supported more populist politics and political use of popular assemblies, called the *populares,* were perhaps grafted onto earlier, past conflicts between patricians and the plebeians.[3] In this way, the patricio-plebeian conflict became an "ideological weapon."[4]

Many of the issues mentioned in these histories would have also gripped contemporary readers in the first century BCE—and been quite familiar from their current lives. Popular struggles over debt, credit, and usury rates in the years after 49 BCE had pushed Caesar to institute his own debt relief and credit measures in Rome. The debt problems that historians such as Livy and Dionysius of Halicarnassus reported on for the early Republic would have hit home for audiences just a few decades after the civil conflicts of the late Republic.[5] Embedded within their myths were also moral warnings about the dangers of abusing regular Romans alongside a celebration of civil diplomacy over violence. At least in these quasi-historical imaginings, the early Republican plebeians had rejected the tyrannical ways of some patricians, organized themselves in secret, and collectively bargained by withdrawing from the city.

Our story starts with a Roman farmer and soldier deep in debt. In 495 BCE, the Senate voted for war against nearby Italic peoples called the Volscians. But this time, not everyone was in support of this call to arms. At Rome, a destitute freeborn farmer entered the Forum and pleaded with the citizens gathered there to listen to his plight as a freeborn man forced into debt servitude as a result of going off to war.[6] It was a story familiar to many, it seems. Although he had faithfully served Rome in all its recent campaigns, he could not pay the taxes due on his farm. He also took out a loan after his farm was raided. When he could not pay back the loan, the man and his two sons were taken away by an unyielding moneylender and placed into debt bondage. They were then beaten when the father refused to follow directions. Standing among the crowd gathered in the Forum to tell his story, the farmer threw off his clothing to show the lashes on his body for all to see.

It was in that moment that long-festering tensions and outrage began to boil over between the patricians and the plebeians. Dionysius derisively notes a madness that possessed the crowd at this time.[7] This turmoil and the farmer's pivotal call to abstain from military service would eventually lead to the so-called First Secession of the Plebs the following year. Myth or not, taking a closer look at the motives, tactics, and achievements of this defining conflict in Rome's early, heavily mythologized past, we can see more than just threats of a strike and the animosity between two different social groups. Likewise, if we review the Struggle of the Orders alongside shifts in labor, economic networks, and demographic changes, issues of the late Republic come to the fore: systemic inequality, increasing biases against tradespeople and commerce, power concentrated among the few rather than the many, debt problems, and a growing suspicion of private associations that met under cover of darkness.

In the fanciful retelling written by the Greek historian Dionysius of Halicarnassus, the public viewing of a Roman citizen and veteran beaten by a moneylender in 495 BCE so rankled the populace that many of those living in debt bondage due to their unpaid balances ran out of the houses of their

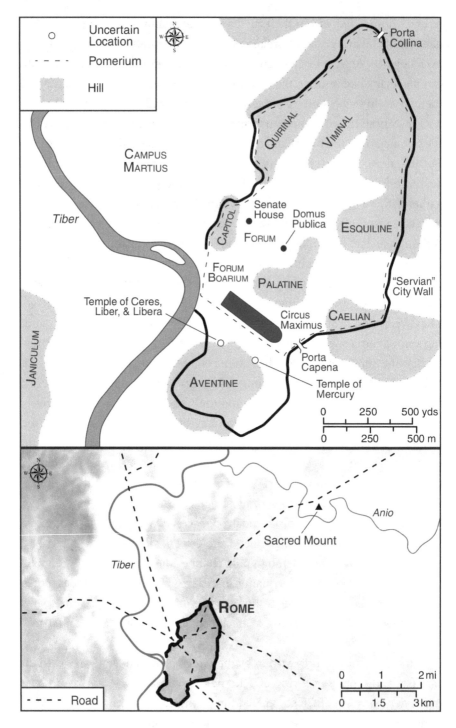

Fig. 4. Map of early Republican Rome during the Struggle of the Orders. (Map created by Gabriel Moss.)

creditors and joined in decrying the practice altogether.⁸ One of the two consuls for that year, Appius Claudius Sabinus, who was the founder of the patrician Claudii family, could feel the ire in the air. Although he had been steadfast that the Senate not succumb to the demands of the plebs, he knew when to exit a volatile situation. He fled from the Forum. Meanwhile, his co-consul, Publius Servilius Priscus, sent a crier to plead with the people not to riot. As a concession, he paused all debt arrests in the city until the Senate could decide the matter. But the fact was that neither of the consuls that year was seen as a defender of the non-elite people of Rome. Priscus rode the figurative fence on many matters prior. Consequently, both consuls were ultimately disliked by the many plebeians outside the senatorial circles of patricians.

In the same year, the Senate announced to the plebs that they should choose a consul from the two currently serving to dedicate the new Temple of Mercury in the southwest Circus Maximus. The senators noted that this dedicator would also be responsible for two other important charges: the city's grain supply and the setting up of a *mercatorum collegium,* a type of religious association of merchants to care for the temple and serve the city.⁹ Rather than give this precious charge to a serving consul, the people instead chose a centurion to dedicate the Temple of Mercury. The space was devoted to the god of commerce and dedicated on May 15. Thereafter, the Ides of May held a special place in the ritual calendar observed by Roman merchants and those engaged in commercial activity. The observance was marked with a sacrifice to Mercury and the god's mother, Maia.¹⁰ There were always links between commerce, religion, and associations. Likewise, the people's choice of a centurion over a consul to do the honor was a social comment on their current dissatisfaction with Roman patricians and the magistracies they monopolized.

In addition to the debates over debt slavery within the city, there was also a growing means for acquiring enslaved persons from outside of the city: war. In raising troops to go against the Volscians that year, Priscus then declared that all the male soldier-citizens who followed him into battle would be free from having their property or bodies seized by the debt collectors. He also permitted the division of spoils—namely, enslaved persons, cattle, arms, and military stores—among these soldiers when victorious in their battles, along with allowing the seizure of hostages from the Volscians and their allies.¹¹ Sabinus, for his part, remained viciously jealous of Priscus. He ordered that these hostages be whipped in the Forum and beheaded for all to see instead of being sold into servitude for profit. Here we see both Livy and Dionysius contrasting the ways that those in power should rule through the use of the patrician exemplars. But the calls upon the military service of the plebs were not yet finished; they lingered into the following year.

The new consuls for the next year, 494 BCE, entered office and again tried to compel service from the rather exhausted plebeian male population. The nearby Italic groups of Aequi, Volsci, and Sabines were all in arms and had to be dealt with. For their part, the plebeians held numerous meetings at night to discuss the levy and continuing problems with debt servitude. Some met on Rome's Aventine Hill and others on the Esquiline, rather than in the Forum.¹² Livy reports that these secret assemblies greatly perturbed the senators, who in turn blamed the lack of consular leadership and the idleness of the plebeians for their behavior. The senators appointed a dictator named Manius Valerius, which satisfied the plebeians, and ten legions enrolled. The dictator and his legions took on the Sabines, while the rest went with the consuls to take on the other groups. But after his later triumph in Rome, the Senate again refused to deal with remaining plebeian debt issues. Valerius berated the senators and then resigned to popular acclaim, while warning that mutiny was on the horizon.

The senators viewed the plebeians as still under military oath to serve and tried to regroup them to fight against the Aequi. Incensed and abstaining from the levy, the plebeians spoke of killing the consuls. The senators grew fearful that if the army were disbanded, there would again be "secret gatherings and conspiracies" of the plebeians. Ultimately the plebs chose to secede and to leave for the nearby Sacred Mount, a place three miles north of the Tiber, rather than serve as soldiers again.¹³ Business and activities in the city came to a halt, and tensions between the plebeians remaining in the city and the patricians only heightened. After the senators sent an envoy, a deal was worked out for the establishment of a new type of magistracy only held by plebeians, called the tribunate. The Senate agreed to their request, and the plebeians returned to Rome. There was also the creation of a new popular assembly that could create legislation, the Council of the Plebs, and two new plebeian magistrates known as aediles.¹⁴ Later, these aediles would become magistrates who cared for the buildings, roads, city games, and regulation of the markets. As accounts of the First Secession indicate, response through swift collective action was a pivotal bargaining mechanism during the Struggle of the Orders. It also provoked a fear that would last centuries among the senators. This elite Roman dread of nighttime meetings, secret groups, and the potential for social discord in the late Republic seems infused like strong tea into the stories of the early plebeians.

Patricians and the Monopolization of Power in the Early Republic

The patricians largely monopolized Roman social, legal, and religious power well into the Republican period. Separation of church and state did not exist in the Roman mindset. Romans believed that the political welfare of the city and its people depended upon its relationship or pact with the gods.[15] Early pontiffs were patrician protectors and interpreters of religion, law, and even time. From early on, the religious power to maintain the *pax deorum* (peace of the gods) depended on the city's elite religious associations or colleges, also called *collegia*. They had particular command over the ability to take the auspices from the sky. These religious colleges interpreted divine will through auspices, communicated piety to the divine through sacrifice, and controlled the religious calendar. Priestly *collegia* were also dominated by patricians in the regal period into the early years of the Republic. Only patricians could hold the top priesthood for men, the *rex sacrorum* (king of sacrifices). This religious official held no other magistracies and was the inheritor of the priestly power of the previous kings—a vestige of the earlier period of monarchy. He lived in a house along Rome's Sacra Via (Sacred Way).[16] His patrician wife was the *regina sacrorum* (queen of sacrifices), with ties to Juno.

Below this priestly king was the head of the pontifical colleges, the *pontifex maximus*, who would remain a patrician until 254 BCE. The major priests who served the Capitoline Triad (Jupiter, Juno, and Minerva), called *flamines*, were also at the time patricians, as were those members of the college of augurs who read the signs in the sky.[17] Elite women were allowed some participation through certain priesthoods and religious events such as one called the Bona Dea festival, wherein women worshipped the "Good Goddess." But even here, patrician families dominated.[18] The college of Vesta—often alleged, according to legend, to have begun under Rome's second king,

Numa Pompilius—was populated by Vestal Virgins who took a vow of chastity for their thirty-year (or more) term. If convicted of violating the vow of chastity, the Vestals faced the customary punishment of being buried alive.[19] This college lived in the House of the Vestals in the Roman Forum, near where the Pontifex Maximus lived, in the *Domus Publica*. The power of the patricians was constantly displayed through these public religious *collegia*, as well as via their covetous oversight of the calendar and in their occupation of sacred spaces in the city fabric. In addition to their monopoly on Roman religious leadership, patricians also held heavy sway over the declaration of war, election of magistrates, and the prosecution of debts at the beginning of the Republic.

What ultimately may have triggered the First Secession were issues of debt bondage and the actions of patrician magistrates. The early Republican system allowed an individual to put himself and even his children up as collateral for a loan and thus become "bound people" called *nexi*. If these persons were Roman citizens, their citizenship remained intact, but their labor stood in for capital with which to pay off their debt. The extortionate moneylenders in the fifth century BCE appear to have abused this system.[20] But we should not think of this as solely a struggle between the rich and the poor. From the beginning, there were indeed wealthy plebeians who helped lead this struggle and ostensibly made it a conflict between orders rather than modern socioeconomic classes. Scholars today are often careful to use the term "social order" over the more modern concept of class. However, the Marxist theorist and ancient historian G. E. M. de Ste. Croix argued persuasively that, while battles between the plebeians and patricians were a struggle between two political orders, this ultimately masked the underlying, concurrent class struggle that lay within.[21]

The Struggle of the Orders represented different things to different people, depending on their wealth level. Not all plebeians were destitute farmers, even if we tend to think of the plebs as a synonym for "the poor." The wealthy among the plebeians wanted the removal of the legal disqualifications and imposed ceiling that kept them from holding political and religious offices. To achieve this, they fought alongside the more economically underprivileged plebeians, who felt financially oppressed through systems such as debt bondage—men who were also exasperated during periods of military service that were well beyond occasional. Ultimately, the patrician Senate's refusal to advocate for the economically underprivileged plebeians induced a portion of the plebs, led by the more economically powerful plebeians, to do something often seen as overtly suspicious throughout Roman antiquity: meet under cover of night. Plebeians began their own nocturnal planning, undertaken in secret on the Esquiline and Aventine hills of Rome. These nighttime meetings set the groundwork for acquiring protection in the face of magistrates and for achieving more political representation. They would also set a precedent for using physical withdrawal from the city as a means of collective bargaining: secession was now on the table.

Early Republican Power Abuses and Assemblies

In addition to the levy and to the monopolization of magistracies, abuses of power by patricians were also a central issue within the Struggle of the Orders. These abuses were underscored and perhaps hyperbolized by later historians as a way of moralizing and pointing out just ways to rule. During this conflict, we are told that Roman citizens began to demand and negotiate for the legal provision of a pivotal civil right: to call on the support of the people if physically abused by a magistrate in the city of Rome. The power of a magistrate to enforce the law as it stood was called *coercitio*, the source of the modern word "coercion." The popular power to counter this magisterial right was then dubbed *provocatio* or *provocatio ad populum*. Today, we might call this the right to appeal to the people.[22] Plebeians were also gaining power through their own magistrates appointed to protect them. Legend held that after the First Secession within the Struggle of the Orders, the plebeians instituted the office of tribune of the plebs. These tribunes oversaw their assembly, called the Council of the Plebs, and were themselves required to be plebeians. There were ten tribunes by 449 BCE. These officials were a route to political power for high-status plebeians. They convened the council, could intervene on behalf of plebeians, made legislation, and were sacrosanct. Perhaps most importantly, they had the power to veto actions of tribunes and other magistrates, as well as senatorial decrees. They also could intercede and stop a Roman from having to serve in the army if unfairly forced to do so by a magistrate.

In addition to the native plebeians, there were other groups growing within Rome as well. Foreign tradespeople lived and worked within the city of Rome as commercial networks expanded across the Mediterranean. Greek traders had already been present in Rome going back at least to the eighth century BCE, but their numbers had grown substantially by the early Republic.[23] Near Rome's cattle market, called the Forum Boarium, Greek and Phoenician influences could also be found, particularly the Ara Maxima (Greatest Altar) that was dedicated to Hercules. Hercules was himself a Greek hero and god associated with commerce connected to the Phoenician and Punic god Melqart.[24] Workshops point to the growth of production and wares at this time. Rather than solely being domestic production spaces for metallurgy, ceramics, and textiles, artisan workshops grew up within and just outside of the city of Rome during the eighth to fifth centuries BCE.[25] Together, this evidence points to a mixture of Greek, Phoenician, and Punic religion, trade, commerce, and culture influencing Rome's own cultural norms and political mechanisms at the time.

Despite concessions, the patricians remained exceptionally powerful, not only within the Senate but also within popular assemblies that made important decisions for the community. At the time of the First Secession, for example, the 193 centuries that made up the Centuriate Assembly stood as the most important popular assembly for making decisions within the state.[26] To convene it, a consul and later a judicial magistrate known as a praetor called the assembly to vote on key matters of war, to hear capital appeals, and to vote on important magistracies such as the consuls, praetors, and, eventually, the censors who took the census. The assembly's meeting was announced by trumpeters, and it met outside the sacred boundary of the *pomerium* in the Campus Martius—the Field of Mars.

The Centuriate Assembly is a fundamental example of how group voting en bloc—versus the individual casting of a ballot for an individual vote—can endow a small socioeconomic group with disproportionate power.[27] To put it mildly, the anatomy and voting procedures of the Centuriate Assembly were complex but are important to understand in order to unpack how elite Roman ideologies and principles became systemic. The voting structure of the assembly privileged land-owning patricians over tradesmen and the wealthy over the impoverished. It also enshrined a bias toward labor and commerce that would continue well into the later Roman Republic, the Roman imperial period (31 BCE–200 CE), and beyond. The modern democratic ideal of every vote carrying the same weight and influence was not at play in Rome's

Centuriate Assembly. Although every century had one vote, not every century had the same number of men within it. Despite the name of "century" suggesting a unit of one hundred men, a century could have more or less within each voting bloc. Just imagine if ten men in a century had the same voting power as two hundred men relegated to another, lower century. Consequently, wealthy centuries of property owners who voted first had the advantage. Property and patriotism were inextricably linked by many elite Romans, who believed that the more property and wealth one had invested in the state, the higher one's level of concern for the welfare of the Republic. To many elite men, more property meant more commitment to the state. For how could someone without land ownership ever be truly tied to or devoted to a place?

Legislative Transparency and the Twelve Tables

In addition to clout via magistracies and many of the popular assemblies, patricians also controlled knowledge of the law in ways that helped them to maintain power—something against which the plebeians protested. The plebeians remained frustrated with the patricians' tight control over the creation of laws, in particular. It was further exasperating to them that the patricians controlled the interpretation of this legislation. After much haggling between the patricians and plebeians in the middle of the fifth century, a board of *decemviri* (ten men) was established in 451 and then again in 450 in order to publish a public and pivotal codification of laws called the Laws of the Twelve Tables. Both the laws and the stories that stem from the creation of this pivotal legislation reveal the biases against plebeians that existed in the early Republic. The famed laws were published on inscribed tablets of either bronze or ivory and placed outdoors for public reading (both aloud for others and to one's self) in the Roman Forum at that time. A later Roman jurist—that is, an interpreter of Roman law—named Pomponius would, in the second century CE, note that these tablets were displayed in front of the speaking platform called the Rostra "to make the laws more open to inspection."[28] Transparency and the public presentation of laws encouraged understanding among the populace, as well as critique. In 451 the first set of ten tables were, upon public assessment, deemed unsatisfactory. Another two tablets were then added in response.

The Laws of the Twelve Tables remained an important set of legislation to know within Rome and beyond. They stipulated trial procedures, spelled out the prosecution of debts and subsequent debt bondage, required women other than Vestal Virgins to have male guardians to oversee their legal actions, discussed property and theft, and listed many types of civil offenses called delicts (similar to torts). They also reinforced Roman elite suspicion of activities in the nighttime, laying heavier capital penalties on stealing pasture land and crops by night. In respect to associations, these laws noted that members of voluntary associations called *collegia* were legally allowed to enter into agreements—as long as they were not counter to the public law.[29] This may or may not have been influenced by Athenian attitudes toward such groups. We are told by a later Roman legal expert named Gaius, who wrote a commentary on the Laws of the Twelve Tables in the mid-second century CE, that the analogous Greek word for a *collegium* was a *"hetaireia,"* the same word used in Greek for political clubs in Athens and elsewhere in the Greek world. The jurist also remarked that the Athenian statesman Solon had made an earlier pronouncement regarding such associations in the city of Athens in the early sixth century BCE. The statesman had announced that these clubs could exist if they did not go counter to the law. Gaius claimed that Solon's law had influenced the later Roman adoption of a similar regulation for their own city.[30]

While the new Roman laws stated that associations were allowed to exist within legal limits, many other portions of the Laws of the Twelve Tables suggest already-evident fears of sedition and secrecy directed at those involved in illicit meetings of private citizens, even if there was a conditional allowance for assembly. It seems the eighth tablet had a section specifically outlawing illicit private meetings that were called a *coetus*.[31] The *decemviri* who drew up the Laws of the Twelve Tables were privileged men with fears surrounding the formation of political groups. The plebeian meetings that had led to the beginning of the Struggle of the Orders had already been occurring for over four decades. From this point on, the holding of possibly seditious private assemblies would increasingly become a source of dread and worry among Rome's ruling aristocrats, a worry reflected in later legislation. As Rome's population, empire, and private associations expanded greatly in the centuries to come, angst over maintaining political and social power remained characteristic of those at the very top.

The stories told about this time continue to moralize about the actions of tyrannical patricians. In the midst of this crucial publication of laws, a patrician from among the Claudian family caused a telling scene—one that once again exposed the disdain felt by some patricians for the plebeians. A patrician senator named Appius Claudius Crassus, who was appointed as one of the board of *decemviri* who had helped to make the new law code, refused to resign his post. But Crassus's disrespect for the plebeians went beyond simply refusing to give up his power on the board. He also viewed plebeians as persons to be controlled, coerced, and even enslaved, as historians in antiquity would illustrate through an anecdote about Crassus's dealings with a woman named Verginia. The patrician had laid his sights on the well-known plebeian woman and was willing to use any means to get her. Verginia was the daughter of a plebeian centurion named Lucius Verginius and betrothed to a former tribune named Lucius Icilius. Like most elite men, Crassus was a patron with many dependents called clients in a powerful system of Roman patronage called the patron-client relationship. He asked one of his clients to claim Verginia as the daughter of one of his enslaved women. This act would make her the client's property as well. The plan was then for the client to give her over to his patron.[32]

The Verginii were only one of the many wealthy and highly esteemed plebeian families gaining notoriety and political clout from the early Republic onward.[33] This is a major reason we cannot see the Struggle of the Orders as a class conflict in the way that Marx and Engels did. The historian Livy says Verginia attended school in one of the many ad hoc booths and tents set up in the Roman Forum for schooling during the day.[34] Entering into the Forum, Appius's client, Marcus Claudius, dragged Verginia to a court tribunal overseen by Appius. This was a conflict of interest, to put it mildly. Although there was a delay in the trial while her father rushed to her the next day, Appius ultimately ruled that she was the enslaved woman of his client. After the unjust verdict was pronounced, a crowd gathered around Verginia and her father, who were near the butcher shops on the northern side of the Forum at the time. Snatching a butcher knife, her father killed Verginia. It was to give her—in his words—her freedom.

The plebeian crowd collectively rushed to protect Verginia's father from arrest and ushered him to the city gate. While the women grieved her fate, the men, including Verginia's fiancé, used the moment to lament the patrician abuse of judicial powers and the need for a right of appeal to the people. Still wielding the knife and leading a group of four hundred civilians in togas, Verginius exited Rome to a hill about twelve miles southeast of Rome with a military camp. A mix of soldiers and civilians then marched back to the city and rounded up more followers as they went to Rome's Aventine Hill and occupied the Temple of Diana.[35] As historian Lisa Mignone reconstructs, the plebeian soldiers and civilians marched conspicuously through Rome in a performance of nonviolence to occupy the Aventine in this secession. As she notes, "This military boycott constituted a sit-in."[36] This meant that yet again, the plebeians were again on strike in 449 BCE.

The initial occupation of the Aventine did not move the patricians to action this time. Escalating the withdrawal, the plebeian protesters again retired outside the city to the Sacred Mount to force the hand of the patricians. Their strike eventually forced the Senate and new consuls into approving the reinstitution of the plebeian tribunes and the resignation of the original board of *decemviri*. The consuls also passed a law making the plebiscites of the Plebeian Assembly binding on all citizens—but with the Senate's approval first. Increased documentation and transparency were a part of these senatorial concessions. Copies of the resolutions of the Senate, called *senatus consulta*, would now be archived in the plebeian-associated Temple of Ceres at the foot of the Aventine, overseen by the aediles. By withholding their labor and civic participation once more, plebeians continued to chip away at patrician power. Patrician control of information and access to law began to ebb, allowing increased plebeian access to legal processes and procedures. Knowledge was power, and the plebeians demanded that legislation such as the Laws of the Twelve Tables be made accessible to the people.

Artisans, Merchants, and Trade Networks in the Early Roman Republic

The first decades of the Struggle of the Orders indicate that the plebeians did not form a monolithic union or even a homogenous social group in terms of wealth, occupation, or status. Despite not being a monolith, they could, as the myths suggest, coordinate en masse or in large, efficacious groups, to lobby for their causes, to strike, or to boycott. Tales of the early plebeians have them engaged in a number of important strategies for the acquisition of their civil rights: nonviolent protest, physical removal to places like the Sacred Mount, the Aventine Hill, and later to the Janiculum Hill, and the physical use of insulating groups of plebeians to safeguard individuals from Roman magistrates in public—that is, a bodyguard. Centuries later, in the late Republic and empire, these methods became important to some groups of merchants and those engaged in commercial transactions in the mid-first century BCE. Yet their actions were much more violent than those of the earlier plebeians. The endorsement of peace over pummeling was perhaps one of Livy's key lessons in his histories.

As we have seen, much of our quasi-historical knowledge of the Struggle of the Orders is based on the exclusive narratives of later historians such as Livy and Dionysius of Halicarnassus, both writing in the reign of Augustus (27 BCE–14 CE). But if we go beyond the internal intrigue of early Rome and the possibly mythical stories that dominated the narratives of these historians, we can begin to use other sources of evidence, such as mentions of treaties and legislation, to see the expanding local and international commercial networks also developing in the early Roman Republic. These early commercial networks will later become important in our quest to sketch out the formation of occupational associations and evaluate their purpose, their reputations, and their suppression in Roman antiquity.

One place to look for evidence of increased economic networking is treaties. Around 509 to 507 BCE, Rome may have signed its first treaty with the Punic city of Carthage, a Phoenician colony within what is modern Tunisia. In his explanation of the tumultuous events of the Second Punic War (218–201 BCE) between Rome and Carthage, the Greek historian Polybius later recounted the numerous treaties between the two states in the early to middle Republic. Supposedly, the first was in 509, and others followed in 348, 279 or 278, 241, and 226 BCE. The treaty of 348 put Roman and Carthaginian traders on equal legal footing for trade and attempted to limit piracy. At the time, the Punic city was the more successful state economically and offered attractive access to the grain market for Rome.[37] This grain market would remain of highest significance to Romans throughout its history.

Grain came at a premium and was a constant concern for Rome. Famine consistently plagued the city, and although the treaty seems more advantageous to Carthage, Rome signed it. The terms addressed Roman trade in the Carthaginian territories of Libya, Sardinia, and Sicily. It stipulated that

Romans were not to engage in trade without a messenger or clerk present. Prices would be controlled by the Carthaginian state. In exchange, Carthage was not to harm the Latin cities already under Rome's control, engage in conquest within the region, or build any forts in the area. Grain shortages in 496 compelled the Romans to vow a temple to Ceres, later dedicated in 493. This building project would involve non-Roman labor. Pliny remarks that the first officially contracted Greek artists to be hired for work in the city of Rome were two sculptors and painters named Damophilus and Gorgasos. These men decorated and put Greek verses on the dedicated temple.[38] The archaeological record reveals Greek artists living and working in Rome long before this, but like many legends, Pliny's story served as a neat, reductive way of connecting Rome to Greece's long history of artists, temple building, and traveling craftspeople.

Grain remained an important staple for all of Rome's existence. Perhaps in 508 BCE, in 492 BCE, 440 to 439 BCE, and many other times in the Republic's first two centuries, Roman magistrates and senators sought out and then secured grain for the populace of Rome.[39] The Roman diet focused heavily on grain, and the commodity was often the impetus for trade, treaties, legislation, and eventually—associations that facilitated a supply chain. In the later Republic, the grain supply was the basis for the creation of more organized corporations of grain merchants, dock workers, barge runners, and other intermediaries who would transport it to Rome. In addition to international treaties with kingdoms such as Carthage, Rome also began to create agreements with its Latin neighbors. These accords secured the legal validity of contracts and reconciled differing legal systems. Such resolutions were necessary to protect the growing number of merchants and tradespeople. They also functioned to encourage exchange through protection and the upholding of legal agreements. This would later be termed the *ius commercii* (law of commerce).

And yet property still trumped commerce as a source of prestige in Roman culture. As we saw with the structuring of the Centuriate Assembly, elite male Romans advocated for an intrinsic virtue tied to agriculture and the ownership of property. Farming one's own land was venerated above business by elites in public and in literature, but this only meant that commerce was undertaken more covertly by people like senators and other elites. In a more clandestine and indirect manner, senators often instrumentalized clients, enslaved persons, and agents to do their business dealings. Similar to elite Greek views expressed in the works of Aristotle and Xenophon, Roman philosophers and wealthy statesmen of the late Republic often looked down on trade and manual labor as "banausic"—a pejorative term used for those who practiced the "illiberal arts" of craft production.[40] For elitist ancient writers, the term was frequently connected to slavery and to a disreputable need to earn wages.

Rome was not the only culture that sneered at manual labor. We can see this bias at work elsewhere, in the classifications of the various types of people in Mediterranean societies created by authors such as the Greek historian Herodotus. In his *Histories*, written circa 426 to 415 BCE, he remarks that there was a commonly held disdain for craftspeople. The exception to this social scorn was in the highly commercial city of Corinth—a great producer of pottery, textiles, olive oil, and stone—where the least amount of stigma was placed on them. Herodotus observed a common contempt connected to artisans across the Mediterranean: "I have noticed that in Thrace and Scythia and Persia and Lydia and among nearly all the barbarians, those citizens, along with their offspring, who learn technical skills are held in less honor than the rest of the people, and those who have the least to do with handicrafts, especially those men who are free to practice exclusively the art of war, are highly honored."[41] Manual laborers were essential workers, but not always respected ones.

The ability of artisans to serve as soldiers was also a question in the Republic. Livy would later comment that, when faced with war against the Gauls in 329 BCE, the two Roman consuls, Lucius Aemilius Mamercinus and Gaius Plautius, had chosen to conscript a lesser pool of men for service in the Roman army. When the consuls entered office, they raised an army that, to Livy's explicit shock, even included a mass of workmen and sedentary artisans. This was a group that, to the historian, was the least suitable for military service.[42] To many elite literati of antiquity, key Roman virtues of masculinity, honor, and patriotism stemmed from owning land, not from trade or dependence on wage labor. Correspondingly, we will see that later occupational associations made up of artisans and tradespeople were not often cast in a favorable light in Roman literature, especially when they assembled for a political cause.

Roman literature created a mirage of anti-commercial attitudes and written biases against tradespeople that can obscure the reality of Rome's underlying, active participation in trade networks since its very inception. Rome's stories of the regal period held that it was one of its legendary kings who had helped Rome to acquire the area that would become Ostia, Rome's port, eleven miles to the west. Rome sat inland along the commercial ventricle of the Tiber River, which carried barges, tradespeople, and wares back and forth along the waterway—this in addition to the network of roads that led into and out of the city. Despite a law passed in 218 BCE that tried to keep senators and their sons from engaging in maritime trade by barring them from owning ships that could hold over three hundred amphorae, we know that senators tried hard to keep their reputations free of the stain of commerce. They used proxies and back channels to continue to participate in commerce, since trade was seen as rather déclassé among senators.[43] Literature and historical accounts may have cast Rome as originally growing from a village of farmers led by Romulus, but make no mistake: it was always a city of trade and exchange as well.

In addition to the maritime networks expanding at this time, the Italian peninsula was a vibrant mélange of peoples and languages in the sixth to fourth centuries BCE, from the Etruscans, to the Oscans, to the Greeks of Magna Graecia, to the Celtic peoples to the north in the Po Valley. As Elena Isayev has recently emphasized, there was regular migration, mobility, and urbanization from below at this time, one particularly engaged in by groups of artisans, traders, elites, and many others in Italy. This culture of everyday movement continued until Rome orchestrated a more centralized control of migration from above in the late third century BCE.[44] And yet Roman and Greek historians often characterized migrations as being more abrupt waves, applying ethno-stereotypes and markers of difference provided by food, beverages, or customs as a way to create cultural binaries—that is, seemingly opposing differences between Greco-Romans and the "other."[45]

Cultural mixing is also revealed through contemporary inscriptions that offer firmer evidence than later, quasi-mythical histories. They indicate that at least since the seventh century BCE, Celtic groups had a presence in northern Italy. Recent studies suggest that these settlements may have increased in number around 550 to 540 BCE, with more groups crossing over the Alps and settling in the Po Valley beyond. Unlike the literary accounts, the archaeological record reveals ongoing interactions rather than distinct waves of

Celtic migration and disruption.[46] Trade then encouraged this steady intermingling of cultures further. From Celtic settlements in modern Austria also came a pivotal commodity: salt. This was an important product to Romans, one that, going all the way back to the first years of the Republic, the government had at times taken over from private sellers, when there was a need to give it to the populace at a lower price.[47] Celtic merchants also trafficked in Baltic amber and many other luxury goods and traded for things like ceramics and amphorae of wine.

Although Gallo-Celtic groups were often characterized by later Greco-Roman sources such as Livy, Plutarch, or Dionysius of Halicarnassus as more "primitive" peoples displaced by hunger, discord, or overpopulation, in actuality Gallo-Celtic groups in Italy were accomplished merchants who in the fourth century BCE looked to expand southward. After Rome's conquest of the Etruscan stronghold of Veii in 396 BCE, the Gallic soldiers saw their chance. Meeting at the junction of the Allia and Tiber rivers, just eleven miles north of Rome, they defeated the Romans at the Battle of Allia. As Livy notes, the defeat on July 18 of that year was so devastating that the Roman *fasti* maintained the date as *nefas* (inauspicious), banning public and private business transactions on that day.[48] Just as they were suspicious of nocturnal meetings and illicit assemblies internally, elite Romans would continue to be skeptical of both tradespeople and the influx of certain foreigners coming into their city in the centuries to come.

Around 390 or 387 BCE, the Gauls infamously sacked the city of Rome. It was a generational trauma that would be mentally and physically remembered by Romans for centuries to come. Rome would not be sacked again until 410 CE. What is less emphasized about the time thereafter is not just the animosity toward the Gauls that continued for centuries to come, but also the fact that groups of laborers helped remake Rome and particularly its walls within a decade—at a high economic cost. The Republican walls, called the Servian Walls, after Rome's sixth king, were begun at this time. In that moment, the seven-mile-long fortification and ditch became—much like the much larger Aurelian Walls begun many centuries later in 271 CE—Rome's largest monument.[49] The walls were an investment in the city and a testament to the growing professionalization of Rome's military.[50] The walls also reveal Rome's increasing reliance on organized labor forces pulled both from the citizenry and from the burgeoning enslaved population.

The organization of workers for these new walls provides a window into Rome's labor supply at the time. In the mid- to late fourth century, the labor landscape of Rome and Italy was shifting drastically. There was, however, one major change: during this time, debt bondage began to decrease as Rome's conquests brought in more enslaved captives.[51] As archaeologist Seth Bernard has proposed, a mix of corvée (that is, compulsory laborers from the citizenry) and enslaved workers filled the ranks of the skilled and unskilled teams used to build the wall—all males ages seventeen to forty-five and numbering 16,300 to 32,000 in total.[52] These unpaid workers were compelled, as Bernard argues, through a complex mix of coercion, debt, obligation, and taxation to create Rome's new city walls. Enslaved persons also factored in. Newly enslaved Veians may have quarried the stone for transport to Rome. The multiyear, forced devotion of civic funds and people to the project then had broader consequences, possibly causing an economic stagnation that would drag down the mid-fourth-century BCE economy.

During the fourth century BCE, the Struggle of the Orders also continued to drag on. The differences between plebeians and patricians further eroded, even as other markers of social difference increased. The conflict was never about freedom and justice for all, but rather about providing power to plebeians with means. A series of laws in 367 BCE had already put limits on usury and the holding of public lands by wealthy Romans. Plebeians also became eligible for certain priesthoods and the consulships. Throughout the second half of the fourth century BCE, the plebeians continued to win more representation through magistracies both old and new. Debt bondage also decreased as a threat to the plebeians. The practice was effectively abolished for free Roman citizens in 326 BCE or 313 BCE by a law called the *lex Poetelia Papiria*. This liberated Roman citizens even further from the threat of bondage themselves, even as they enslaved others at an ever-alarming rate. Chattel slavery rather than debt bondage would be a defining feature of labor issues and organization in the middle and late Republic.

Labor Changes at the End of the Struggle of the Orders

In Rome within the late fourth century BCE, there were also increasing concerns about another group: manumitted persons (previously enslaved persons) in Rome called *liberti*. Legislation concerning the taxing of manumission at the time points to the fact that manumitted persons were a growing social order. These men and women entered society with the rights of Roman citizens, but with limits on their ability to hold office. As with all Roman women, manumitted women also could not vote. *Liberti* retained legal and social obligations due to their patron even after manumission, and often endured a social stigma stemming from their earlier enslavement. The increasing roles played by these manumitted persons are glimpsed at in the waning decades of the Struggle of the Orders.

At this time, a former scribe and *libertus* brought transparency to the inner workings of the secretive Roman pontifical associations through a rebellious act of what might be called vigilante justice. The scribe's name was Gnaeus Flavius, and as Cicero would later remark, he "pierced the eyes of crows [that is, outwitted those in the know] and published the calendar of court days to the people and in this way stole the knowledge of the legal calendar from the astute legal experts."[53] The legal calendar marked out which days were either good or bad for legal action. Even two hundred years after Rome had become a republic, this calendar was still overseen by a small coterie that made up the *collegium* of pontiffs. The incident indicates that the Struggle of the Orders was about diffusing power to plebeians through their collective actions, but it was also about publishing information for public knowledge.

Toward the end of the legendary conflict between plebeians and patricians, the potent religious *collegia* finally became integrated. Through the advocacy of the plebeian tribunes, the two major priestly colleges ultimately allowed plebeian pontiffs and augurs by increasing their overall numbers in 300 BCE. But the struggle was not completely over; there was one last strike to be waged. In 287 BCE, the final secession of the plebeians allegedly took place over the very issue that had begun it: debt. Although details are murky, Pliny the Elder and a later epitomator of Livy note that the plebeians left for the Janiculum Hill across the Tiber, a space altogether outside the city walls, to protest the handling of debts.[54] They were once again leveraging their demographic power through physical withdrawal. A plebeian dictator, Quintus Hortensius, was elected to deal with the crisis. He passed the law known as the *lex Hortensia,* which made the plebiscites passed in the Plebeian Assembly binding on all Romans, without the need for the Senate's approval. After between three and five plebian secessions (depending on the historian writing), the Struggle of the Orders was over.

Conclusions from the Struggle of the Orders

What is fact and what is fiction about early Rome? Examination of the quasi-mythical tales of the Struggle of the Orders alongside archaeological evidence for Rome's social, economic, and labor transformations during its first few centuries as a republic do not provide many concrete answers. The stories do point to the myriad, real prejudices held by elite and propertied Romans in a highly stratified society increasingly engaged in commerce, exchange, and the intermixing of peoples from outside of Rome. This lore surrounding the early plebeians may also indicate at least the potential of collective action, secession, and peaceful strikes as bargaining tools in ancient societies, at least by the time of the late Republic, when many of these stories were written down. These collective memories of Rome's early days may also be viewed as moralizing tales that encouraged more nonviolent negotiation tactics over the civil violence engaged in between *optimates* and *populares* that we will soon discuss. Even if the early stories about the Republic are largely mythical, they taught core moral lessons and transmitted at least some hint of plausible, collective social actions to later Roman audiences.

What we can state definitively is that the success of the plebeians and the end of the formal Struggle of the Orders in 287 BCE did not magically transform Rome into a democracy.[55] Rome remained a city and a society ruled by an oligarchy that outwardly displayed prejudices against trade. Now that oligarchy just had more wealthy male plebeians at the helm. While these men achieved greater parity with the patricians at Rome, social inequality, slavery, and a distinct xenophobia directed toward certain cultures and foreign groups expanded. As the next chapter examines, private associations of tradespeople and artisans also began to form and increase during these pivotal last three centuries BCE. This growth in associations happened first in the eastern Mediterranean, so as to navigate new commercial networks and provide things like entertainment and food more easily.

Tradespeople in the Italian peninsula and Rome also began to create small associations at this time. Some inscribed their existence into the historical record through inscriptions in stone or contracts written on papyri. In Italy, there were also involuntary associations of enslaved persons called *familiae* created by enslavers that increased in number within Italy. As the next chapter explores, at various times in Sicily and in the Italian peninsula, some of these groups realized the distinct advantages of collective action—acting together and leaning on prior organizational structures—as a tactic for breaking free from human bondage altogether. Rather than withdrawing from Rome to bargain for their rights and representation, as the plebeians may have, groups of enslaved workers in the late Republic would use their organizational skills to resist their captors and rebel against the Roman state. They did this through careful planning, strong leadership, and collective might that converted their prior labor organization in bondage into a weapon for coordinated action.

2

We Are Spartacus: Labor and Resistance in the Late Republic

IN THE LATE REPUBLIC, A GLADIATOR from Thrace named Spartacus commanded a highly organized revolt of enslaved persons against Rome from 73 to 71 BCE. This was no small rebellion. Although the numbers given by ancient sources are often problematic to trust, they note that Spartacus commanded a staggering number of soldiers: between 70,000 and 120,000 at the rebellion's height. It is no surprise that from Karl Marx to modern movies, the story of Spartacus has captivated audiences. However, to understand the mechanics and logistical success of this impressive resistance to Rome, we first need to appreciate the shifting status of labor and its organization in Italy at the time. We must also situate Spartacus and his rebellion within the context of the expanding trade networks, burgeoning occupational associations, and forced organization of enslaved persons in the Mediterranean. The Third Servile War (73–71 BCE) led by Spartacus did not occur in a vacuum. It was a product not only of changes in the number of enslaved persons within the Italian peninsula, but also an increasing realization among free and unfree peoples of the power of collectives.

In the middle to late Republic (c. 300–31 BCE), many variant types of occupational and commercial associations emerged in response to the Hellenistic empires and then to the Roman one. They relied both on free and unfree workers, organized either voluntarily or involuntarily into their own groups, for a range of purposes. In the case of the Third Servile War led by Spartacus, he drew on the close internal bonds formed previously by enslaved associations called *familiae,* in order to spark a resistance that would conjure a quite real fear in the heart of many elite Romans. Looking at the three Servile Wars of the late Republic underscores the capacity for ancient enslaved persons to organize and resist bondage in antiquity. But understanding earlier labor organization draws attention to the fact that leaders of the Servile Wars may have productively drawn on already-existing corporative structures and associative bonds to aid in their epic—and coordinated— struggle for freedom.

Entertainment Associations and Collective Bargaining

Associations were important mediators embedded in and often facilitating the networks that crisscrossed the Mediterranean and beyond. In the eastern Mediterranean, we can recognize this growth in associations particularly within the burgeoning trans-Mediterranean entertainment industry. Due to the popular hunger for theatrical entertainment and religious festivals that flourished after the death of Alexander the Great in 323 BCE, there was expedited development and patronage of associations of elite theatrical performers, which may present the earliest parallel to today's trade unions. In the Italian peninsula and Rome as well, associations of scribes, actors, and poets would also form to provide music, present performances, and exhibit theatrical shows for the growing calendar of annual festivals enjoyed by the people. This tendency to create groups and to rely on one's association was a social feature of the era. And the affinity for traveling entertainment troupes that began to gain steam at this time only encouraged the trend.

In the western Mediterranean during the second century BCE, there is an increase in evidence for other types of professional associations as well. Groups of cooks banded together to provide culinary services for hire in the marketplaces of ancient cities. Professional bakers allegedly were brought to the city of Rome in 168 BCE. The increase in Roman imperialism in the East and the massive influx of enslaved labor to Rome and the Italian peninsula was due to Rome's conquests and the fact Romans had no qualms with enslaving the conquered. There was thus an increasing reliance on forced corps of enslaved *familiae* in addition to voluntary associations. These organized "families" were associative units structured from above by enslavers and used to work on farms, to function as shepherds in places like Sicily, to perform domestic functions, and even to participate in a new form of popular entertainment gripping the city of Rome from the mid-third century BCE onward: gladiatorial combat. This intensifying system of both voluntary and involuntary associations within the Roman economy began to provide an underlying associative framework for many workforces laboring in the Mediterranean.

Associative changes were not the only ones afoot in Rome and Italy. Eastern conquests also brought waves of new peoples, goods, and religious beliefs to the city. This was, at pivotal times, met with a reactive xenophobia that impelled elite Romans to try and safeguard traditional ideals and religion. New legislation limited certain types of worship of foreign cults, modifying the freedom of assembly by certain groups. In 186 BCE, the Roman state would eye with suspicion the popularity of the worship of Bacchus and the connected religious associations that formed to worship this god of wine and drunkenness. The subsequent senatorial ban on Bacchic rites and the gathering of his worshippers is an instructive moment. Here we can start to outline how elite Romans began to react legally to their reservations surrounding nocturnal activities, foreigners, and any possibility of popular discord. Anti-assembly legislation would—well into the high empire—be recurrently deployed, to maintain state control from above by deactivating the private associations formed from below.

If we look to the Greek world for a view of new associations, the earliest professional organizations that we might view as analogous to the modern labor union were formed by entertainers connected to the theater.[1] Their development was driven in part by high demand: in the earlier fifth and fourth centuries BCE, there had been a popular clamor for Greek dramatic performances of tragedy, comedy, hymns to Dionysus called dithyrambs, and other types of dramatic performances that were being held on growing festival circuits where theatrical performances often were staged. Although cities had long contracted with well-known individual actors to perform dramatic works at their local festivals, the early decades of the era we call the Hellenistic period (323–31 BCE) in the East saw the banding together of performers for collective action, as a means of ensuring that favorable, secure working conditions were established as they traveled to various cities to perform. The essential function of this labor association was to fight for and improve the rights and pay of its members.

By the early third century BCE, groups called the *technitai* (practitioners) of Dionysus, in particular, had established formidable associations, often referred to today as acting troupes, that fiercely advocated for their members. Contracts for the practitioners of Dionysus often came with what we might today call artist riders that listed their demands and secured their places on a festival circuit that wound throughout the Greek world and part of the Roman one. These unions of performers were particularly visible where rulers, such as the Ptolemies in Egypt, acted as their patrons. In this way, these groups were different from modern labor unions: powerful monarchs often used the fame of these performance troupes to their own advantage by advertising their patronage of them at festivals. This also demonstrated how state or monarchial patrons could work with associations to provide entertainment to the people.[2]

The professionalization of the entertainment industry increased during the Hellenistic age and transformed the organization of entertainers, musicians, costumers, scenery-makers, and eventually athletes into popularly known workers in a burgeoning business sector. This important associative network continued well into the late Roman period. Popular demand for actors and performers at festivals ranging from the *Soteria* of Delphi to the *Dionysia* of Samos to the *Ptolemaia* in Alexandria drove these professional performers to create independently organized associations often called *koina* or *synodoi*. Some ultimately united as practitioners called *technitai*. These groups later spread to Magna Graecia in southern Italy and to Sicily, influencing the organization of the entertainment industry in Rome as well.

What made these ancient quasi-unions different from other associations at the time? According to contracts and agreements established through letters and often published as copies on inscribed stone, itinerant *technitai* could secure special dispensations. This included asylum rights that prevented one from being seized, or freedom from taxes.[3] Foreign travelers needed protections in the ancient Mediterranean, and these unions of entertainers often used elected secretaries to write to and work with assemblies in local cities, festival organizers, and the monarchs who required their services. While many independent groups formed private labor unions, an increasing number of wealthy Romans also saw the compulsory organization of enslaved labor into groups as a means of satisfying the growing demand for a new type of entertainment gripping Italy: gladiatorial matches.

Even today, traveling entertainers continue to desire representation and collective protection from exploitation. In 1939, the American Guild of Variety Artists (AGVA) was founded to protect touring American actors, dancers, and performers on the circuit of traveling variety shows. This labor union grew out of the public demand for burlesque and variety shows as well as the need to protect stripteasers, dancers, and performers who were forced to endure long work weeks for low wages. Today, the AGVA continues to help with contracts, set wages, specify work conditions, set up secure travel and publicity, offer health benefits, and provide a number of other member services. Since antiquity, the entertainment industry has had a unique popular leverage that often makes work stoppages more successful. Gaining the support of the people by depriving them of popular entertainment until demands are met was—and still is—a viable labor tactic for entertainment and sports groups.

Like many ancient associations, the *technitai* of Dionysus were highly systematized and hierarchical. These organizations relied on their own elected officials and internal magistracies. The titles for the magistrates of the *technitai*, such as archon, often imitated the magistracies of the Greek polis and provided internal prestige and reputation. They had their own protocols, guidelines, and officers, and often another trait common to premodern associations in particular: a religious component. The *technitai* had ties to Dionysus, the Greek god of wine and patron of the arts, as well as to Pythian Apollo. Although inscriptions often focused on this religious element, scholars have emphasized that the principal function of the secretaries of the *technitai* was business. As Mali Skotheim has reconstructed, the primary task of these groups was risk mitigation, since, as professionals moving from place to place, they were "legally and financially vulnerable."[4] Many *technitai* maintained extensive archives of correspondence and had libraries to maintain and prove their legal rights, enforce contracts, and perpetuate their knowledge base. As we will see later for compulsory associations formed by the state in the late Roman Empire, knowledge organization and cultures of documentation within associations were methods for providing legal security, risk mitigation, and continuity over time. In the case of the *technitai* of Dionysus, these performers traveled widely and needed to make sure that they were protected and paid for their services properly and punctually.

Associations of Entertainers at Rome

Theater was not always a part of the Roman social scene. Livy notes that the city of Rome had its first theatrical performance in 364 BCE, following a bout of plague that had devastated the populace. Even after religious officials engaged in a sacred *lectisternium*—a kind of religious banquet intended to propitiate the gods, who were represented in the banquet by icons on couches—the sickness continued. According to the historian, the desire to appease the divine impelled the Romans to welcome their first public stage performances, which were allegedly introduced to them by the Etruscans.[5] From here, groups of theatrical entertainers in the city only grew and became more visible, in part through their clubhouses. The actors in the theater were in Latin called *histriones,* and by the late third century BCE, writers, secretaries, and, at that time, poets were—along with the *histriones*—allowed a special dispensation to meet within the confines of the Temple of Minerva on the Aventine Hill.[6] There may be a continuity with the later *collegium poetarum* (association of poets) known in the second century BCE. Like many groups, this one had an official *schola* (meetinghouse). Theirs was within the Temple of Hercules and the Muses. This conspicuous clubhouse stood near Rome's Circus Flaminius in the Campus Martius. This special privilege of assembly within a sacred space, extended to the group by the Senate, came following the contributions of a poet and dramatist named Lucius Livius Andronicus during the tumult and uncertainty in the later years of the Second Punic War.

The long career of Lucius Livius Andronicus is a prism through which we can isolate and track many of the social and economic changes in Rome over the course of the third century BCE. The young Andronicus was born free. He was perhaps enslaved sometime after 272 BCE, when the Romans seized his hometown, an important port city in Italy's heel called Tarentum (modern Taranto).[7] This critical addition to Rome's expanding Italic power came three years after the conclusion of a war during which the Tarentines had invited Pyrrhus, the king of the Greek kingdom of Epirus, to intercede on their behalf. This had resulted in the exhausting Pyrrhic War (281–275 BCE), ultimately won by Rome. In addition to Tarentum's well-known intellectual capital, stemming from its connection to Pythagoras, the city was famed for the production of expensive purple dye, pottery, wine, textiles, salt, and shellfish. Following its subjugation, its valuable double lagoon port system became a boon to Roman commerce.[8] As Andronicus's praenomen, Livius, indicates, he was enslaved but then at some point manumitted by his enslaver. This was likely the consul Marcus Livius Salinator. Perhaps this was because he had earlier served as a professional teacher of Greek and Latin for the children of the family.[9] The enslavement and eventual manumission of many Greek teachers who educated Roman students would become a common practice in the Republic.

At this time, transformations in other areas of Roman popular entertainment led to shifts in labor demands. Romans decided to use predominantly enslaved workers to fulfill the clamor for the new gladiatorial contests in particular. Although Romans had likely encountered them earlier, in Etruria, it was not until 264 BCE that gladiatorial contests came to Rome. In that year, Marcus and Decimus Junius Brutus, brothers from the famed Junian clan that had allegedly helped to found the Republic, brought three pairs of gladiators to perform for the funeral of their father. Valerius Maximus states that the exhibition was held in the Forum Boarium (the cattle market at Rome), while others locate it at the tomb itself.[10] The much later, fourth-century CE source Ausonius notes that these were Thracian gladiators. This gladiatorial type, the Thraex, equipped with high shin protectors called greaves, a small shield, and a short, curved sword, was a common type.[11] Gladiatorial types often assumed ethnic stereotypes and had distinct features that people could recognize.

It is likely, although not certain, that these first Roman gladiators were either enslaved prisoners of war or enslaved persons purchased specifically for funeral displays. This was a practice that would only grow in popularity in the coming years. Alongside these gladiatorial fights, spectacles began to be staged featuring persons fighting exotic beasts. These bouts represented and visualized Rome's expanding empire for the people of the city. For his triumphal games in 252 BCE, Lucius Caecilius Metellus arranged a battle in the Circus between a collective of *operarii* (workmen) of ambiguous status and either 140 or 142 elephants imported from Sicily.[12] Rome increasingly relied on enslaved labor in its gladiatorial matches and beast fights (called *venationes*), the latter of which took off after 186 BCE. Eventually, owners of entertainment troupes began to organize these fighters into compulsory groups called *familiae*. Although these families of enslaved gladiators and beast fighters were created from above, as we will see, it appears that many within them created close bonds that generated solidarity and—just maybe—allowed for quicker activation of gladiator rebellions in the late Republic.

Entertainment and Labor during the First and Second Punic Wars

The year 264 BCE was remembered as pivotal for Rome's expanding empire. The treaties with Carthage ultimately did not prevent the Punic sea power and Rome from coming to blows. In the First Punic War (264–241 BCE), Rome faced the Carthaginian Empire and its mix of mercenary and conscripted troops for the first time, predominantly on and around the island of Sicily. And Rome was victorious. Historians in antiquity pinpointed this moment as a transitional one for Rome. Picking up where the Sicilian historian Timaeus had left off, a Greek historian named Polybius commenced his own histories of Rome at this date. Polybius had experienced Rome's expansion as one of the thousand Achaean military hostages brought to Rome after the defeat of the Macedonian king Perseus in 168 BCE. As such, Polybius knew firsthand the waves made by Rome in the Mediterranean, and wanted to explain how it had come to gain such supremacy there.

During the First Punic War, Rome's armed forces metamorphosed and enlarged in order to take on its new foe. Rome's naval fleet went from a small number of ships used to fend off pirates or to transport delegations to a much more intimidating naval presence. After raids in 261 BCE, the Roman consuls of 260 famously ordered one hundred quinqueremes (ships with five banks of oars) and twenty triremes (ships with three banks of oars) to be built in just sixty days.[13] But a key outcome of the First Punic War was not only more ships, but also more land, taxes, and prisoners. Rome annexed its first province, Sicily, and would eventually establish a magistrate called a praetor as its head. At this time, a province was more a magisterial assignment than a geographic place. Roman ships also increasingly imported grain from the island of Sicily. In the years following the First Punic War, the island began to pay taxes in grain (that is, in kind) that could help feed Rome's army as well as its citizens. This was done by tapping into a preexisting "agricultural tithe" system used by Carthage, particularly for the system implemented early on by the city of Syracuse.[14] First Sicily and then the province of Sardinia-Corsica, starting from around 238 BCE, would pay import taxes in grain. Bread continued to be a primary state concern, as it had been for centuries.

Following the First Punic War, Rome also further evolved its own dramatic and literary cultures. In 240 BCE, Livius Andronicus put on Rome's first dramatic, narrative work in Latin for the games called the *ludi Romani*. This was just one of many written pieces we are told he composed. Andronicus also created a Latin translation of the *Odyssey*, in which he gave Odysseus a name that would be used for centuries to come: Ulysses. The incorporation of ritual games, new literary works, and performances into the Roman ritual calendar increased during the Second Punic War against Hannibal, Hasdrubal, and the Carthaginian army. Confronted by external chaos, Rome used the ritual calendar to create games and festivals to propitiate the divine with increasing frequency. This intensifying festival calendar also required more labor organization. The magistrates known as curule aediles took over the presentation of the theatrical *ludi scaenici* in 214 BCE, and new games called the *ludi Apollinares* were vowed to Apollo in order to invite his goodwill during the Second Punic War. In 212 BCE, four years after the devastating Battle of Cannae, these important games were overseen by the urban praetor.[15]

Organizing games and ritual was not just the responsibility of curule aediles and urban praetors from above. If we look to the level of the *vici* (neighborhoods) of Rome, it is likely around this time that freedman magistrates called *vicomagistri* increasingly began to supervise their neighborhoods and their neighborhood shrines, underscoring the growing importance of identity and organization at the level of the urban neighborhood unit. People, and even whole occupational categories, were increasingly tied to these neighborhoods. The *vicomagistri* officially oversaw the preparations for the winter crossroads festival called the Compitalia. This annual celebration honored the very streets and intersections of the city. These magistrates could also be called upon by the state to arrange for sacrifices at the many local shrines during times of crisis, or to use the socio-geographic unit of the neighborhood for handing out subsidized grain to people.[16] Over time, the social unit of the urban neighborhood came to function as a way not only to organize, but also to mobilize, Rome's populace.

A final result of the Second Punic War was that it brought changes to the status of Rome's artisan labor force. The use of enslaved labor from abroad became more pronounced at this time of expansion and imperialism. Polybius and Livy note that two thousand artisans from New Carthage, in what is now modern Spain, were sent to Rome to work as *servi publici* (state-owned enslaved persons) within what would be called the *familia publica* (publicly owned slave units). They were forced to work for the city, with an incentive of eventual manumission.[17] But even after manumission, these freedmen remained tied to the state *familia publica* and often took the name of the town as part of their own names.[18]

Manumission continued to be a coercive tool used by enslavers and the Roman state in the Second Punic War. In 214 BCE, eight thousand enslaved men were manumitted and given citizenship in exchange for their service in the Roman army, while that same year, elites were required to supply enslaved men to row in Rome's naval fleet.[19] Likewise, Carthage was also a society dependent on chattel slavery and debt bondage. During the Second Punic War, it too drew on enslaved labor, purchasing five thousand enslaved men to row in the galleys of its naval ships.[20] The use of enslaved labor in the Second Punic War is often overlooked in favor of valorizing the tactics of Roman generals such as Scipio Africanus, because it was indeed rare to enroll enslaved persons into the Roman military. Regardless, their largely invisible labor was a significant contributor to Rome's ability to win their second confrontation with the formidable Carthaginians.

Following the war against Hannibal, a number of state hostages began to be taken out of the city of Rome, where they were often held as political prisoners, and embedded in Latin colonies or Italian cities, as assigned by the Roman Senate.[21] These political prisoners were accompanied by large retinues of predominantly African enslaved persons to attend them. In 198 BCE, there was an insurrection in the town of Setia, forty miles south of Rome, by not only the hostages and their enslaved retinues, but also additional Punic prisoners of war.[22] The hostages sent out enslaved men to seek support from other enslaved persons in the nearby Italic towns of Norba and Cerceii. The revolt seized Setia but could not expand its reach, because two enslaved persons arrived in Rome as informers to tell the praetor about the conspiracy; he then gathered an emergency group of soldiers, headed to Setia, and arrested the leaders, while also punishing thousands more.

When word reached the praetor that a similar revolt was being planned for the nearby city of Praeneste, five hundred men connected to the conspiracy were executed. Fears inspired by the influx of new enslaved persons—many of them with strong ethnic and linguistic ties to each other—spread to Rome. Night watches were instituted in the neighborhoods of the city, along with orders to keep hostages under house arrest. This denied the hostages access to assembly in public places. Prisoners of war were chained up in city prisons and watched closely. Enslaved persons of the same cultural background could be eyed with suspicion within the household. In the first century BCE, the agronomic writer Marcus Terentius Varro would even warn that grouping together enslaved persons of the same background could lead to "domestic quarrels" and problems controlling them.[23] Fear and suspicion of enslaved persons meant that their actions, their gatherings, and their lives were often under surveillance by enslavers, even in a domestic setting.

The Status and Organization of Enslaved Persons in Italy in the Middle Republic

Slavery was a deplorable part of Roman society from its very beginnings. But there were acts of resistance against this system. Understanding not only its growth and impact, but also how it was organized, can provide some insight into how involuntary associations functioned from above and how later rebellions of enslaved peoples may have relied in part on this internal structure to organize defiance. In the decades after the Second Punic War, Rome classified large swaths of the population as property, and thus as commodities to be bought, sold, counted, and organized. In contrast to the modern democratic notion of equality before the law, Roman legal and judicial systems favored people with higher status. Legal penalties and punishments were often meted out based on a person's civic status, gender, and even reputation.[24]

After around 286 BCE, enslaved persons were chattel governed by a property law called the *lex Aquilia*. In Roman legal thinking, the murder of an enslaved person brought injury to the property of another, and thus was a civil rather than criminal matter. Alternatively, killing a free man was classified as the criminal act of either murder or homicide committed through negligence.[25] As with the public enslaved persons often used for the upkeep of the city's infrastructure and in many other urban positions, enslaved persons in households and on farms were also placed into involuntary groups of *familiae*. Those working in an urban or domestic space were referred to as the *familia urbana*. Families engaged in agricultural or pastoral labor, referred to as a *familia rustica*, were often herdsmen and agricultural workers.[26]

The legal status of those born into slavery followed the status of the mother. We should not take the influence of this legal decision lightly. For instance, in early America, the Roman approach to dealing with the offspring of citizen men and enslaved women would have a huge impact on the southern colonies. In 1662, the Virginia assembly stated it was following the "wisdom of the ancients" by declaring that children inherited the status of their mother. As historian of the American South Catherine Clinton has noted, Virginians and many other southerners "invoked Roman custom to protect property interests" and, in the process, also increased the number of enslaved persons born directly into the household.[27] Romans called a person born into slavery a *verna*. It was common for *domini* (male enslavers) to sexually assault and rape their own enslaved persons, whether male or female. A *domina* (female enslaver) could also force enslaved persons to perform or submit to sexual acts. Whereas Roman citizens' bodies were seen as protected, enslaved bodies were vulnerable and largely unprotected from abuse. Roman law enshrined and protected this attitude. The later social legislation of the emperor Augustus decreed that fathers could freely kill a daughter and adulterer if they were caught in the act. Meanwhile, their husbands could only kill the adulterer if the person was dishonorable, an enslaved person, or a prostitute.[28] Enslaved persons navigated different expectations and consequences than Roman citizens, and their bodies were not treated as their own.

Occupational Associations in Italy in the Middle Republic

Associations often form in reaction to economic or social demands—or both. People tend to band together to address a shared need or common identity. We saw this in theatrical entertainments with the voluntary creation of *technitai* for staffing theatrical performances. Likewise, Romans would do much the same with the formation of involuntary gladiatorial *familiae* to fight in the escalating number of annual games. Associations were also formed in order to address new culinary tastes, elite desires, and commercial demands.

Like today, certain places throughout the Mediterranean world were known for specific foods and beverages. Just north of Rome lay the previously Etruscan city of Falerii, famous for its tasty sausages. The earliest Latin inscription for an occupational association was found on the capitol here, on a little bronze plaque once attached to a votive offering and dedicated to the Capitoline Triad of Juno, Jupiter, and Minerva.[29] The second-century BCE dedication was commissioned by an association that had been sent to Sardinia. This association of cooks boasted—as ancient cooks often did—of their ability to facilitate good living and entertainment during festivals, through their ties to the fire bestowed upon humankind by the god Vulcan. Dedicatory inscriptions offered a chance to show gratitude to the divine, but make no mistake: they also functioned as a medium for bragging about the status of people or their association.

In the Roman world, as in the Greek one, on special festival days, for dinner parties, or for a sacrifice, skilled cooks could be hired at the marketplace and the Roman Forum.[30] In Rome, the first indoor market for the selling of meat and other foodstuffs such as vegetables existed by 192 BCE, if not earlier.[31] This market was located at first in the northwestern portion of the Forum Boarium. As was typical across the Mediterranean, when people bought foodstuffs, they could also hire a cook to prepare them. Later inscriptions of the Roman imperial period note the existence of associations of cooks in Rome, often called a *corpus* or *collegium cocorum,* some of which had their own scribes and even treasurers.[32] It is impossible to say whether the second-century BCE cooks of Falerii functioned like a modern union, but it is highly probable that as a collective, they were better able to set wages for hire and to establish themselves as an association that was directly consulted and hired for various festivals. At Rome and at the city of Praeneste, twenty-three miles to the southeast, other associations increasingly began to note their occupations, with a growing sense of pride in inscriptions, alongside their religious ties to certain gods. But not all Roman elites took kindly to the proliferation of new groups and their introduction of new and possibly disruptive deities.

Growing Xenophobia and Anxiety over Private Associations at Rome

After defeating Macedon in the Second Macedonian War in 197 BCE, the Romans infamously and rather falsely declared the Greeks "free" at the convening of the Isthmian Games the following year. The Greeks were in fact anything but liberated. The next century and a half would see Rome expanding aggressively into Macedon, mainland Greece, and Asia Minor through a mix of military campaigns and, as in the case of Pergamum, bequeathment to Rome. Along with the wealth that came with expansion into the eastern Mediterranean also came elite anxiety over safeguarding the ways of the Roman ancestors. There was suspicion of both the spread of foreign luxury in the city and of private cults that might undermine the Republic and interfere with its functioning.

This suspicion is evident from later literary sources, but also in the legislation of the time. From the Second Punic War into the second century BCE, Roman laws limiting luxury, reported by writers such as Aulus Gellius and Macrobius, appear to have been prevalent but rather impotent. The passing of these laws does, however, signal some Romans' displeasure with the changes in Roman society in terms of food, textiles, furniture, customs, and religion.[33] The hostile rhetoric aimed at foreign migrants and the palpable anxiety of many traditional elites about the extravagance of exotic goods and services coincided with the growth of collectives of tradespeople coming into the city of Rome and Italy at the time. According to Livy, in 187 BCE, the first professional enslaved cooks arrived in Rome after Gnaeus Manlius Vulso won victories in the East in Asia Minor. The Romans had previously regarded these individuals as menial laborers. With the rise in importance of the Roman banquet at this time, cooking went from being denigrated as low-status work to being reclassified as an *ars*—a valued skill that was part of a more respected profession.[34]

New associations meeting in the city of Rome were on the rise at this time too. We know of only a few who were recognized by the state formally and recorded in historical accounts. One of them was a result of Andronicus's literary services to Rome during the Second Punic War. In gratitude to him, an association of scribes, actors, and poets was allowed a special dispensation to have a state-sanctioned meeting place in the temple of the Roman goddess Minerva, starting around 207 or 206 BCE. They had a Latin name and a Roman goddess as their patron deity, rather than being labeled the *technitai* of Dionysus, as they were in the East. This was an attempt to Romanize this well-known union. As Erich Gruen has argued, their Dionysiac heritage was at this time shed in favor of a connection to Minerva "not because they required protection, but because the act signified the appropriation of Hellenic traditions for Roman national purposes."[35] After all, religious piety was for the good of the state.

Romans had embraced some foreign cults in the previous century, but with caveats and hesitation. The Great Mother Cybele had been imported, along with her priests, from Phrygia in Asia Minor. This translation occurred during the Second Punic War against Hannibal around 205 to 204 BCE. The prophetic Sibylline Books had dictated that this action would happen at a time of crisis, and it was at first housed in the Temple of Victory on the Palatine Hill. But even then, her cult was tightly regulated from above. Cybele and her priests, the *galli*, were in many ways a necessary but highly contained foreign pathogen in the city. By law, Cybele's priests were not Roman citizens, were confined to their temple precinct, and could not convert Romans.[36] In 191 BCE, Cybele's newly dedicated space was given a Latin title, the Temple of Magna Mater on the Palatine, rather than being called the Temple of Cybele. All of these changes in nomenclature and the civic limits placed on religious groups reveal some degree of unease with foreigners forming their own religious associations following the Second Punic War.

Elite Roman beliefs in the corrosive nature of foreign excess, residual fears of internal sedition from war, and a growing suspicion of burgeoning private associations at this time allow us to contextualize the Roman reaction to a new foreign group: the cult of Bacchus. In prior decades, the worship of Bacchus had spread north, from southern Italy to Rome. Livy says that a Greek priest brought the orgiastic Bacchic rituals to Italy, and that these included ever-suspicious nocturnal rites. These rites were inflamed by nighttime indulgence in wine and feasts, which broke down Roman gender norms and ideas of modesty among the participants. Consequently, in 186 BCE, the consuls turned their attention to the disturbances caused by this internal *coniuratio* (conspiracy). Livy makes wild accusations of murders, poisonings, false wills, and other criminal behavior all coming from the same, as he terms it, *officina* (workshop).[37]

In reaction, the Senate drew up anti-assembly legislation dubbed the *senatus consultum de Bacchanalibus*—the senatorial decree regarding the Bacchanalia— and promulgated it throughout the city, its Latin colonies, and its Italian allies (called *socii*) in the Italian peninsula.[38] The first step the law took was targeting physical assembly places by outlawing any meeting space for the worship of Bacchus, such as a temple, house, or clubhouse. An additional result was the banning of the group's nocturnal banquets, filled with wine and loose morals. Appeals went to the praetor, who then judged them with the aid of at least one hundred senators. Next, the law attacked the leadership hierarchies so common to all types of associations, by prohibiting men and women from serving as a head administrator or priest. It also abolished the group's use of a common treasury, internal oaths, and the coming together of five or more people for the rites. In his assessment of the Roman state's reaction, Jean-Marie Pailler remarked: "The Bacchic movement was reproached mainly for assuming *de facto* for itself an overall autonomy regarding the *res publica*, as if it aimed to function like a 'state within the state.'"[39] As Aristotle had also advised, Greek and Roman elites preferred groups that functioned to support the state and its laws, rather than ones perceived as giving individuals an alternative to it.

The Growth of Occupational and Business Associations Outside of Rome

While Rome grappled with foreign groups and new religious rites in the city, Roman troops won the Third Macedonian War (171–168 BCE) following the Battle of Pydna in 168 BCE. And while suspicion of new cultic rites might have been on the rise in the city of Rome, elsewhere, groups of opportunistic merchants and businessmen were themselves increasingly using the structure and benefits of flourishing collectives to their advantage for trade. Religious worship was a common feature for each of these new collectives, but underneath this pious veneer, many of them also profited in business ventures connected to Roman imperialism. An illustrative example of this can be found on the island of Delos.

In 167 BCE, Aemilius Paullus and his army sacked seventy cities in the Greek region of Epirus and took 150,000 captives.[40] In the same year, Rome made the Aegean island of Delos a tax-free port, albeit under Athens's oversight. Although some Italian merchants had lived on Delos in the century prior, Rome's removal of taxes opened the island up to an escalation in Italian, Roman, Syrian, Tyrian, and other merchants and tradespeople forming their own associations to facilitate commercial networks and trade with Asia Minor to the east and Rome to the west.[41] Unlike the collectives of Hellenistic entertainers who had banded together to fight for fair wages and negotiate contracts, these were less akin to labor unions formed from below and more analogous to small business associations today.

On Delos and elsewhere, these merchant associations often had overlapping ethnic and commercial interests, as well as a focus on a patron or tutelary deity, like most associations in antiquity had. For merchants and businesspeople, this often meant worshipping the god Poseidon (Neptune to the Romans), Hercules, Mercury, or Apollo. The Tyrian merchant association on the island chose to worship Hercules-Melqart, the patron deity of Tyre.[42] Similarly, the association of merchants at Rome had been attendant to Mercury's temple on the Aventine since the fifth century BCE. And in 112/111 BCE, the freedman magistrates of the merchant association of Capua are first noted by an inscription. Only a few years later, they are being referred to as the Masters of Mercury. Merchants and commercial agents not only worshipped the gods through their associations; such merchant associations also spread religious worship elsewhere as they traveled along commercial roads and waterways.[43]

In terms of meeting places, many of the Delian associations used clubhouses built specifically for meetings and banquets. Others simply met in a sanctuary at a shrine or altar, or congregated within a space at a marketplace such as the agora. These associations courted wealthy patrons who could endow them with money, status, and connections. The best known is the Delian *koinon* (association) of the *Poseidoniastai* (worshippers of Poseidon), who originally hailed from the Syrian city of Berytus (modern Beirut, Lebanon). These Syrian businesspeople were a group of merchants, shipowners, and warehouse-keepers who, in 153/152 or 149/148 BCE, honored their patron, the Roman banker Marcus Minatius.[44] Having a wealthy banker as a patron might have gotten them better loan rates with low or no interest. In return, they honored him as one was supposed to in antiquity: with statues and events held in his honor.

What types of goods did these Delian merchants trade in? Italian associations of wine and olive oil merchants living on Delos proliferated, but so did human trafficking; the strategically located island was a premier site for the auction of enslaved persons.[45] During the reign of Augustus, the geographer and historian Strabo noted that Delos could handle the selling of ten thousand enslaved persons per day, most likely in spaces such as the agora of the Italians.[46] Cilician pirates often captured and brought enslaved Syrians and other peoples from the region to the island to be bought and sold at auction. The Delian population who lived and worked there was itself a mix of ethnic backgrounds and statuses, possessing memberships in various groups. A notable majority of the agents working on the island (persons often used as proxies for their patrons and enslavers in commercial transactions) who identified as *Romaioi* (Romans) were in fact either enslaved men or freedmen of Greek and Syro-Phoenician origins.[47] The Delian economy and its success were heavily dependent on both slavery and the merchant associations that facilitated the buying, selling, and transport of human bodies across the Mediterranean.

Familiae, Resistance, and Organized Labor in the First and Second Servile Wars

Roman imperialism, rapid expansion, and the selling of captives were the engines behind the increasing dependence on slavery in Italy. Between 297 and 167 BCE, Rome reportedly enslaved 672,000 to 731,000 war captives.[48] Another 55,000 were taken from Carthage after its destruction in 146 BCE following the Third Punic War (149–146 BCE), and an untold number were enslaved (and some slaughtered) during Rome's sacking of the Greek city of Corinth that same year.[49] These enslaved persons were increasingly reassigned to a variety of occupations and positions while being sold and redistributed throughout the Roman Mediterranean. In Italy, they were particularly used for work in agriculture. On the island of Sicily, grueling agricultural labor on large estates and pastoral work as shepherds and herders lay ahead for many captives who had formerly been soldiers.

This influx of enslaved persons and their harsh treatment resulted in three large-scale revolts by enslaved peoples during the period from 135 to 71 BCE. Today, these are known as the First Servile War (135–132 BCE), the Second Servile War (104–100 BCE), and the Third Servile War (73–71 BCE). The first two took place primarily on Sicily, and the third on the Italian peninsula. Scholars have long recognized that the massive number of enslaved persons coming into Italy during the first and second centuries BCE was a major catalyst for these episodes of resistance to the Roman state. But, as we will now briefly explore, preexisting labor organization, leadership, and collective action were instrumental to these uprisings as well. The speed and the success of these rebellions were, I suggest, in part due to an early reliance on and deployment of the social unit of the gladiatorial *familia* and its underlying corporative structure. This is particularly true for the Third Servile War (also called the Spartacan War). The enslaved *familia* was a basic cohort for cohesion, day-to-day organization, and—when the time came—permitted a coordinated action against its oppressors.

In 135 BCE, the first of the three Servile Wars commenced. A later summary of Diodorus Siculus tells us that the war was due to both the huge influx of enslaved persons and their harsh treatment by wealthy equestrian landowners. Their bodies were habitually marked and branded by their enslavers, and they were given only minimal amounts of food and clothing on which to subsist. In response, these enslaved peoples organized themselves into what Diodorus dubbed miniature armies of brigands dispersed across the island, each working as bands.[50] These enslaved shepherd-soldiers were not acting as inept mobs; they developed some sense of cohesion and established networks for communication both prior to and during the war. And it is telling that the epicenter of the nascent uprising was at the level of the household.

The start of the rebellion near Enna, in the central part of the island, was begun by the enslaved persons of a particularly brutal *dominus* named Demophilus and his wife. Likely acting as a *familia*, they chose as their leader a man originally from Apamea in Syria named Eunus, who belonged to another wealthy Roman. This group first rose up and killed Demophilus and his cruel wife (although sparing their daughter). Eunus then created a royal council that systematically armed six thousand to serve in his army. The bands of enslaved persons on the western coast chose a Cilician named Cleon as their leader. Each group took part in coordinated movements as separate but intentional units, as scholars such as Roberta Stewart have pointed out, before joining forces with Eunus at their head.[51] Ancient sources undercut Eunus's leadership by casting him as a charlatan cult leader who relied on religious devotion to inspire men to follow him through signs and miracles. He did fashion himself as a Hellenistic king in the mold of the Seleucids through his choice of name (Antiochus) and by minting coins. However, to dismiss him as merely a charismatic magician and pseudo-king disregards his organizational skills during the First Servile War and the rebellion's influence.

In Roman literature, writers cast the First Servile War's coordinated but unsustained success as a "contagion" and its rebels as a "mob" that had to be contained and then remedied.[52] Not all Romans reacted positively to those who attempted to cure the situation by addressing its root causes rather than simply punishing the rebels. For instance, at Rome in 133 BCE, the tribune Tiberius Gracchus recognized the dangers of the buildup of enslaved persons on large Roman estates and attempted a reform that would redistribute public lands called the *ager publicus,* which had been encroached on and taken over by expanding, large farms akin to plantations. What began with the swing of a wooden chair leg ended with Gracchus and many of his supporters abruptly being assassinated in the city of Rome, and many of their bodies cast into the Tiber. Furthermore, literary accounts calling the First Servile War a "contagion" downplay the fundamental structural components and evident martial coordination we glimpse at in the sources. From the basic social unit of a single Sicilian estate and its *familia,* the movement expanded and created its own internal hierarchy.

At the end of the First Servile War, Cleon died in battle, and Eunus was eventually imprisoned in the central Sicilian city of Morgantina, where he died from lice. But their actions inspired others, particularly the synchronization of the revolt. Uprisings of enslaved persons at Sinuessa, Minturnae, Rome, and the island of Delos similarly troubled the Romans. In 134 BCE, enslaved workers in the mines of Laurium in Attica revolted against their overseers as well. The systematic gains made by Eunus's troops appear to have motivated others to undertake collective action and to resist their enslavement—a sentiment that posed a risk to the stability of the Roman state and its economy. This wave of imitative rebellions demonstrates that there was also a functioning network of communication bringing news of the events on Sicily to other enslaved persons throughout Italy and the Mediterranean.

Less than three decades later, from 104 to 100 BCE, a Second Servile War gripped Sicily. This occurred in a period of upheaval during which Gaius Marius served as consul for successive years, while Rome became distracted by a war to the north against the Teutones and the Cimbri. The Bithynian king Nicomedes rejected Marius's request for allies to supply troops to Rome, stating that the Bithynians were already being enslaved by the Roman tax farmers sent out to the provinces. In response, the Senate declared that

Roman allies should no longer be enslaved. In Sicily, the praetor began to carry out these manumissions widely, much to the dissatisfaction of the owners of the enslaved who were being freed by the decree. The elite enslavers begged him to stop turning their chattel into *liberti* (freedmen). When a number of Sicilian enslavers approached the praetor after over eight hundred of the enslaved had gained freedom in just a few days, the magistrate listened to their pleas. However, the abrupt and illegal halt to the manumissions in Sicily caused widespread discontent and plans for a new rebellion among those who had hoped for liberty. The enslaved persons within the *familiae* of two rich brothers then banded together and killed their masters at night.[53] In these origins of the Second Servile War, we can detect a focus on the conspiratorial elements that caused elite Romans such anxiety. We can also see the important role pre-organized labor played in these uprisings.

Much in the manner of a large association with its own set mechanisms for voting and electing officials, enslaved persons during the Servile Wars banded together and then replicated the structures of both the Greek polis and the Roman state, albeit on a smaller scale. Diodorus notes that, once the enslaved rebels in the First Servile War had reached six thousand strong, they formed a popular assembly that he calls an *ekklēsia*—a term for the popular assembly in a Greek *polis* and, in later epigraphic and literary sources of the early empire, a label also used for certain associations and collectives.[54] During the Second Servile War, the convened *ekklēsia* of enslaved persons voted in a king named Salvius who, in the style of Eunus prior, renamed himself Tryphon to evoke ties to the Seleucids and Hellenistic kingship. Later, about thirty thousand troops were trained and deployed, eventually joining with another rebelling group of enslaved persons led by a certain Athenion, whom Salvius Tryphon later detained and then released. Salvius Tryphon established his own capital, with a palace and advisors, at Triocala in western Sicily, where he adopted the visual signs of power accorded a consul: a Roman *toga praetexta* of the kind worn by senators, and lictors carrying fasces who preceded him.[55]

Not long thereafter, Tryphon died after a battle. But the war continued, causing famine in the city of Rome. This was a potent reminder of Rome's dependence on Sicily's wheat for its bread supply. Egypt was not yet a part of the Roman Empire, and thus the city greatly depended on the island. Rome directed its ire at both the enslaved persons who had risen up and those communities in the East that it saw as the root cause of the uprising. Aaron Beek has argued that Rome in part blamed those in the regions of Asia Minor for the sedition occurring in Sicily, and sent Marcus Antonius (grandfather of Marc Antony of the Second Triumvirate) on a Cilician campaign to punish them in 102 BCE.⁵⁶ The Sicilian revolt was finally put down by Gaius Aquilius, Marius's co-consul, in 101. Afterward, Aquilius tried to send one thousand war captives back to Rome to participate in the beast fights that were increasing in popularity in the city. In 104, an aedile had put on Rome's first beast fight with multiple lions, and fighting elephants would soon become all the rage in the early first century BCE. However, we are told that, to a man, the Sicilian prisoners committed suicide rather than perform as beast fighters for the pleasure of Roman crowds hungry for spectacles. The events at the end of the Second Servile War indicate that the growing appetite for organized games continued unabated into the first century BCE, causing an increase in the number of enslaved persons sold into familial troupes and trained within a flourishing new type of school: the gladiatorial training camp.

Collective Action and Mobilization under Spartacus

Roman accounts of the Third Servile War (73–71 BCE) reveal the convergence of socioeconomic trends in Roman society relating to slavery and entertainment with numerous elite fears connected to independent groups and sedition.⁵⁷ This context set the stage for the last of the three large slave wars. Roman male elites continued to experience anxiety about the possibility of nocturnal planning by seditious groups—whether foreign cults or enslaved *familiae*—that might undermine the established social order and the Roman state. At the same time, large groups of enslaved persons realized that, with proper organization and leadership, they could formulate, mobilize, and function as alternative states. And finally, an increasing number of enslaved gladiators were being placed in training schools embedded in the Roman countryside, eventually to be sold and deployed in games, in reaction to the growing demand for spectacles in Rome and elsewhere in Italy.

The "Spartacan War" checked all of these boxes. Almost two hundred years later, Plutarch's account of the war in his *Life of Crassus* notes that Spartacus was a nomadic Thracian. Thrace was the Balkan area west of the Black Sea, consisting of parts of what are now modern Bulgaria, Greece, and Turkey.

We are told that his prophetess wife came from the same background. She was said to be subject to a "Dionysiac frenzy"—a harbinger of foreign danger that certainly would have evoked the senatorial fears and actions taken against the Bacchanalia over a century before.[58] Spartacus was brought to a gladiator training camp at Capua, a town in Campania in southern Italy, on the Via Appia. Training schools for gladiators had been located there since at least the second century BCE. These troupes, owned by Roman elites rather than the aristocrats of Capua, often performed in the Capuan amphitheater just beyond the walls of the city and elsewhere in Campania and at Rome.[59] Spartacus's troupe, owned by Gnaeus Cornelius Lentulus Vatia, may have largely consisted of Thracians and Gauls.[60] As will be discussed in the next chapter, Caesar later had a gladiatorial troupe of about one thousand gladiators housed at Capua.[61] We are told that seventy-four to seventy-eight gladiators escaped from Vatia's school and, together, collected more enslaved persons from the surrounding *ergastula* (workshops). But what is it about the organization of the gladiatorial school that might have facilitated a labor uprising and escape like the one undertaken by Spartacus and his fellow gladiators?

There was a distinguishable hierarchy within ancient gladiatorial training camps. Troupes were run by a gladiatorial overseer stigmatized as legally infamous and thus legally restricted. He was called a *lanista*. These head trainers could also rent out the troupes of gladiators (called *familiae*) to any game organizer (called an *editor*) who wished to pay the price to put on games for the community. Gladiators trained and lived at gladiatorial training camps called *ludi*. In 2011, a gladiatorial training camp was found at Carnuntum in Pannonia (now in modern Austria), but there were many others in cities such as Rome, Pompeii, and, of course, Capua. As with other servile *familiae* and *collegia*, gladiators drew on them for a sense of identity and likely for camaraderie as well.

Gladiatorial troupes could be further subdivided into named *decuriae*.[62] There were also more informal subunits within the gladiatorial *familia*. In the Ludus Magnus at Rome, four to five gladiators roomed together in a cell, much as the smallest subunit in the Roman army, a *contubernium*, consisted of a tent of eight men. Roommates and tent-mates often formed close bonds. Although they were in compulsory groups, these troupes do seem to have been regarded with fondness by some of their members. A graffito from the Quadriporticus of the theater at Pompeii notes that the gladiatorial *familia* of

Fig. 5. Grave of the gladiator Saturninus from Asia Minor, n.d. Rijksmuseum van Oudheden, Leiden. (Photo: Carole Raddato.)

an elite man named Pomponius Faustinus had signed it as a group. Similarly, in the second or third century CE, in the city of Smyrna in modern Turkey, a *familia* of gladiators did something associations often did: it set up an epitaph for a deceased comrade, in this case, a Thraex-type gladiator named Satornilos or perhaps Saturninus.[63] Many gladiatorial troupes had internal magistrates and religious affiliations, just as voluntary associations did. Inscriptions indicate that even veterans of the troupe and those freed from slavery could continue to be associated with their gladiatorial *familiae* following manumission. Between 120 and 81 BCE, at Puteoli, not far from Cumae, a group of *retiarii* (a gladiatorial type who fought with spears and nets) made a dedication in stone to the god Mercury. The stone lists perhaps six magistrates, three of whom we know were freedmen.[64] However, such troupes present a paradox. As Garrett Fagan has explored in his analysis of the gladiatorial training camp, the gladiatorial troupe is akin to an oxymoron, since it was "a community of trained killers who lived and worked together, only to turn their skills on each other."[65] And yet, it was their close living quarters, organization into troupes, and coordinated training that likely made possible the successful beginnings of the Spartacan War.

The extant accounts of the outbreak cannot tell us much about whether a *familia* acted as one unit, but it does hint at the collective action of the whole *ludus*. In Plutarch's account, two hundred men originally planned to escape from the Capuan school, although less than half were able to. This is slightly smaller than the estimated size of the *ludus* as a whole in Pompeii, which likely held around 250 gladiators.[66] Plutarch describes them grabbing knives and skewers from the school kitchen and, once they had seceded from the school, choosing three leaders. In Appian's account, the rebel gladiators take refuge on Mount Vesuvius, where they organize themselves further, with Spartacus leading and fellow gladiators Oenomaus and Crixus acting as his seconds-in-command.[67]

As a former soldier, Spartacus knew that provisions and organization were crucial, but the suborganization and provisioning of the gladiatorial *ludus* likely informed his knowledge about many of the jobs he needed to create to arm and mobilize his troupes and conduct their early raids. We are told that Spartacus had weapons forged and supplies collected for distribution to his soldiers. He also stopped merchants from trading with them in gold and silver, only accepting iron and copper, because these metals could be melted down for weapons and armor.[68] In his reconstruction of the Spartacan War, ancient historian Barry Strauss remarks that "[Spartacus] modeled his army on the legions, at least in some respects," and that insurgents seized upon the trappings of Roman power: military vexillations, eagles, and the fasces.[69] Most analyses of Spartacus depict him as formulating a micro-version of the Roman army and state. Yet, more credit needs to be given to the preexisting and underlying group structures and organization of the *ludus* and how they shaped rebellions. It is this associative infrastructure that was also familiar to Spartacus, and that he was likely modeling as well. He may have drawn on the labor model organized within the *ludus* and then expanded on it to help organize his troops in the aftermath of their escape from the gladiatorial school.

In the end, after over two years of fighting throughout the Italian peninsula, Spartacus and his troops were defeated by the Roman army. In 71 BCE, the former gladiator took a spear to the thigh in battle against Crassus and his troops. His body was never recovered, but the Spartacan troops fled into the mountains and split into four distinct groups that continued to resist until only six thousand were left. The Romans took the remaining Spartacan soldiers prisoner and then crucified them, likely along the Appian Way. This mass crucifixion was used as a demonstrative punishment, intended to deter any enslaved persons or seditious groups that might be considering rebellion. It was a ruthless communication that Rome would not tolerate treason. The Spartacan War increased the already evident fear of internal sedition held by wealthy enslavers. It also convinced Romans that gladiators should be both legally and physically policed through a mixture of diminished social status and tighter guarding.

Spartacus and the Tumult of the Late Republic

In the Mediterranean during the middle and late Republic, popular desire for entertainment stimulated new types of labor collectives. Some were free and some were unfree. While a few, such as elite Greek performers, created associations for protections and collective bargaining that relied on the growing festival circuits connecting Mediterranean theaters, others, such as cooks, slave traders, and poets, formed their own associations to serve common religious, commercial, and social interests. And yet, as we have seen, involuntary associations also played a big part in the history of the middle and late Republic. The placement of gladiatorial training camps in Campania may have in part facilitated the outbreak of the Spartacan War and informed its early successes by providing a preexisting structure of leadership, friendship, and coordination. The Spartacan War and the two prior Servile Wars that occurred in the second and first centuries BCE did not occur in a vacuum.

And yet, as the Roman associative fabric expanded below, unease grew above, principally at the level of the elites within the Roman Senate who were themselves also wealthy landowners and enslavers. For their part, they turned to legislation as a means of extinguishing the threat of social upheaval. The restrictive senatorial decrees concerning the Bacchanalia in 186 BCE and their tight oversight of foreign cults point to Roman xenophobia at the level of the Senate, while also gesturing to the shifting demographics and interests among the populace below. Tensions between social orders and between enslavers and the enslaved were pronounced at this time. And this was not just among Bacchic cults in Rome or in Campanian gladiatorial training camps. Dominic Machado has argued that in the Roman military at this time, there was also a notable uptick in Roman soldiers pushing back against their commanders through mutiny. Machado shows that the rise in late Republican mutinies by soldiers should be seen within, as he terms it, "a broader context of dissent."[70] Whether it was due to the Italian allies fighting against Rome for citizenship and rights in the Social War (91–87 BCE), the three Servile Wars, or the Republic's increasingly tense political competitions between powerful men like Marius and Sulla, all led to the same outcome: Rome was a society in flux. However, this flux cannot simply be cast as a contagion spread by a disorganized mob of rebels. These rebellions often relied on organized labor from below practicing methods deployed by groups in Roman society since the early Republic.

As powerful men competed for control of the Republic in its last days, regular Romans increasingly turned inward, to the collective identities offered by various associations to fulfill certain religious, economic, and social desires not being met by the state. These groups could be used for trust in commercial deals; to provide burial assurances in a society without universal healthcare or life insurance; or to create their own demimonde through regular communal events, such as dining parties, worship, and social interaction among members. As we will see in Chapter Three, during the last days of the Roman Republic, these new associations would also become key players in Roman politics—as both a source of fear and a font of opportunity for politicians looking to acquire manpower and protection.

Unease with *collegia* among Roman senators would only be reinforced by their political mobilization for violent ends in the mid- to late first century BCE, during the Catilinarian conspiracy of 63 BCE. It would then reemerge with the ascent of a man who would fully realize the clout that came from marshaling these groups as a personal militia: Publius Clodius Pulcher. Under Clodius's patronage, both Roman occupational associations and gladiatorial troupes would soon play a crucial role in the battle for control of the Republic being waged between competing political factions. As a result, the Roman Senate and its consuls would become ever more suspicious of the meeting of associations in inns and bars across the city. Many would question whether their existence was warranted at all.

3
Freedom of Assembly during the Fall of the Republic

IN EARLY JANUARY OF 58 BCE, a newly elected tribune of the plebs named Publius Clodius Pulcher closed the sundry shops and workshops of the city of Rome.[1] With commerce and production paused, he could rally together an impromptu crowd in the Roman Forum at a speaking podium known as the Aurelian tribunal. The crowd was a mix of shopkeepers, enslaved persons, freedmen, and many other attendees, who gathered to hear the political promises being made by the notorious middle-aged magistrate, who courted the populace rather than the established elites in Roman politics.[2] Although new to the tribunate, Clodius was well known for his rebellious actions. Just a decade previously, during an invasion of Armenia, he had allegedly encouraged Roman troops under the command of his brother-in-law, Lucullus, to mutiny.[3] Most recently, he had dressed as a woman to infiltrate the all-female religious celebration known as the Bona Dea festival, held in Rome at the house of Julius Caesar and his (now ex-) wife. Following a highly public trial for this offense, Clodius was ultimately let off the hook, likely aided by a tactic common in late Republican politics: bribery. During the trial, he had developed an animosity toward the orator and former consul Marcus Tullius Cicero, who gave evidence against Clodius. In addition to these earlier controversies, Clodius also had a new identity and lineage to tout: he was now a plebeian rather than a patrician.

Clodius was born to the patrician family called the Claudii, the youngest child of six. However, in 59 BCE, as a man in his mid-thirties, he was allowed to enroll as a plebeian.[4] He was adopted and then quickly released from patronage expectations to a plebeian named Publius Fonteius, in the process shedding his patrician heritage to become an alleged man of the people. This adoption made Clodius eligible to stand for election as a tribune and to work toward new legislation evocative of measures promoted earlier by populist tribunes known as the Gracchi. Of particular resonance was Gaius Gracchus's use of his tribunate in 123 BCE to pass a law that provided grain to the people for below-market value.[5] Cicero later remarked on this law in his defense of Publius Sestius in 56 BCE, two years after Clodius's tribunate. He said that the *boni* (good men)—otherwise known as the wealthy optimates— were hesitant to give out grain, lest the plebs be led "from industry to idleness."[6] Even today, this is still a conservative argument for eschewing social welfare programs.

Like the Gracchi, Clodius aimed his populist politics at the city's nonelites. That demographic had changed in its makeup in the decades since those revolutionary tribunes. Clodius chose to place more emphasis on the currently and formerly enslaved than the Gracchus brothers had. He specifically courted freedmen, enslaved persons, artisans, gladiators, and both the free and the unfree enrolled in Rome's occupational associations. Cicero claims that, speaking from the tribunal on that January day in 58 BCE, Clodius levied his supporters under the guise of dividing them into new *conlegia* (a variant spelling of "*collegia*"). These associations, which systematically enrolled their new members neighborhood by neighborhood, were being further split into subunits called decuries. It was with these newly reorganized bands of associations as his clients that Clodius is alleged to have armed his supporters and begun inciting violence across the city.[7]

At the time of Clodius's tribunate, Rome's various occupational associations and neighborhood clubs were already resentful of the Roman Senate and its self-serving laws and policies. In 64 BCE, the Senate used its legislative power to disband *collegia* that the senators viewed as being counter to the *res publica*—that is, adversarial to the Republic.[8] A few associations integral to the functioning of the state, such as those of the construction workers and the statue-makers, were allowed to continue. No ban ever completely removed all associations in existence. This underscores the necessity of certain associations to the Roman state. The ban of 64 BCE was apparently not upheld and enforced across the empire. Many *collegia* and other types of associations continued to prosper outside Italy, particularly in the East, despite the legislation.[9] The ban was perhaps most concerned with squelching civil discord in Rome and the Italian peninsula rather than across the rest of the empire. In addition to disbanding various associations, the prohibition addressed another common way in which regular people gathered: the games. The celebration of the games known as the *ludi Compitalicii* was also prohibited.[10] The commentator Asconius explained the link between these two popular institutions, remarking that the magistrates of *collegia* had taken to giving the Compitalia games, in the same way that the neighborhood superintendents once had.[11] Neighborhoods, associations, and collegial leadership were firmly linked. Associations and public games were also increasingly being cast by senators as the epicenter of social discord.

Into the late Republic, the Compitalia remained an important neighborhood festival held near the start of the year. Legend maintained that the celebration stretched back to Rome's sixth king, Servius Tullius. A brief but failed attempt had been made by a tribune of the plebs to revive the festival in 61 BCE, but this was stopped by one of the consuls. Nevertheless, this late December or January celebration remained important to the populace. After the raucous December festival for Saturn known as the Saturnalia, it started off the new year with revelry and involved the individual neighborhoods (called *vici*) of the city. It was led and celebrated chiefly by enslaved and freedpersons, groups of whom often oversaw the altar at the crossroads (the *compitum*) for each neighborhood. Collegial and neighborhood identities, which had never been mutually exclusive, further coalesced during the celebration. When Clodius took office in December, he seems to have permitted the immediate resumption of these games on the Kalends of January—January 1, 58 BCE—under the guidance of one of his clients, a scribe named Sextus Cloelius.[12] Only a few days later, on January 4, Clodius halted business and called together his supporters in the Forum in order to divide shopkeepers, freedmen, and enslaved persons into organized *collegia*.[13] He was no doubt riding a wave of popular emotion and gratitude in the days following the reinstated games. After almost six years, the ban had been repealed, and Clodius was the man responsible for reinstituting both the clubs and the neighborhood merriments.

Where did Clodius get the inspiration for his methods? A rather overlooked source is likely the Third Servile War. Although Spartacus had died in service to the rebellion, the models provided by his mobilization of gladiatorial troupes organized within the gladiatorial school, his call to collective action, and his populist tactics made a strong impression on the politicians of the late Republic. Many later co-opted the gladiatorial leader's methods for their own ends, until the Republic was no more. Judging from his incitement of mutiny and his courting of the currently and formerly enslaved, Clodius had carefully observed the events of the Third Servile War only a short time before. Although he is often cast as the dastardly visionary who first realized the intrinsic power of the *collegia*, he actually had historical inspiration. We see this perhaps most strongly in his use of gladiatorial troupes to intimidate his enemies and act as his own personal bodyguard.[14]

The use of gladiatorial troupes as instruments of political will was not altogether new. Gaius Julius Caesar had already used his aedileship in 65 BCE, with all its expensive games and sponsored entertainment for the populace, to acquire 320 pairs of gladiators for his own use.[15] Seeing Caesar's growing *familiae*, the Senate had quickly moved to pass a law forbidding such large troupes within the city of Rome, in the name of public order. In response to the senatorial limits placed on them in Rome, Caesar notably kept his *familiae* in Capua, where he visited them regularly. The specter of the dangers of the gladiatorial schools of Capua rose again when Lucius Sergius Catilina, known as Catiline, instigated a notorious conspiracy that was carried out in 63 to 62 BCE. In the midst of this sedition, it was ordered that the many *familiae* of gladiators still held at Capua's schools be redistributed to other municipalities, out of fear that they might join Catiline's supporters.[16] In the decades that followed, the apparition of the Spartacan rebellion was constantly reappearing, both in the decrees of the Senate and the actions of major political players. Although there may not have been another major Servile War during Rome's subsequent history, that does not mean that enslaved people did not play key roles in organized popular uprisings and the rejection of the state. In the late Republic, some resisted through their associations and, on occasion, through larger popular disturbances.

In addition to the continued anxiety surrounding the use and abuse of gladiatorial troupes, there was also the example provided by Spartacus's employment of enslaved persons as followers, which may have motivated future popular leaders to do the same. By extension, Clodius also appears to have looked to another growing demographic group in Rome for support: freedmen. Clodius looked back to the recent past for inspiration here, too. In the decades prior, the dictator Lucius Cornelius Sulla had strategically deployed manumission in order to build a large clientele of freedmen. From 82 until 81 BCE, Sulla proscribed over five hundred Roman citizens in retaliation for the actions of Marius and his followers. Proscription was a political tactic that stripped citizens of their legal and corporal protections and turned them into outlaws and enemies of the state. Their sons and grandsons could no longer become politicians and participate in elections, making it a means for halting political opposition by leading Roman families. Proscription was also a strategy for acquiring money and land, while also "making a desert and calling it peace."[17] The property of the proscribed—including their *familiae*, made up of enslaved persons and property—was seized by the Roman state.

Sulla saw in the proscriptions a plan for increasing the number of clients tied to him through bonds of patronage. The historian Appian notes that Sulla manumitted ten thousand enslaved persons from among the proscribed. It is likely that this manumission occurred after they had been made part of the *collegia* of public enslaved persons, the *servi publici*, who worked in groups to maintain the city's infrastructure. These newly manumitted freedmen then took Sulla's name, Cornelius, acquiring social ties to him and owing him legal allegiance as their patron.[18] There was often an ulterior motive for manumissions in the late Republic. Sulla became notorious for using freedmen as agents. Federico Santangelo has persuasively argued that Sulla was the first major politician to depend heavily on freedmen, particularly during his proscriptions.[19] There was also some sort of system of organization underlying the upheaval of Sulla's confiscations. Cicero later remarked that the wealthy often depended on relationships with *societates* (associations), enslaved persons, freedmen, and clients.[20]

These associations were not fully activated or exploited under Sulla. In 79 BCE, Sulla retired from the dictatorship, disbanded his legions and lictors, and exited Rome for a country life in the south, in Puteoli. There he wrote his memoirs in the company of actors and theater folk, aided in his writing by copious amounts of wine.[21] To his credit, Sulla did finish those memoirs before he died, even amidst all that alleged debauchery. He also penned his own epitaph, placed in the Campus Martius in Rome, in which he noted that no other man had done more good things for his friends or harm to his enemies.[22] The lesson of the former dictator was clear: keep your clients close and your enemies suppressed. This advice was heeded by later tribunes who also counted on the support of freedmen and enslaved persons.

During the Compitalia in 67 BCE, the tribune Gaius Manilius, allegedly reinforced by a gang of freedmen and enslaved persons, proposed a law that would allow freedmen to be redistributed to the tribe of their patron when voting in the Comitia Tributa (the tribal assembly).[23] Unless granted special exemption, freedmen were relegated to voting only in the four urban tribes. Consequently, their votes were limited and less potent. However, Manilius's law would have given them greater influence. Although ultimately stopped, Manilius and his cohort rioted and blockaded the capitol. Despite the defeat under Manilius's aegis, the supression of the growing freedman vote through assembly restrictions remained an issue—one that Clodius would later take up as part of his political agenda in 52 BCE. Defenders of the elite cause, men called the optimates, reacted with horror. Cicero claimed that passage of Clodius's laws giving equal suffrage to freedmen would result in the freeborn being "subject to their slaves."[24] Early Republican fears of plebeian power now shifted to an aristocratic panic over the increasing influence of freedmen and the enslaved.

There is much slander and invective laced in Cicero's rhetoric about enslaved persons and their "mobs." There is also a perceptible angst over those in power being subject to "the other." Brigades of enslaved and freedpersons were also named as a threat during the Catilinarian conspiracy. Catiline, who had counted himself as one of Sulla's allies, appears to have mimicked many of his patronage prototypes too. But when Catiline undertook his own conspiracy against the state, he looked not only to enslaved persons and the freedmen of his co-conspirators as his instruments, but also to broader yet overlapping networks of artisans. This was a group that included many freeborn persons, as well as freed and enslaved persons, in its ranks. The enslaved persons and freedmen in the *familiae* of Catiline's key allies, Gaius Cornelius Cethegus and the praetor Publius Cornelius Lentulus Sura, were mobilized and combined with the artisans, going street by street to achieve their ends.[25] In addition, we may be able to make inferences as to their core constituents and supporters from the meeting places of the conspirators. It was alleged that, under the cover of night on November 6, 63 BCE, Catiline had gone to the private house of one Marcus Porcius Laeca, in the scythe-makers' district.[26] We do not know exactly where this area of the city was, but the clustering of similar commercial shops and industrial workshops was common in the neighborhoods of many Roman cities across the Mediterranean. In a telling comparison, Cicero would later note that Clodius's creation of *collegia* at the Aurelian tribunal recalled the earlier "troops of Catiline."[27] Catiline's "troops" were also greatly shaped by preexisting involuntary and voluntary associative configurations that were more akin to *collegia* than to a standing army.

Courting associations was already an important part of political canvassing and winning elections. In the pamphlet on electioneering that he wrote in the mid-60s BCE, Quintus Tullius Cicero had already advised his older brother, Marcus Tullius Cicero, that it was important to cultivate the leading men of *collegia* and of the city's neighborhoods and wards during his campaign for the consulship of 63.[28] There was often overlap between the two groups, a trend illustrated by both the clustering together of artisans and of members of certain religious affiliations. In the late 60s BCE, growing numbers of enslaved and manumitted Jews were residing in Rome, many of whom lived across the Tiber after having been brought back by Pompey following the conclusion of his eastern campaigns in Syria and Palestine. Along with other conquered and enslaved peoples in a triumph often forced to wear labels as to their origins, they were paraded through the streets in Pompey's triumph of 61 BCE. This was a visual embodiment of conquest. These Jews formed synagogues, likely classified under Roman law as *collegia*, as will be discussed more in Chapter Five. The later Jewish author and visitor to Rome, Philo (c. 20 BCE—c. 50 CE), noted that many manumitted Jews lived in the neighborhood across the Tiber.[29] This was alongside the small population of Jewish Romans who had already been living there since around the middle of the second century BCE. At times, neighborhood alliances and associations intersected in important ways.

Associations and their freedmen were sleeping giants of late Republican Rome, even if they were not a majority. By the imperial period, freedpersons amounted to perhaps 7.5 to 8 percent of the city's population.[30] Although some lacked means, many were not impoverished. Within many associations, there was a spectrum of wealth and status among the members, who could range from equestrians all the way down to enslaved workers.[31] Although enslaved persons and women were not always the primary constituents of many of the elite *collegia,* ambiguities exist about membership demographics, as will be discussed in the next chapter. While membership and monthly fees would have prohibited some from entrance into certain prestigious *collegia,* it is by no means definite that all associations even had initiation fees. Many, such as the much later *collegium* of Diana and Antinous in the second century CE, had only modest ones. This association, which included enslaved and freedpersons as members, charged an entrance fee of 100 sesterces along with an amphora of a good wine, plus a monthly membership fee of five asses.[32] For comparison, a typical quarry worker at the Mons Claudianus in Egypt's eastern desert earned 47 sesterces per month in the same time period.[33]

Other surviving membership rules for associations indicate that the wealthier members could be bound by the rules of the association to help impoverished members. A Ptolemaic-era religious association at Tebtynis in Egypt fined members for not aiding a fellow member in need who was asking for money at the side of the road.[34] Membership costs, fees, and expectations depended on the type of association. Onno Van Nijf characterizes the *fabri*—the construction worker associations that peppered cities of the West and were allowed to remain even after the association ban in 64 CE—as "an elite group of Roman craftsmen—employers rather than employees."[35] But it seems some did get their hands dirty. In Chapter Five, we will discuss Pliny's request to Trajan for an association of *fabri* to act as a fire brigade. Today, we would classify many of these groups as business or professional associations, rather than as labor unions that served the interests of everyday workers. However, in antiquity, a variety of associative structures and members existed. And sometimes, associations consisted of a mixture of lower-level workers and their employers. It is nearly impossible to calculate the number of *collegia* members in total, or to discern each one's status with any certainty from the extant membership lists and inscriptions alone. The picture is too fragmented and the spectrum too broad to attempt any homogeneous characterization of all associations in Rome and elsewhere. But herein lies the strength of the underlying associative networks expanding throughout the Mediterranean at the time: associations were flexible socioeconomic and religious units for creating trust, mitigating risk, providing security, and fostering comradery.

Many freedmen of all economic levels belonged to associations, as both employers and employees. At Rome's port at Ostia, for instance, 40 percent of the people listed in the extant inscriptions recording *collegiati*—various members of associations—are freedmen.[36] These association members were what Paul Veyne, deliberately avoiding the anachronism of a middle class, dubbed the *plebs media:* workers with surplus money who did not necessarily live in luxury, but who were of middling means.[37] Membership in an association was a vital route to social mobility for freedpersons. Both within and then beyond their associations, association membership offered a path to belonging, especially for those marginalized by Roman law and society. Clodius's law allowing the reformulation of the *collegia* (referred to as the *lex Clodia de collegiis*) reopened a pivotal path for many, particularly for freedmen in Rome. As tribune, Clodius passed a number of other laws aimed at the populace as well, particularly one authorizing the distribution of grain to all free citizens. Dio reports that, following the passage of this law, a number of enslaved persons were manumitted expressly in order to capitalize on this allowance to the free population of the city, and thus taking the burden of feeding them off of patrons.[38]

Not long after his closing of the shops in January of 58 BCE, Clodius successfully forced his rival, Cicero, into exile. With Caesar away on campaign in Gaul and with Cicero gone, Clodius now saw himself as Pompey's direct political rival. In August of 58, an enslaved man from among Clodius's clients apparently dropped a dagger in the Temple of Castor, where the Senate was meant to gather. He had been tasked with assassinating Pompey, who, as a result, holed himself up in his house for many months. Despite Cicero's exile, his friends continued to support him at Rome, but Clodius used his own followers to stymie the orator's return. In January of 57, there was an attempt in the popular assembly to initiate a vote to bring Cicero back. Clodius used his followers and borrowed *familiae* of gladiators from both his brother and a current praetor, Appius Claudius Pulcher, in order to obstruct the meeting of the assembly and prevent the vote. Cicero again points out Clodius's deployment of enslaved people to occupy public spaces for a nocturnal attack.[39] This was a means of delegitimizing Clodius's support base and suggesting that they had been coerced or paid, rather than truly representing the will of the people. One of the tribunes for the year, Titus Annius Milo, pursued legal action against Clodius for his use of gladiatorial henchmen. But Milo failed to prosecute the violence successfully, even if the skirmish in the Forum had resulted in a serious assault on two tribunes and their supporters, with many dead. Cicero's brother had even hidden himself among the corpses. Instead of using the law, Milo then adopted Clodius's own methods: raising personal troupes of gladiatorial *familiae* to fight fire with fire.

Elite Roman men continued to use *familiae* of predominantly enslaved gladiators as militias, but we must also consider the use of actors and theatrical players, many of whom likely belonged to their own voluntary associations. The clashes, riots, and clamor of the Clodian years often occurred during times when games and theatrical shows were being held in the city. The theater marked a space for public gathering and popular discourse, as it had for centuries, but was particularly important in the years of the late Republic. In July of 57 BCE, possibly during the *ludi Apollinares,* Clodius assembled a crowd upset about the price of grain who terrorized the spectators in the theater.[40] However, use of the theater was not just a tactic of the populists. Even Cicero's return was sold to the people in part by the famous tragedian actor Claudius Aesopus. Cicero admits that Aesopus spoke to the people more persuasively through the lines of Accius's *Eurysaces* than he himself could have done to argue for his return. The orator conceded that the will of the people was most effectively voiced at *contiones* (public speeches like the ones Clodius regularly called), in the assembly, and during gladiatorial games.[41]

Many of the festival actors, like those in the Greek chorus, the musicians, and the various other *technitai* often used in sponsored games, were still organized into their own associations in Rome and elsewhere in the Mediterranean. Many, such as the *societas* of Greek singers (known from a Roman inscription dated to around 100 BCE), had freedman magistrates; a named *designator* (or *dissignator*) to arrange their contracts, wages, and performances; and specific burial sites set aside for their members.[42] The associative population of Rome was not limited to the shopkeepers and manual workers defamed by Cicero as part of Clodius's entourage. Labor unions of artists, particularly the ones hired to perform in the then-temporary theaters and amphitheaters of Rome, were also important political players who took partisan stances and favored certain politicians. Rome did not receive a permanent theater until 55 BCE, thanks to Pompey, nor a permanent amphitheater until 29 BCE, thanks to the Augustan general Titus Statilius Taurus. While there was much benefit in providing permanent spaces for theatrical performances and games in the city, there was also great reluctance to do so.

Despite Clodius's objections, Cicero's exile did not last long. In September of 57 BCE, the statesman came back to the city in what he viewed as a triumphant return. He soon addressed an immediate concern of the people: grain. Clodius's broadening of the *annona* had contributed to a grain shortage in the city, and there may have also been famine elsewhere, affecting the supply. The orator repaid Pompey for helping with his repatriation by supporting the triumvir's allocation as caretaker of the grain supply. But Clodius came up with a new plan. In the subsequent year, 56 BCE, Clodius became aedile and enlisted his henchman Cloelius, who had previously overseen the Compitalia for him, to lead his followers to the Temple of the Nymphs and burn it, likely in order to destroy the archive that held the list of persons given free grain.[43] The possible involvement of the *collegia* is obscured here by the sources' use of disparaging and vague language labeling those involved as gangs, bands, hired workmen, and thugs, rather than naming these groups as official associations per se.

In early 56 BCE, the Senate stepped in. A decree of the Senate dissolved political associations called *sodalitates* as well as their subgroups, *decuriae*. This was followed by a law passed by Crassus as consul in 55, the *lex Licinia de sodaliciis*. This law attempted to stem the practice of bribery during elections at Rome. Rather than banning all political clubs, the law likely made members who used these collectives to engage in bribery vulnerable to being prosecuted in a trial, which could result in exile.[44] Occupational *collegia* are not specifically cited here, but the targets and aims of the legislation are murky, and *collegia* too were often subdivided—as they were under Clodius—into *decuriae*. It appears that the core objective was to halt politicians from using certain outside groups, which had been formed solely as political clubs that then pressured the tribes to vote in a certain way.[45]

The streets both inside and outside Rome were dangerous for certain politicians in the years thereafter, as alliances were shifting or falling apart. The First Triumvirate, revived at Luca in 56, was reduced to only two members by the death of Crassus in the Battle of Carrhae (Harran, Turkey) against the Parthians in 53. Back at Rome, gladiatorial bodyguards had become more standardized. They continued to be employed by both the *populares*, like Clodius, and the *optimates*, who championed more traditional leadership, like Milo. In an infamous meeting of the two groups in early 52 BCE, Milo and his hefty retinue, including two well-known gladiators named Eudamus and Birria, ran into Clodius on the Appian Way.[46] The two groups met about twelve miles from Rome near the city of Bovillae and the Temple of Bona Dea. Milo's men far outnumbered Clodius's and, in the upheaval, Clodius was stabbed and then carried to a tavern, where Milo's men ultimately finished the job. His body was found by a senator and brought to Rome, where his widow stirred up his supporters, comprised of plebeians and enslaved persons. Clodius's body was conveyed to the Forum, where a crowd had gathered, and was spontaneously burned on a pyre in the Senate house. The flames then razed the Senate house to the ground. To bring order to the city in the aftermath, Pompey became sole consul and exiled Milo.

The fear-inducing specters of Spartacus, Catiline, and Clodius reappeared a final time when Julius Caesar crossed the Rubicon in early January of 49 BCE. Caesar was still in Gaul, but needed to be able to stand for the consulship of 49 in absentia to protect himself from prosecution. When he was blocked from doing this, Caesar eventually marched from Cisalpine Gaul into Italy, essentially declaring civil war by not disbanding his troops. Upon hearing this news, Pompey may have been reminded of the last days of the Spartacan War. After all, he had been the one to order the slaughter of the Spartacan survivors he encountered in northern Italy, upon his return from Spain in 71 BCE. Soon after the start of the civil war with Caesar, one of the consuls for 49, Pompey's ally, Lucius Cornelius Lentulus, then raced to Capua, called together Caesar's gladiators in the Forum, and offered them their freedom in exchange for serving in the resistance against Caesar.[47] To sweeten the deal, Lentulus also offered them horses. But such a lowly (one might say Clodian) move was disdained by his elite friends back at Rome.

Pompey decided to instead take Caesar's one thousand gladiators from the training camps of Capua and redistribute them to the servile *familiae* of top elites, two gladiators apiece, as Cicero informed his friend Atticus in a letter.[48] If Cicero is correct that these same gladiators were then redistributed by Pompey to elite families, this represents a return to the tactic of separating and redistributing *familiae* in order to smother rebellion and conspiracy.[49] Although the Capuan gladiators were stopped from joining battle, Pompey was unsuccessful in the larger war. He lost his struggle against Caesar in the months thereafter, eventually being murdered near Pelusium in Egypt after his loss at the Battle of Pharsalus in 48 BCE. Ever the Pompey supporter,

Lentulus was taken prisoner after that battle and later executed while imprisoned in Egypt. The Pompeians had never used those Capuan gladiators, but maybe they should have.

After Pharsalus, Julius Caesar's legal agenda in Italy after 48 BCE indicates that he too learned lessons from the preceding decades of Republican turmoil that had facilitated his own rise to power. Caesar sent eighty thousand Roman citizens to foreign colonies, particularly Carthage, Urso, and Corinth. Suetonius says this left the urban plebs "exhausted."[50] Ancient historian Evan Jewell has pointed out Caesar's use of colonization as "social engineering" that likely drained the urban freedmen and many impoverished freeborn from Rome, and sent them elsewhere.[51] This functioned as a kind of pressure release valve, one similar to Pompey's Capuan gladiator approach or even the Roman use of exile—except that in this case, freedmen were allowed important roles as municipal magistrates in these colonies. Caesar also promulgated a new and telling law: that the number of freeborn shepherds (as opposed to servile ones) working with livestock and herds should not fall below a third of the overall number.[52] In other words, Caesar capped the number of armed enslaved persons roaming and networking in the Italic countryside. Perhaps the lessons provided by the two Servile Wars, borne from Sicilian shepherds and servile *familiae*, entered his mind.

This memory, and Clodius's instrumentalization of the *collegia*, may have also influenced another of Caesar's decisions: a ban on all *collegia* except those deemed licit or of ancient origin.[53] The dates on this law are a bit unclear. It may be that Caesar's imposition of a prohibition on *collegia* followed an important valuation carried out by the dictator in 46 BCE. This was the first census of Rome to assess its population neighborhood by neighborhood, apartment block by apartment block. The results of the census lowered the number of people eligible for the grain dole from 320,000 to 150,000.[54] One wonders if there were additional motivations for this fine-grained census-taking in Rome's neighborhoods besides just the grain dole, namely, the closer examination of associative ties. In the colonies and municipalities, there also appear to have been halts put on associative behaviors. The charter for the Roman colony of Urso in modern Spain, drafted by Caesar in 47/46 BCE and later enacted by Marc Antony in 44, following Caesar's death, included a clause that stopped colonists from organizing "any assemblage or meeting or conspiracy in that colony."[55] This essentially meant revoking the *ius coeundi*—the Roman right of assembly—for associations.

Caesar tried to limit the power of additional known threats in other legal ways, particularly by placing limits on who could fill the local magistracies in Roman towns. A law called the *lex Julia Municipalis,* passed around that time, limited who could serve on local municipal councils. A bronze tablet from the southern Italian town of Heraclea—the so-called *Tabula Heracleensis* of 45 BCE, which bars gladiators, actors, sex workers, criers, organizers of games, funeral workers, and others of ill repute from entering the municipal council—likely preserves part of Caesar's municipal law. Ideas about Roman honor, and the socio-legal stigma of *infamia* (infamy) attached to those in the arena and on the stage who sold their bodies for profit, served as the public justification for these people's political exclusion from local town councils.[56] But the fear of bribery and social discord associated with many of these occupations may also have been a motivation. These professions' close ties to games, populist politicians, and the *collegia* of the late Republic may have hastened the imposition of legal limits on their political careers that then kept them out of power.

The legal agenda of Caesar in the years before his assassination on the Ides of March, 44 BCE, gestures toward a coordinated plan to disband associations, squelch popular pushback, and restrict the opportunities available to popular but historically lowly figures. This was accomplished by a man who, as aedile, had seen the power of games, grain handouts, and associations firsthand. His laws bolstered the freeborn in Italy, attempted to avert possible future slave rebellions in the countryside, and tamped down on the chances of *collegia* rising up again. Caesar's ban on associations was more widespread than any previous ones and likely affected numerous associations across the empire. These associations were now judged on two metrics in order to exist: whether they were ancient or of utility to the Republic. Regardless of the law, some associations in Asia Minor and elsewhere continued to meet. However, provincial governors and Roman administrators now had a key piece of legislation at the ready to use to disband disorderly groups and require their subservience to the state in order to survive. But not every association fit easily into these new legal boxes. Jewish collectives in the Mediterranean seem to have been placed in the category of *collegia,* but escaped the ban and were permitted to exist as *collegia licita* (lawful associations). Roman legal definitions for associative bodies were quite broad and elastic. And, as Josephus indicates over a century later, the Jews never forgot that they had been afforded a loophole in Caesar's restrictions in Rome and across the empire.[57]

Julius Caesar ushered in a new era of labor oversight, organization, and registration. Although we do not have an exact date for its promulgation, the *lex Julia de collegiis* banning associations became an instrument of "law and order" in the legal toolbox of Roman magistrates and their enforcers.[58] While Caesar tried to stem the rising tide of unruly involuntary and voluntary associations, he could not protect himself from the plots hatched by his senatorial colleagues. He was assassinated on the Ides of March, 44 BCE, near the Senate house in the complex of the theater of Pompey. It was a conspiracy planned from above by senatorial schemers, rather than from below by the much-feared artisans. Graffitied messages on the tribunal of the praetors had apparently urged on the assassins, particularly Brutus, to take care of Caesar. Appian relates that when Cassius questioned Brutus about these mysterious inscriptions, he asked: "Do you think it is artisans and shopkeepers who have written those clandestine messages on your tribunal? Or is it rather the noblest Romans?"[59] The shopkeepers and the manual laborers of Rome had been Clodius's constituency; however, the death of Caesar was a product of the senatorial elite rather than the long-vilified manual laborers of Rome.

During the civil war that followed Julius Caesar's death, there was a pause in the regulation of associations. A period of restructuring and closer oversight would later resume under Caesar's successor and adopted son, Octavian-Augustus, from 27 BCE on. This included a renewed ban on *collegia,* which should make us wonder whether the association-busting done under Caesar was altogether effective, or even obeyed, in the years after its passage. Inscriptions provide some insight into the continued citation of legal allowances. Sometime in the reign of Augustus, an association of musicians at Rome called the *collegium Symphoniacorum* noted that, according to the *lex Julia,* they had the Senate's permission to meet for the sake of putting on games.[60] And yet, the vast majority of *collegia* from the Augustan period onward either fail to mention this permission or else seem not to care much about it.

Citing permission to assemble and touting it visually on stone inscriptions appears to have become points of pride for some *collegia*. In reality, associations were most often tolerated in Rome and elsewhere in the empire until there was a reason to disband them, often in reaction to fears of violence, discord, or popular dissatisfaction, in particular cities. As Rome hurtled into the early empire of the first centuries CE, magistrates in cities from Pompeii to Alexandria dealt with threats to their governance by attempting to disband associations. Nevertheless, the desire and the will to gather, to mitigate economic and social risks, and to find community through common occupations, religious beliefs, and socioeconomic needs would continue in full force throughout the ports, cities, taverns, and workshops of the Roman Mediterranean.

4
Anxiety and Associations in the Early Roman Empire

DURING THE REIGN OF THE EMPEROR NERO in 59 CE, rioting broke out in the amphitheater of Pompeii.¹ During the games, inhabitants of Pompeii and the nearby town of Nuceria came to blows, threw rocks, and then seized daggers during the exhibition of gladiatorial matches put on by a Roman patron named Livineius Regulus. There was a strong local rivalry between the Pompeians and Nucerians.² The uprisings in the amphitheater that day ended in bloodshed and sanctions. Many of the maimed Nucerians were brought to Rome, including women and children, and the matter was laid before the emperor. After all, only two years prior, Nero had settled a number of Roman veterans in Nuceria. The emperor had close ties to the former soldiers placed in the colony there. But Nero delegated the matter to the Senate, which in turn tried to hand the issue over to the two consuls, who then gave it back to the Senate. Ultimately, Livineius and others who had incited the violence received the punishment of exile. More crucial and devastating to the Pompeians was that they were barred from holding gladiatorial displays for ten years, and all illicit *collegia* were disbanded.³

The ban on gladiators was likely lifted early. Beast hunts and athletic competitions continued regardless of the penalty, but Roman senatorial fear of private groups acting in a coordinated manner in times of discord or upheaval was again made evident. State paranoia over some types of assemblies does seem a consistent worry in periods of resistance. As ancient historian Brent Shaw has commented in his evaluation of rural markets in North

Fig. 6. Fresco from the house of Actius Anicetus, Pompeii, likely depicting the riot of 59 CE in the amphitheater of Pompeii. Museo Archeologico Nazionale, Naples. (Photo: Erich Lessing/Art Resource, NY.)

Africa, "The Roman state, as most other central states in antiquity, had an almost morbid fear of any unofficial assembly or association."[4] This elite fear was often only evident in times of disharmony or in provinces known for pushing back against Roman governance. The civic restrictions the Roman senators decided to impose on Pompeii for that day were dire, but they were not a novel political reaction to urban violence, as we have seen in previous chapters. Such penalties were likely familiar to those Romans who had read or heard about the final years of the Roman Republic and were akin to the laws imposed early in Augustus's rule.

Why had the Senate singled out the Pompeian *collegia*? Who was their target in such broad anti-association legislation? Some modern scholars think that the ban was directed in large part at the Pompeian *collegia* of *iuvenes* (youths)—groups of predominantly male young people who frequently had paramilitary matches in Roman cities throughout the western Mediterranean. In the East, comparable associations of youths already existed in the form of the ephebes and of the slightly older youths called *neoi*. During the imperial period that began with Augustus, youth associations became more prevalent in the towns of Italy, Africa, and the western Mediterranean, serving as an early introduction to martial training and combat. However, they became known for engaging in raucous or disruptive behavior at times. In a legal opinion included in Justinian's *Digest*, the Severan-era jurist Callistratus noted that the young people of certain turbulent cities were known to incite mobs.[5] If caught for this offense—and if they had never previously been punished—they were either to be whipped or forbidden from attending civic spectacles. But if these youths kept up their unruly behavior, they could be exiled or killed for their seditious actions. In the provinces, punishment was usually meted out by the governor, who, as we will see, had great power over the formation and assembly of associations.

Youth associations' reputation for riotousness and agitation at games and among the urban populace may be one reason for a senatorial decree (cited in an inscription from 138 or 139 CE under Hadrian) that explicitly granted the *neoi* of Cyzicus, a city on the Sea of Marmara, the right to gather as a corporative body.[6] Contemporaneous regulations from the Italian city of Lanuvium in 136 CE reveal that the *collegium* of Diana and Antinous also received a decree from the Senate allowing it to convene as an association. In regard to such licenses for gathering, Jinyu Liu has noted that twenty-three additional *collegia* we know of between 136 and 251 CE allude to explicit permission to meet in some manner; but this was still only a small sliver of all total associations across the Mediterranean.[7]

Even if not all associations seem to have applied for such a license, certain places and groups fell under direct suspicion of the authorities due to their history of violence. Youth associations were already under scrutiny, and the city of Cyzicus had a history of uprisings. In 20 BCE, there was a notorious episode involving the beating and killing of Roman citizens, who were protected from such treatment by law. This caused Augustus to revoke Cyzicus's status as a free city, although it appears it was later reinstituted. For associations known for rabble-rousing in particular cities, licenses or permissions may have been sought. But for many groups, such as the association of fishermen in Cyzicus, who were also an active group alongside many others in the city, they may not have felt the need either to pursue or publish notation of a special state license. This was likely because they did not fall under the same suspicion of the state by nature. Or it may be that many noted collectives, such as those found at Pompeii, were not formal or legally regulated associations at all.

Like most ancient collectives, youth associations had a religious aspect and an internal hierarchy in terms of leaders and officers. Each usually worshipped a common patron deity and had its own named magistrates.[8] Some had members who were women, and some even had female leaders.[9] Ancient historian Mark Vesley has argued that this is where many of the known female gladiators of the imperial period may have first trained, rather than in gladiatorial *familiae*.[10] Such youth associations, which put on their own games called the *Iuvenalia*, made a comeback in Italy due to Augustus encouraging freeborn youths to engage in military training and games.[11] Although freeborn, they were often coached in gladiatorial combat methods; however, these were amateurs who did not become lifelong professionals. Later in the imperial period, there is also evidence for crossover between youth associations and the theater. Pantomimes were given special membership in some of these *collegia*.[12]

Were these youth associations the impetus behind the Pompeii riot? Scholars have alleged that it was such associations from Pompeii that were fighting the youth associations of Nuceria in the amphitheater at the time of the riots, even if they were not named directly.[13] It is more likely, however, that there was a move to limit games and *collegia* at Pompeii because disbanding illicit associations was now one of the first standardized steps in squelching popular discord from above. Another graffito, etched on the façade of a Pompeian house, may refer to the bleak aftermath of the riot, which left a mark on the whole community. It remarks: "Campani, you perished with the Nucerians in a victory."[14] Accompanying the graffito was a drawing of a gladiator with a palm raised in victory.

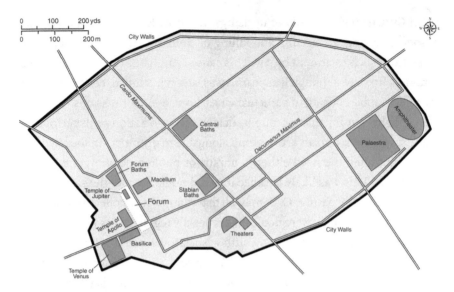

Fig. 7. Map of Pompeii in the first century CE. (Map created by Gabriel Moss.)

Pompeii was a town filled with variant types of associations. At the time of its destruction in 79 CE, just twenty years after the famous riot, the town of Pompeii had between twenty-seven thousand and thirty thousand inhabitants.[15] It was a relatively small city—especially when compared with the one million people likely living and working in Rome in the early imperial period—but nonetheless an important one. There is evidence for forty-five associations in Pompeii at the time, of which twenty-eight mentioned in inscriptions and graffiti appear to have been predominantly occupational associations—from garlic sellers called *aliarii*, to bakers, to cleaners called fullers, to musicians called *scabillarii*.[16] These groups also sometimes engaged in political lobbying. The fishermen of Pompeii, for instance, used graffiti to urge the election of a new aedile. This was the magistrate who would be intimately involved in overseeing the terms of their business dealings and the price for fish set at the market.[17] These were groups with social, political, and commercial interests, particularly when it came to market regulations.

What were the size of these associations? By law, any *collegium* had to have three members to qualify as such. However, the actual membership number was, on average, often much higher. Modern scholars have estimated that if each Pompeian association included around one hundred members, then 22.5 to 30 percent of the city's population was part of an association, with 45 to 60 percent of Pompeii's men possessing a membership.[18] From electioneering to burial insurance, we have already seen that associations could provide a range of attractive services to their members. Associations served the interests of many within both large cities and small towns. However, they were not always seen in a favorable light from above.

Associations and Their Regulation under Augustus

To understand the aftermath of the Pompeii riots, we must go back to the beginning of the imperial period and apprehend the mindset of a young Octavian regarding associations. Following the assassination of his adopted father on the Ides of March in 44 BCE, he had come to the fore and been a part of the Second Triumvirate. This was a group of three men composed of Octavian, Marc Antony, and a Caesar supporter named Lepidus. And yet, like the demise of the First Triumvirate of Pompey, Crassus, and Caesar years prior, there would ultimately only be one man left standing. With his trusty lieutenant, Marcus Agrippa, Octavian was victorious against Antony and Cleopatra at the Battle of Actium in 31 BCE. The forced suicides of Antony and Cleopatra in 30 BCE then paved the way for Octavian to annex Egypt as a province and to reformulate the state in new and important ways. In 27 BCE, the Senate had granted Octavian the honorific title of Augustus (Revered One), and in 2 BCE, he was even given the formal title of "Father of the Fatherland."

Along the way, Augustus's use of the self-justifying rhetoric of "public welfare" or "public utility" increasingly provided the legal rationalization for the actions of the emperor and the state. Augustus put in place a hierarchy of social needs. He broadcast the message that maintenance of the public welfare would be touted as of a greater socio-legal necessity than the "welfare of private individuals."[19] In theory, the public needs of the many supposedly outweighed the wishes of the private individual. In reality, Octavian-Augustus used law and the direct patronage of certain associations to champion particular social groups, increase oversight and surveillance, and above all mitigate possible dissent. Augustus was not the first to underscore the need for groups to provide a public good to merit their existence. Cicero had begun to develop this notion as a civic metric, that is, a measure of who contributed to a city, in the last decades of the Republic. The notion simply became more standardized and accepted into the imperial period.

In the Principate, public utility went hand-in-hand with the emperor as a caretaker, an architect, and a father of the country. In an observation that likely reflected his own day, the later first-century commentator Asconius remarked that the *collegia* that survived the Augustan ban were those that exemplified public utility.[20] But who fit this definition? Associations of building contractors endured and were reorganized in Rome under Augustus in 7 BCE. There is also strong evidence throughout Italy and the western Mediterranean for associations of textile workers and possibly timber merchants. Augustus saw the building industry as a civic necessity, and his allowance of construction associations aligns with his revamping of the administrators who took care of the city's buildings and infrastructure.[21] Paternal oversight was part of the deal if these associations wished to continue to function, particularly those in the city of Rome. If we think back to Augustus's encouragement of *collegia* of youths throughout Italy, we can already see that the emperor used direct patronage of certain associations for his own political objectives and to protect himself.

Augustus protected himself through the creation of new associations as well. There was no formal, publicly funded police force for the city of Rome during the tumultuous era of Catiline and Clodius in the middle of the first century BCE. Augustus wanted much more surveillance of the city and security for himself (and his interests) at the ready. This is why Rome became a city occupied by garrisoned soldiers. In 27 BCE, Augustus created a Praetorian Guard that was nine cohorts strong, with three of these cohorts attending the emperor and billeted in the city at any one time. The rest were placed in Italian towns nearby. Augustus may also have stationed an urban cohort in Lugdunum (modern Lyon) to protect an important mint there. The princeps organized Rome into fourteen districts and gave the city its first state-run police force by recruiting Italians to fill three urban cohorts of five hundred men each. In 6 CE, he then formed seven cohorts of 560 freedman each called *vigiles* (watchmen). They had barracks and designated watch stations in the city and acted as fire brigades in seven of the fourteen districts. Each cohort later had four doctors attached to it, along with torch-holders and even a trumpeter. In the early empire, there were as many as 3,920 freedmen sub-organized into smaller units called centuries. At the top, the *vigiles* were overseen by an equestrian prefect who reported to the city prefect.[22]

Later evidence tells us more about these paramilitary groups living and working in the city. In the watchhouse of Cohort VII of the *vigiles* in Trastevere across the Tiber, which was excavated in the nineteenth century, surviving graffiti dated to 214 to 245 CE tell us about the lives of these urban firefighters and patrolmen who could also be used as a police force or guard. Archaeological evidence also reveals that religion was tied to their workspace; there was a genius—a kind of religious spirit of the firehouse—that unified the cohorts.[23] In the years that followed, emperors from Claudius to Vespasian deployed brigades of *vigiles* in cities to protect the grain supply, oversee the coinage, and watch the people.[24] The fire brigade or night watch could serve as a ready security force on hand if needed. Thus, these patrolmen came to be known as a group that could be used to secure a city, but emperors knew that in the wrong hands, they could also aid a rebellion.

In addition to the notable increase in associations of contracted builders, appointed city administrators, and groups of garrisoned soldiers and guardsmen in the city of Rome, there was also a surge in the use of involuntary labor associations composed of *servi publici* (public enslaved persons) under Augustus. The imperial family came to use their enslaved *familiae* for both personal and state functions. Take, for instance, the water supply for Rome and its upkeep. When Augustus's trusted general and friend Marcus Agrippa became aedile in 33 BCE, he had already been employing his own enslaved persons to oversee and clean the aqueducts, basins, and water sources in and around Rome. When Agrippa died in 12 BCE, he left these private "water men" to Augustus, and they were absorbed into the *familia Caesaris:* the groups of enslaved persons and freedmen who served the emperor.[25] When Augustus later died in 14 CE, these enslaved water workers then formally became part of the broadening network of organized, servile families being deployed as *servi publici* to oversee Rome's public services. But Rome was not alone in depending on enslaved associations for the upkeep of cities. Such publicly held enslaved persons also worked for municipal governments in many other cities across the Mediterranean, frequently overseen by municipal councils. Often, the organization and approach taken by the *princeps* was exercised in miniature in the provinces.

Changes to the associative fabric extended to Augustus's reorganization of the Roman festival calendar and the organization of games. It was not enough to simply systematize and surveil the neighborhoods, the streets, the buildings, and the people. If late Republican events had taught Augustus anything, it was that he also needed to control the times, popular venues, and communication instruments provided by the arena, the theater, and (to a lesser extent at this time) the hippodrome. These venues provided important sites for communication between ruler and ruled, but could also be flashpoints for social upheaval. As such, Augustus began to monopolize the patronage of the festivities and civic games put on in Rome. The imperial family increasingly paid for these games and employed its own groups of gladiatorial troupes and beast hunters.[26] Augustus had learned lessons from the gladiators that were weaponized by aristocrats in the late Republic. Private gladiatorial schools in Rome may have been banned under Augustus, and definitely were by the reign of Domitian.[27] In the early empire, emperors set up their own imperial training schools in the city, overseen by appointed administrators known as the procurators of the gladiatorial families.

Imperial control over the games and entertainment associations at work therein extended to attempts at controlling the crowd and those entertainers with whom they interacted as well. Augustus was wary of the changes and shifting trends on the city's stages. Sometime at the end of the first century BCE, a new wave of entertainment focused on a type of dance called pantomime began to grow in popularity, particularly in Italy and in Rome. Already, these early pantomimes were gaining popular followings, along with a reputation for lewd or immoral behavior. One wonders whether, like the gladiators, these emerging pantomimes and their troupes of chorus performers and flautists were seen as possible threats to be isolated and contained in their own legal and social categories. Augustus was harsh on the "lawlessness of the actors" and even exiled a pantomime named Pylades for making a lewd hand gesture at him.[28] For Augustus, laws framed in the language of honor and morality were often the means through which he created and maintained the socio-legal sequestration of possible threats to his own power. Declarations of dishonor were, like laws prohibiting assembling, often a cover for his true fear: dissent.

Marriage was a key issue to Augustus, and one he used to separate out and isolate professions cast as dishonorable. Legislation in 18 BCE and 9 CE used marriage to define these social orders more stringently. Augustus prohibited men of the senatorial order, their children, and their grandchildren from marrying formerly enslaved persons, those who currently or formerly performed on the stage, or those with the legal stigma of infamy.[29] Those convicted of certain crimes or who practiced infamous professions incurred this legal stigma, which affected their reputation and their legal protections. A law of 4 CE also kept gladiators and beast fighters from becoming full citizens with suffrage upon their manumission.[30] These professional entertainers would never be persons with full civic rights. Instead, these former fighters only achieved the same status as captured foreigners. Notwithstanding his obsession with social eugenics, Augustus did provide a loophole for elites in this case, by allowing equestrians and others of high status to fight as free gladiators called *auctorati*. However, Suetonius notes that this practice of allowing high-status gladiators was soon ended by a decree of the Senate.[31] With few exceptions, the games and the theater continued to be cast as moral danger zones that, to the emperor's mind, needed to be heavily regulated and cordoned off. It is no wonder, then, that many entertainers turned to their associations for protection, rather than relying on a society that both celebrated and shunned them.

Groups who participated in the circus were also active at this time. The charioteers who competed in the circus during the Augustan era had long been organized into *factiones* overseen by faction masters, who were usually of equestrian status. Wealthy equestrians with what amounted to their own personal charioteer associations contracted with organizers of games (called *editores*) to employ their still-private factions of charioteers, horses, veterinarians, and attendant staff. As Chapter Seven will examine more closely, a vast majority of the charioteers and many of the workers in these factions were originally either enslaved or from enslaved families. Their predominantly servile and manumitted statuses are indicated by the 229 known instances of charioteers that survive, as compiled by Gerhard Horsmann.[32] In addition, Augustus continued the work of Julius Caesar in improving upon the seating and decoration of the Circus Maximus in Rome, meant for the display of these competing factions and the enjoyment of the public. Taken as a whole, Augustus's legislation indicates that the perceived threats posed by gladiators and those connected to the games, the theater, and the circus were partially diffused through direct patronage and further asphyxiated by new laws imposing social limits.

While many associations may have been technically banned under Augustus, the stability under his long reign of over four decades did provide fertile space for growth in the festival and athletic circuits. During his life, Augustus enjoyed athletic and theatrical displays and—like the Hellenistic monarchs before him—viewed them as a method of entrenching his imperial rule. New studies of associations of competitors undertaken by Bram Fauconnier have demonstrated that during the Augustan period of the early empire, emerging agonistic and festival circuits developed and became more engrained, particularly in the eastern Mediterranean. The growing networks of associations of actors, musicians, and athletes possessing special privileges and wages then traveled along these set circuits.[33] As Augustus lay dying in Nola in 14 CE, the seventy-five-year-old emperor even used some of his last words to cast himself as an actor, inquiring whether he had played his part in life well. All the world was a stage, and Augustus knew that many would remember his performance.

Associations and the Freedom of Assembly under the Julio-Claudians

Several potential heirs had died prior to Augustus. Ultimately, the Roman princeps was forced to leave control of the Roman Empire to his reluctant stepson, Tiberius. The fifty-five-year-old, originally from the old patrician, Claudian family and the first son of Livia, Augustus's widow, solidified the creation of the Julio-Claudian dynasty. This dynasty would continue many of the policies of its founder. Tiberius's reign (until 37 CE) would further illustrate the persistent tensions between the state and the populace in terms of associations and their perceived threat. There were also new groups forming in many cities across the empire. Although likely unknown to Tiberius, a man named Jesus of Nazareth was crucified at Golgotha outside the city walls of Jerusalem late in his rule. Groups of early Christ-followers espousing his teachings began to form their own assemblies, often referred to as *ekklēsiai* or, occasionally, synagogues.[34] Their demographics and internal organization at this time are murky, but there is no evidence or mention of them petitioning for a special state license to meet as an official association.

Emperors after Augustus, however, continued to monitor certain spaces seen as rife for seditious associations. They were wary of known places for gathering, such as taverns, and passed legislation that made these spaces less attractive as places of assembly. Tiberius stopped the sale of baked goods in bars called *popinae* and assigned the magistrates called aediles to watch over them closely. This was one of many legal attempts to indirectly halt assemblies in bars and what we might call public houses.[35] Taverns and pubs would continue to be spots for associations to meet well into the modern era. Theatrical spaces also continued to fall under suspicion from the emperors, particularly as groups of stage performers mobilized people in ways that frightened the emperor and government. In the city of Rome, where we continue to have the best evidence for such popular discord and rebellious movements, it was the fame of certain pantomimes that could be the match that lit popular fires.

Soon after Tiberius's ascent, the so-called pantomime riots of 14 and 15 CE took place in Rome. These series of popular upheavals stemmed in part from newly formed games after the death of Augustus, creating fresh opportunities for social gathering. A new group of elite priests of Augustus was appointed after the emperor's death, along with the creation of a festival and games to be held annually in October in honor of Augustus: the *ludi Augustales*. The calendar and Roman religion again preserved Roman memory and justified imperial rule. Within these games, the dramatic art of pantomime became wildly popular. Pantomimes continued to gain popularity and thus to accrue soft power among the people in the early empire. Apparently, in 14 CE, a pantomime set to perform at these games withheld his performance because he wanted more pay. He went on a one-man strike by withholding his appearance and, in turn, the people took the side of the pantomime. They rioted until the tribunes convinced the Senate to up his wages.[36] Certain entertainment figures were lightning rods who had the ability to mobilize the people in ways viewed by elites as dangerous. Some clearly also had the ability to advocate for higher wages by withholding their performance.

The "disorderliness of the stage," as the former consul and historian Tacitus dubbed it, broke out again in 15 CE. This time, the riots resulted in the deaths of civilians, several soldiers, and even a centurion; in addition, an officer of the Praetorian Guard was wounded. Although Augustus had kept actors from being whipped, except in specific circumstances, during his reign, the Senate tried to overturn this prohibition, to no avail. However, the Senate did manage to set price ceilings on expenditures for entertainment, to put a stop to senators going into the houses of pantomimes (and thus teaming up), to prevent equestrians from fraternizing with these theatrical leaders, and to allow praetors to exile unruly spectators.[37] Just as Augustus had thought, keeping the upper orders from interacting and assembling with these ambassadors to the people was one technique for maintaining public order and halting treasonous plans. A core question is whether official associations of actors, pantomimes, and musicians led the crowds into the fray. Ambiguous language by elite Roman historians trying to demean these movements as riotous mobs makes it hard to tell the level of organization on the ground. However, under Augustus, there was an association of musicians, who had petitioned the Senate for the right to gather "for the sake of the games" and had received a license to do so.[38] Entertainment associations were integral to the underlying labor organization that underpinned spectacles and yet, as emperors well knew, could mobilize a crowd quickly and effectively.

Under Tiberius, individual pantomimes and actors greatly benefited from the patronage of the emperor's son, Drusus, and from many other elite men of the time, but many likely also had associative memberships. The social lines Augustus tried so hard to draw in the sand were quite blurry—demarcations that existed in law, rather than being reflected in lived experience.[39] Into the empire, pantomimes continued to grow in acclaim and to form their own specialized unions. Pantomimes were also represented within the later associations of pantomimes and mimes known as the Parasites of Apollo. Although the exact time of their formation is hard to pinpoint, we know these mime troupes connected to Apollo came about by and likely before the reign of the emperor Claudius (r. 41–54 CE). The groups were economically similar to, but much less socially prestigious than, the theatrical performers known as the *technitai* of Dionysus. In terms of religion, they focused their dedications on the god Apollo rather than on Dionysus. Other performer groups similarly proliferated. A first-century CE inscription from Calabria notes a named group of "Ionic pantomimes" who created an association in southern Italy.[40] Entertainers continued to benefit from collectives immensely, whether in the eastern or western Mediterranean.

Not every group had the right to assemble under the new emperor, however. Tiberius broke up cults perceived as contaminating the populace with non-Roman behaviors in the city of Rome. In 19 CE, a resolution of the Senate expelled worshippers of Isis and Jews collectively. The resolution dictated that four thousand freedman Isis followers and Jews of military age be taken to Sardinia and employed there to extinguish brigandage. Sardinia had become a kind of ancient Australia just off the coast of Italy. This was because the worshippers had, in Tacitus's assessment, been "infected by those superstitions."[41] Suetonius also attributes the banishing of "foreign cults" (as he calls them), particularly the Egyptian and Jewish ones, to their being viewed as "superstitions."[42] The allegation that religions were disruptive, illegitimate, or *superstitiones* would later be leveled against early Christ-followers and their emerging associations as well. The Senate noted that the rest of the Isis worshippers and Jews were either to cease worship altogether or leave Italy.

Like many legal expiations and bans on assembly, Tiberius's policies did not span the whole of the Mediterranean. They mainly focused on the maintenance of order in Rome and Italy. Questions also linger as to the motivations behind them. In Jewish historian Josephus's account, the Tiberian expulsion of the Jews was a reaction to the mistreatment of a convert named Fulvia by four Jewish men.[43] Tiberius's eviction of the Isis worshippers is blamed by Josephus (without support from other sources) on the betrayal of an equestrian woman named Paulina.[44] Ultimately, the true impetus for Tiberius's actions was—as Mary Smallwood has argued—probably rooted in the reason Dio gives for Tiberius throwing out the Jews: the false imperial Roman perception that many Romans were being converted to Judaism at the time.[45] Roman authorities often looked askance at alleged missionizing by foreign religious groups.

Women, Trade, and Occupational Collegia

A key question that too often goes unasked is whether women were allowed into the unions and associations that formed in the Roman Mediterranean. No extant Roman legislation barred women from participating in voluntary associations. It was not illegal for women to be in an association. Although inscriptions indicating women's membership in associations is rare, it is not unheard of. Take, for instance, a burial area for a collective of female mimes at Rome:

> For the members of the association of female mimes.
> (This burial plot is) 15 feet in the front and 12 feet deep.[46]

Scholars today are often in doubt about the presence of women in associations because it is rare to find their names explicitly mentioned in the surviving membership lists of occupational *collegia*.[47] This is a salient reminder that we probably only have between 1 to 4 percent of the literature and inscriptions that actually existed in the ancient Mediterranean. An exception is the associations with more focus on female deities, rather than on commerce. In those groups attending to Isis, Magna Mater, Vesta (the Vestal Virgins), and, of course, Bona Dea (Good Goddess), women played more prominent roles, and such groups could be all-female.[48] But whether this was the only route allowed women within associations is more uncertain than it may at first seem from the inscriptional evidence.

The scarcity of women in surviving inscriptions is deceptive. Once again, the absence of evidence is not necessarily evidence of absence. The dearth of explicit references to women in associations even led the celebrated historian Paul Veyne to argue unequivocally that all members of Roman *collegia* were men. He further said that such associations were either religious or professional, and were confined to one town.[49] Each of these statements is reductive and imposes false binaries within Roman society. There were many exceptions—particularly the idea that associations were either male or female, religious or professional. Language complications muddle the issues of gender and associative membership. The visibility of women may be obfuscated by how the Latin and Greek languages work when addressing a group, since the use of a masculine plural is used as the default, even for groups that had both men and women. However, there are rare but telling examples of women as both textile dealers and tailors. At least one, a freedwoman at Rome named Avillia Philusa, was a member of a textile association.[50] The extent to which collective language erased women's membership in associations may never fully be known, but must be taken into account.

It would have benefited some working women with vulnerable socio-legal designations to be members of associations. Female mimes, actresses, and musicians in particular may have sought out associations for the group protection they offered. As we have seen, Roman law provided minimal security for those cast as disreputable in these kinds of commercial roles. Augustus and Tiberius had also done much to make the lines between reputable and disreputable professions even clearer.[51] We can see the consequences of dishonor for women in the telling literary examples that survive. They illustrate reasons why an entertainment association might provide a safe haven for female entertainers often seen as synonymous with sex workers. In 54 BCE, Cicero glosses over the rape of a female mime at Atina, a town about eighty-five miles southeast of Rome.[52] Into the empire, Syrian female musicians collectively known as *Ambubaiae* and other women connected to the amphitheater or the circus were commonly grouped with sex workers by elite writers such as Suetonius.[53]

Even when disparaged, male writers outside their ranks saw these women as forming recognized associations. In his *Satires*, Horace cites the *collegia* of *Ambubaiae* and the networks within which they operated: "The *collegia* of Syrian flute-players, the drug sellers, the beggars, the female mimes, the jester actors and all that type of person are despondent and mourning at the death of the singer Tigellius."[54] By establishing even informal *collegia*, performers and entertainers seen as lowly and legally infamous in Roman society might have been able to create some degree of solidarity and redress for their members: people who stood outside the discriminating boundaries of Roman honor.[55]

For wealthy women in the elite orders of Roman society, their connections to *collegia* seem to be more as patrons than as members. Into the empire, affluent women began to attach themselves to *collegia* through patronage bonds. Although being formally named as the patron of an association was often a male role, women in the first three centuries CE in particular began to be given the title. In a second-century inscription from the Italian city of Firmum Picenum, we get a reference to a woman named Alliena Berenice, who served as a patron for the local associations of builders and textile merchants: "Gaius Vetus Polus erected this for his most virtuous wife along with Gaius Vettius Polus, in honor of his mother, Alliena Berenice, daughter of Titus, the most pious patron of the association of builders and textile dealers. The place was designated by decree of the decurions."[56] Ancient historian Emily Hemelrijk has shown that official female patrons of *collegia* were usually of high status—often women from the senatorial or equestrian order. However, another, less prestigious honorific, "mother of the association," could be given out to sub-elite and freedwomen connected to an association as well.[57]

There were women connected to *collegia* in other roles beyond patron, even if an honorary title was not listed in inscriptions. At Pompeii, one of the most well-known women with a connection to a *collegium* was Eumachia, a priestess, civic benefactress, and woman with ties to the Pompeian *collegium* of fullers—that is, the group who laundered clothing and cleaned wool.[58] Even if they did not call her a patron, they gave her a statue, an action that speaks to some sort of social contract or understanding between honorand and dedicator. We can see a similar process for a priestess named Claudia Iusta, who was honored in 79 CE with a statue by the "tree carriers" connected to Magna Mater in Regium Iulium in southern Italy. The same group at Brixia also honored a woman named Aemilia Synethia. What women like Eumachia, Claudia, and Aemilia illustrate is that not just wealthy male patrons and magistrates were sought out by associations. Women were also courted for their capital and connections.

Associations and Public Order under Gaius and Claudius

Tiberius died at Misenum in March of 37 CE. In his place, the well-known son of Germanicus and Agrippina the Elder (Augustus's granddaughter) succeeded him as the third of the Julio-Claudians. He was named Gaius, but is known today largely by his nickname from the camps: Caligula ("Little Boots"). We hear little about his policies concerning voluntary associations in the city of Rome itself. Elsewhere in the Roman Empire, however, it was often up to Roman governors to lay down policies either for or against associations. Of particular interest was always the province of Egypt, which was an imperial province with garrisons overseen by an equestrian administrator called a prefect. A notorious assembly policy was enacted there by Aulus Avilius Flaccus, the prefect of Egypt (32–38 CE), who began his rule under Tiberius and ended it under Gaius. Flaccus, who was from a high-level equestrian family, had close ties with the children of the Julio-Claudian family, having been taught alongside Augustus's grandchildren. He also shared the

Julio-Claudian fear of group action. He likewise upheld many of their anti-assembly policies during his governance of Roman Egypt.

An Alexandrian philosopher, scholar, and Jew named Philo tells us a great deal about the man in his treatise *Against Flaccus,* in which he remarks on rioting in the city of Alexandria in the summer of 38 CE. Philo's treatise was likely written after Flaccus's arrest in the fall of 38 CE, but before Gaius's ultimate assassination in 41 CE.[59] What is important is that, in his defensive writings and during his delegations to Rome to speak with the emperor, Philo tried to establish that Jews did not engage in the seditious or drunken type of assemblies that Roman emperors and governors most feared and often legislated against. Through the example of Alexandria, we can perhaps see how governors could implement and intensify anti-assembly policies in their provinces at certain times. Such interventions could have broad repercussions within a province—something we will see exemplified by Pliny in Bithynia less than a century later.

The spark for the rioting in that fateful summer was a visit by Herod Agrippa. The Jewish king stopped in the Egyptian city while returning home to Palestine. After the royal was roundly mocked in the gymnasium, a crowd clambered into the theater of Alexandria around dawn and demanded that Flaccus have images of Caligula put up in the prayer houses of Jews—despite their rejection, on religious grounds, of such idolatry. Flaccus heard, and then instituted, the crowd's demands, which were submitted (as was usual) from the communicatory platform of an urban theater space. The desecration and confiscation of Jewish prayer spaces ensued, along with other horrendous actions against the Jewish population. During this attack on the Alexandrian Jews, they were largely relegated to what is perhaps the first known instance of what would be called, from the late Middle Ages on, a *ghetto*.[60] Jews were consigned to a sector of the city called the Delta quarter. This portion of the city was likely established in the early Hellenistic period as a sort of Jewish area and a privilege. What later changed under Flaccus was that all Alexandrian Jews were, at least according to Philo, being restricted within and forcibly pushed to that quarter in 38 CE—a quite different situation than before, even if there was legal continuity regarding residence rights.[61]

What was the state of associations in Roman Egypt during the riots in Alexandria? In early imperial Egypt, associations continued to proliferate despite the prior bans under Julius Caesar and Augustus. As Ilias N. Arnaoutoglou has argued, when Egypt was annexed, it is likely that preexisting associations were considered sufficiently antique, according to the rules of Augustus, so as to continue to exist. Newer ones perhaps took advantage of a loophole that we hear about much later in the legal evidence, which allowed associations to form and meet under the pretext of *religio*—for religious purposes. In the early third century CE, during the reign of Caracalla, the jurist Marcian noted that the common people, collectively called *tenuiores*, were permitted to meet only once a month for a small monthly fee, in order to forestall the formation of illicit *collegia*. He also mentioned that associations formed for religious purposes were still allowed as long as they did not go against the ban on illegal associations.[62] Marcian states that soldiers were notably not sanctioned to form their own associations, even for religious reasons. This policy may date from the reign of Augustus, although we are not sure. Numerous inscriptions reveal the existence of military associations both before and after the juristic opinion, regardless of the policy.[63] This suggests that anti-assembly legislation was often in place, but not always stringently enforced except in periods of great social or political upheaval, it seems.

Why did Philo need to mount a defense of Jewish associations? The later religious loophole cited by Marcian is important to note because Philo tells us that other political clubs of Alexandria and the synods were constantly holding their meetings under the pretense of offering sacrifice, when they were in fact mainly interested in drunken feasting on couches that led to political intrigue.[64] This influenced Flaccus's long-standing but rather ad hoc policy decision, even before the rioting, to prohibit assemblies of "promiscuous men" gathering in every quarter of the city, as well as his bans on political clubs and synods. Philo's inclusion of the detail that many of these groups claimed they assembled for the sake of sacrifice is likely meant to signal to his readers exactly how some new Alexandrian drinking clubs were able to skirt the earlier Julian law: by declaring a religious purpose for their assembly.

In his writings, Philo works hard to portray Jewish associations as learned, authentically religious, and antique. That is why, in his writings describing his embassy to Rome to speak with Caligula, he noted that Jews were previously protected under Augustus and Tiberius, and that their laws were in alignment with "quiet and stability."[65] Philo did everything in his power to argue that Jewish associations were not the cause of public disorder. In the end, Flaccus would be arrested in the fall of 38 CE and exiled before later being executed. His policies largely remained, despite Jewish and Alexandrian delegations being sent to the city of Rome to speak to Caligula in 39 CE. The Jews of Alexandria would have to wait for a new emperor in order to get a new hearing on their rights within the Egyptian city.

Around noon on January 24, 41 CE, officers of the Praetorian Guard lay in wait following the conclusion of the Palatine Games in order to assassinate Caligula.[66] His uncle Tiberius Claudius Caesar Augustus Germanicus—a man whom we call Claudius—became the new emperor. In Alexandria, the Jews took up arms and rebelled upon hearing of Caligula's death.[67] Claudius would listen to the pleas of the Jews of Alexandria and restore many of their rights, asking the Alexandrians to respect their antiquity and religious beliefs. However, he took a different stance on Jewish associations and their perceived threat in the city of Rome itself. After all, the assassination of one's predecessor has a way of striking fear into the heart (and paranoia into the mind) of the next ruler. Dio tells us that, while Claudius did not ban Jews from the city of Rome altogether in 41 CE, he prohibited them from holding meetings.[68] Additionally, the new emperor also disbanded the "political clubs" that Caligula had allowed to be reintroduced.[69] At first, Claudius's policies were not about religious persecution, but rather about extinguishing even the slightest flicker of sedition and pushback against him. Dio remarks that, as part of this bundle of restrictions, the emperor also closed the taverns in the city where Roman clubs often gathered to eat and drink, even placing constraints on the sale of hot food as well.[70] Time and time again, legislation governing taverns, a prime location for associations to gather their ranks and make plans, occurs in times of political uncertainty. Claudius was falling back on old approaches to political transition that were by now quite familiar.

The tension between Claudius and the Jewish groups in the city of Rome reached a breaking point after rioting in 49 CE, when it does seem they were expelled from the city altogether.[71] A highly contentious passage in Suetonius blames their expulsion on the rioting incited by followers of a man named Chrestus.[72] Although there is evidence of "Christus" sometimes being spelled in this manner, this may or may not be an allusion to groups of early Christ-followers. Claudius's restrictions against Jews were not empire-wide, but were instead intended to focus on his immediate vicinity, Rome, in order to protect him and stave off political unrest. For the roughly one million people living in the city of Rome in the early empire, there were often different associative experiences, policies, and enforcement levels in regard to assemblies than there were for the fifty to sixty million people in total living across the Roman Empire in the first century CE. In cities such as Alexandria, Pompeii, and Rome, riots and perceived threats to social and political order could still trigger enforcement of anti-assembly laws that, at most other times, were largely skirted or ignored entirely.

Religion and Freedom of Assembly in the Early Empire

Particularly in the case of rioting or in times of political transition, rights to assembly were often the first things to be targeted and revoked. Both the baby and the bathwater were thrown out by emperors and governors (or prefects) due to an abundance of caution. As we will discuss further in the following chapter and have already seen with Jewish associations in Alexandria, there was an enormous Roman legal umbrella that governed myriad types of associations, largely en bloc, with a few loopholes regarding those formed for religious purposes and burial. This meant that certain groups, such as Jews, attempted to separate themselves out from disruptive associations and argue that they were peaceful, sober, and not a threat to public order. In the late first and second centuries, emerging groups of Christ-followers would later defend their existence similarly and argue for their right to assemble. However, while the Jews could argue that they were an ancient and thus long-standing group, the Christ-followers could not present that same defense.

There was an early imperial struggle to justify the nature and existence of new Christian congregations assembling in various Mediterranean cities. We see this most clearly within the late second-century CE work the *Apology*, written by a Christian named Tertullian. The writer had grown up in the North African city of Carthage, a town with its own raucous amphitheater built in the late first to early second centuries CE. Like Philo, Tertullian was well versed in Roman law and rhetoric.[73] And like Philo's defense of Judaism, his defense of Christianity went to great pains to employ legal language and to differentiate Christian groups from the "illicit factions" that were well known for causing discord both at the games inside the amphitheater and out in the streets. The *Apology* refers to Christians as both a *factio* and a *corpus* that met together in a common religion, meaning there is likely an allusion to the loophole mentioned by the jurist Marcian, which may have existed since Augustus, to allow associations meeting for the sake of religious piety to bury their dead—the so-called *collegia tenuiorum* (associations of the impoverished).[74] But as with Egypt under Flaccus, provincial context and histories of uprisings were always key. Chapter Five will look at the difficulties facing early Christ-followers, particularly in areas of Asia Minor, in achieving status as a legitimate association in the midst of continued strikes, collective actions, and other disruptive popular and commercial activities during the high empire.

Into the imperial period, associations—both licensed and unlicensed, formal and informal—continued to gather in amphitheaters, theaters, taverns, homes, and many other spaces within the cities of the Mediterranean. This was in addition to those wealthier associations lucky enough to have a clubhouse or prayer house. Whether they self-professed as *collegia, factiones, corpora, thiasoi*, or any of a litany of terms for collectives, they were often treated similarly by Roman authorities during the institution of a ban emanating from the emperor, senate, or governor—whether or not the collective thought of itself reflexively as an association or a political club. As this chapter has alleged, from Augustus's policies onward, these groups were increasingly cast from above (but often not from below) as sources of violence or possible sedition when assembled, even if legal loopholes were created. This is why Tertullian had to reject the connection of such a reputation to the new Christian congregations in North Africa and elsewhere. The Augustan litmus test of antiquity or contribution to public welfare made Christ-followers a hard sell for many emperors and governors. But the North African writer points out that Christians avoided spectacles in the amphitheater and thus should not be seen as an illicit faction.[75] Historian of early Christianity Eric Rebillard has argued that Tertullian's defensive words firmly and quite intentionally alluded to the earlier *lex Julia* under Augustus that banned associations.[76] Augustus's policies surrounding *collegia* set long-standing legal precedents that could often lie dormant, only to be activated and enforced more stringently when rebellion or urban conflicts arose.

5
Strikes, Riots, and Associations in the Roman Imperial Period

ON JULY 16, 116 OR 117 CE, in the reign of the Roman emperor Trajan, a wealthy grandmother named Eudaimonis penned a letter on papyrus to Aline, her pregnant daughter-in-law. In it, she told Aline that she hoped she would have a boy and also let her know about troubles afoot. Aline's husband, Apollonius, was a magistrate who oversaw an area close to one hundred miles away from his hometown and much of his family. Apollonius not only supervised the Apollonopolites-Heptakomias nome in Upper Egypt, he also owned a number of wool-weaving workshops back in Hermopolis, where Aline often resided near her mother-in-law. About to give birth and taking leave from overseeing the workshops, Aline had left Hermopolis to be closer to her husband. Apollonius was already exhausted and dismayed from having to deal with the repercussions from the Kitos War, a rebellion of Jewish groups in Cyrene, Cyprus, Judaea, and Mesopotamia that lasted from 115 to 117 CE. This was only forty years after the conclusion of the First Jewish War in Judaea that had begun under Nero and was then ruthlessly ended by Vespasian and his son, Titus. While her son and daughter-in-law were away, Eudaimonis was left to direct the enslaved girls at their weaving workshops. In her letter, she laments a labor shortage; she cannot find enough staff for the workshops, since they are all already working for others. Perhaps most intriguingly, she notes that the workers from their workshops have taken to the streets of the city to demand higher wages.[1]

Egypt was no stranger to worker strikes. In fact, the first strike ever recorded appears to have occurred under the pharaoh Ramses III, over twelve hundred years before Eudaimonis wrote her letter. Twenty-nine years into his rule, around 1157 or 1155 BCE, during the New Kingdom period, the artisans and laborers in the workmen's village of Deir el-Medina laid down their tools and went on strike due to a lack of rations, late pay, and bad working conditions.[2] These artisans were integral to the decoration and upkeep of the necropolis known as the Valley of the Kings. Prior to the strike, a scribe named Amunnakht had written (on a pottery fragment called an ostracon, the ancient version of scrap paper) that the grain payments for their work were twenty days overdue. The events of the actual strikes staged not long thereafter were then recorded by the same scribe, this time on papyrus. Leaving the village and declaring, "We are hungry!" the workers sat down, without displaying any violence, at the back end of the Temple of Thutmosis III. Much as "strike" became the term for workers refusing to work in the eighteenth century, notation of the withdrawal of a worker group, often to the back of a temple, became the shorthand for Egyptian worker strikes.

Despite being yelled at by state officials browbeating them to carry on, they refused to work. While they were subsequently given rations (consisting predominantly of a type of wheat called emmer), delivery was inconsistent, and the system remained faulty, unreliable, and unsatisfactory. Further strikes occurred in the weeks that followed. After numerous strikes and attempts by some to leave the community altogether, the workers peaceably sat behind another temple, the Temple of Merneptah. They stated: "We are here because of the famine and thirst. We are not accustomed to not having unguents, fish, and greens. Write to the pharaoh our perfect lord, take note of our words, and write to the vizier, our superior, because we are in need of our provisions."[3] Hunger and bad pay, as it turns out, were powerful motivators for withholding labor.

In ancient Egypt, workers could withhold their labor and use high demand for their services to their advantage. This inspired a corresponding fear from above. As Sitta von Reden has discussed, before the Roman annexation of the province, Ptolemaic Egypt struggled to retain free contractual labor.[4] It is likely that, as with the workers of Deir el-Medina, worker groups who "sat down in the temple" or who fled individually to one for protection were in fact engaging in known methods for withholding labor and striking. Temples were sacred spaces where asylum—what we would today call sanctuary, in places like a church—might be granted to those who needed protection from prosecution or violence. As a group of farmers fleeing to a temple did in 257 BCE in Ptolemaic Philadelphia, laborers used asylum to their advantage.[5] Into the Roman period following the annexation of Egypt as a province, loan lenders and overseers drew up contracts that, by asking them to waive their right to asylum, kept workers and loan recipients from being able to flee into temples.

To safeguard against this tactic, it appears that business owners may have used oaths and loan contracts to keep workers from leaving, striking, or even seeking asylum in a temple so as to avoid work. But Eudaimonis's letter reveals more than just the long history of small-scale strikes and wage disagreements in Egyptian culture. It also suggests that labor organization, worker solidarity, and mobilization such as walkouts can and did happen outside the bounds of a formal association such as a *collegium*—at the level of the workshop or, as we have previously seen in the case of slave rebellions, among enslaved *familiae*. The unity of workers did not depend on or need to be formalized through a written charter, the payment of membership dues, or the building of a clubhouse in order to be "real" for those in antiquity. However, into the high empire of the first and second centuries CE, hundreds of inscriptions demonstrate that copious associations did choose the route of a more formal organization, with their own rules and regulations. These associations proliferated across the Mediterranean in the Roman imperial period and often announced their identities through writing inscriptions.[6]

In the midst of this thriving associative order, imperial and municipal anxieties over the formation of certain types of associations persisted, from the Pompeii riots of 59 CE through the bitter end of the Severan dynasty in 235 CE. Although the degree of actualized state enforcement of legislation is still often questioned and debated, municipal laws, inscriptions, literary evidence, and juristic opinions all point to a continued wariness of private associations at the government level. For instance, a Flavian era municipal law, from the town of Irni (in what is now modern Spain), demonstrates a sustained sentiment, among at least some provincial towns, that they needed to control the right of assembly locally. The same is true of the letters between the governor Pliny and the emperor Trajan regarding the creation of a fire brigade at

Nicomedia in the province of Bithynia, an area today in northwest Turkey along the Bosporus and Black Sea. These letters affirm an imperial fear that, particularly within the region of Asia Minor, associations could get out of hand and cause political discord.

These fears were perhaps confirmed by the occurrence of events such as the bakers' strike at Ephesus in the mid- to late second century, as well as by other labor strikes in the area during the high empire. Amid this tense relationship between the state and associations, we must also situate the growth of Christianity and the suspicion surrounding new and emerging groups of Christ-followers. Such Roman elite anxieties were neither new nor surprising. However, while some associations were marginalized, others were brought deeper into the fold. The Roman state began to cultivate closer relationships with certain associations that were tied to key supply chains and seen as essential to state needs, such as those integral to the grain dole and the production of bread. The inefficacy of assembly legislation, alongside the increasing necessity of securing supply chains, may have led to the growth of a policy that more directly bound corporative bodies to the state. Associations in what we now call the *corporati* system proliferated in late antiquity.

Fear of Assemblies under the Flavians

In 68 CE, almost ten years after the riots in the amphitheater at Pompeii, Nero was forced to commit suicide. With his death, the Julio-Claudian dynasty ended. After a tumultuous year of four emperors, a new era of rulers, collectively called the Flavians (69–96 CE), emerged. This dynastic line included Vespasian and his two sons, Titus and Domitian. Vespasian was a military man who did not claim a divine lineage from Venus, as Augustus had. He was instead born to a wealthy family of the equestrian order in the central Italian city of Reate at the end of the Augustan period. Vespasian was someone who knew the power of money, and that he needed to refill the coffers of the Roman Empire. His father had belonged to the groups of tax collector/contractors in Asia that had been hated in that province since the Republic. These were the *societates publicanorum* (companies of tax farmers), whose members we call publicans. They were businessmen who bid on contracts to collect taxes in certain provinces. Although Julius Caesar had greatly modified this tax farming system to be more localized, by placing the collection of direct taxes largely under the purview of local councils, tax farming continued for the collection of indirect taxes. This occupation was still notorious well into the imperial period. But perhaps his father's business dealings had taught Vespasian about the need for diversified cash flow to fund things such as construction and entertainment.[7]

During his reign, Vespasian imposed new taxes on everything from urine to the Jews, a people recently defeated in the First Jewish Revolt (66–70 CE). The latter was the so-called Jewish tax, which was initially used to fund the rebuilding of the Temple of Jupiter Optimus Maximus on Rome's Capitoline Hill. Construction at this time was financed not only by money from the Jews conquered in the rebellion in Judaea; their bodies were also used as forced labor in several building projects. In 67 CE, early in the revolt when Nero was still in power, Vespasian had sent six thousand Jewish male captives to dig a canal at the Isthmus of Corinth (a project that was later abandoned). He also sold off 30,400 Jewish enslaved persons for profit. The historian Josephus says that ninety-seven thousand Jewish captives in total were enslaved in the revolt.[8] Among these were the twenty-five hundred whom we are told Titus compelled to fight as gladiators in games at the amphitheater of Caesarea (in what is now modern Israel). Thus, forced labor was used not just for excavating canals and erecting buildings, but also for entertainment. A number of Jewish captives were brought to Rome. As Kathleen Coleman has suggested, the huge workforce required for certain building projects may even have meant that Jewish workers contributed to the construction of the new massive Flavian amphitheater, today called the Colosseum.[9] The spoils taken from Jerusalem likely helped to finance this amphitheater.[10] The colossal space, made to accommodate fifty thousand spectators, was dedicated in 80 CE, under Vespasian's son, Titus. It was a monument to Rome's imperialism and a testament to its enduring hunger for spectacles.

Inscriptions offer small windows into the expanding commercial networks and associations of everyday workers who facilitated Flavian economic policies, many of which encouraged the import and selling of goods from the East. Such associations continued to use kinship language—calling one another brother, sister, family—and could adopt military nomenclature to denote suborganizations within their associations. We can see this reflected in an epitaph commemorating two second-century CE *piperarii* (pepper dealers), who were either literal or collegial brothers who worked within the larger cohort of pepper dealers in Rome:

> To the divine spirits.
> Publius Veracius Firmus, heir, made (this) for Publius Veracius Proculus and Publius Veracius Marcellus, most dutiful brothers of the cohort of *piperarii*, (within) the century of Firmus.[11]

These pepper dealers were likely connected to the spice warehouses called the *Horrea Piperataria* within Rome, completed under the last Flavian emperor, Domitian. As Raoul McLaughlin has explored in connection to Rome's Indian Ocean trade, these state warehouses, begun under Vespasian, were important to the imperial fiscus. If they were like the Roman grain houses, they may have held as much as nine thousand tons of spice.[12] These businessmen handled just some of the selling off of the imported pepper from the East (and perhaps other spices such as myrrh and frankincense) to secondary dealers in Rome, who could then put these products on the luxury market. Commercial *collegia* remained important mediators in various long-distance trade markets well into the late empire.

New associations of all types gained members from a spectrum of backgrounds, possessing varying degrees of wealth. And as Richard Last and Philip Harland have pointed out, "unofficial associations" flourished at this time. They define these associations as "small, relatively informal and noncompulsory groups with memberships usually ranging between ten and fifty members, but some were larger."[13] Such collectives met regularly but were not directly sustained by imperial or civic patronage. Others wished to enter into conversations with imperial or civic authorities on some level, and to get special privileges. A Flavian-era association of demolition workers at Rome dates to 79 to 81 CE, and an inscribed copy of a letter of Vespasian notes that associations of physicians at Pergamon (located in what is today the province of Izmir in Turkey) were given special dispensation to assemble in specified spaces such as temples and sanctuaries.[14] The inscriptions and papyri of this time point to a golden age of associations populating many Mediterranean cities; still, at the top, state and local municipal fears over the meeting of groups whose interests ran counter to the desires of the state would never fully cease.

Although there is a lack of verifiable evidence for Flavian emperors taking direct action against associations, the wording and spirit of the earlier Julian laws against *collegia* continued to be in effect and to resonate into the next dynasty. This can be glimpsed in the Flavian-era municipal laws engraved on six bronze tablets found in the modern Spanish province of Seville in 1981. Today, we call these the *lex Irnitana*. These municipal laws for the Spanish town of Irni date to 91 CE, during the reign of the last Flavian emperor, Domitian. One section of the law directly deals with any meeting of an "assembly, club, or association," stating: "No one in this municipality shall create a gathering, nor shall that person have a club or an association for that reason, nor shall there be a conspiracy, nor shall anyone do anything through which one of these things occurs."[15] The considerably high penalty for an illegal assembly was a fine of 10,000 sesterces. This was not a modest sum to pay. For comparison: a modius (8.62 liters) of wheat flour cost around 10 sesterces at Rome at the time, and a Praetorian Guardsman made around 8.2 sesterces a day.[16] That is a lot of bread for regular Romans to hand over as a consequence for forming an illegal assembly.

Was Irni a rarity among Roman municipalities or the norm? In other words, can we really take this provincial charter as being representative of most other municipalities and their laws at that time? Many municipal charters replicated legal language and provisions established in the capital, Rome. And if we think back to the municipal charter from Urso (also in Spain) dated to 44 BCE, it already had a similar clause barring colonists from organizing a meeting for the sake of conspiracy. Private meetings held at night, in taverns, or even just conducted in a disruptive manner possessed quite negative connotations and, since the Republic, had been seen as seedbeds of conspiracy.[17] Disruptive assemblies were more feared by elites than the mere existence of an association. It is likely that, in the first century CE, municipal charters became standardized to include language banning meetings aimed at hatching conspiracies. Although evidence for the enforcement of such laws is sparse, they gave local town councils the legal wherewithal to disband groups considered disloyal, seditious, or disorderly, if need be. Roman peace promoted stability and trade, but nonetheless rebellion—such as that which had occurred in Judaea—was clearly not out of the question. In the eastern Mediterranean, and in the area of Asia Minor in particular, there appears to have been a history of discord and labor upheavals that was of specific concern to imperial officials.

Associations, Riots, and Strikes in Ephesus

The port city of Ephesus lies on the Ionian coast of what is now modern Turkey but what was then the Roman province of Asia. Ephesus sat at the junction of a number of important caravan routes and on a primary sea route connecting Rome to the East. In modern parlance, we might today call it a union town. Many of its workers relied on the fishing economy, made their living by providing goods and services, or depended on the revenue brought in by tourism generated both by entertainment, such as festivals, and by pilgrims coming to visit the famed Temple of Artemis.[18] Originally built in the sixth century BCE, the temple was considered a Wonder of the World. Like at Ostia, Ephesian inscriptions and graffiti reveal that many locals also belonged to occupational associations formed for a range of professions: physicians, leather-workers, dough-makers, businesspeople who worked at the slave market, wool-workers, and wine-tasters, among many others.[19]

The population is estimated as having been between 200,000 and 250,000 in the first century CE, when the Christian apostle Paul is alleged to have visited the city on a number of missions. The timeline reconstructed from the Acts of the Apostles, the most detailed source for these visits, places his last missionizing trip to the city around 53 to 55 CE.[20] A particularly telling run-in with the silversmiths of the city is most likely to have occurred in the first half of 55 CE, four years before the riots in the amphitheater in Pompeii under Nero. And yet the context of Paul's visit was likely influenced by the fact it was most likely written down by an evangelist and writer named Luke in the early second century. In a section on Paul's Ephesus trip recounted in Luke-Acts, we are introduced to a silversmith named Demetrius who makes small handicraft shrines sold to pilgrims and others visiting the Temple of Artemis. Upset by Paul's condemnation of idols made by human hands, Demetrius calls together the silversmiths and affiliated artisans of the city to discuss how Paul's proselytizing is harming their own business interests. Paul's message and missionizers were affecting their bottom line, and something needed to be done.

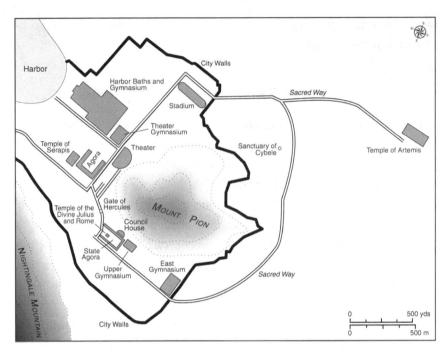

Fig. 8. Map of Ephesus in the first century CE. (Map created by Gabriel Moss and derived from "Ephesus" © Biblica Inc., 2023, licensed under CC BY-SA 4.0 at https://open.bible/maps/.)

The frustrations voiced by these artisans appear to have been largely directed at the economic impact of Paul and his followers on the souvenir economy surrounding the temple.[21] However, their displeasure spread to the populace and was transformed into religious outrage as well. Dissatisfaction then turned into collective action, with rioting and the familiar use of a theater as a courtroom. The crowd grabbed Paul's Macedonian companions, Gaius and Aristarchus, who often traveled with him, and dragged them to the large civic theater. In what was likely a wise move, Paul did not venture there to be judged by the court of Ephesian public opinion. We are told that a Jewish man named Alexander was also seized and falsely blamed for the actions of Paul and his group. Amid the calls for justice in the theater that day, an official scribe stepped forward to tell the crowd that they were in danger of being held accountable for rioting, and that they must depend on the law courts to bring Paul and his followers to justice.[22] He pleaded with the theater crowd to disperse and rely instead on a "lawful assembly," likely because the current gathering would certainly not be considered within the bounds of a licit gathering by Roman law. Arguably, this was the main reason for anti-assembly legislation such as that penned by Caesar or found in the charter at Irni. The scribe then summarily dismissed them in a manner that might suggest either his authority as an official scribe for the city or his role as scribe for a large association—perhaps even one for the silversmiths or artisans. Scribes were frequently employed by both municipal governments and private associations. These important clerks and copyists were often well--versed in Roman law as well.

If we compare the disruptions in Ephesus to the riots at Pompeii just a few years later, we can see that the writer of Acts may also have had in mind the well-known Julian law on associations. He was likely familiar with the state's tendency to disband associations and punish the people at times of civic discord. But were the silversmiths in Acts even a formal association? Merely referring to the silversmiths in the plural does not necessarily tell us that they were an official or licit association. However, inscriptions provide evidence for their group identity. An inscription from Ephesus dating to 250 to 260 CE also refers to the silversmiths in the plural and notes their dedication, likely of a statue, to a proconsul named Valerius Festus in a highly public area between the stadium and the theater. Silversmith associations are similarly referred to in the plural elsewhere, in places like Macedonia, where a treasurer of the silversmiths mentions them in his epitaph.

In Ephesus, a silversmith named Marcus Antonius Hermeias threatens on his tomb inscription that any disturbance to his and his wife's grave will result in a fine of 1,000 denarii, to be paid to the Ephesian silversmiths.[23] Hermeias's epitaph is dated to around the time of Claudius, just before the events in Acts, but numerous other inscriptions point to the fact that the most common way for the silversmith association to refer to itself was simply as "silversmiths." In addition to the strong evidence presented by inscriptions, the speed with which the Ephesian silversmiths and connected artisans came together and then mobilized in collective action suggests the presence, at least to some degree, of an underlying associative network. Just like today, or even in the case of Clodius, associative networks streamlined communication and the gathering of groups in a way that is hard to discern in literary accounts describing crowds or mobs in an ambiguous but decidedly pejorative manner.

In addition to the rioting of the silversmiths, some of our best evidence for labor strikes in antiquity—or the fear of their occurrence—also comes from Asia Minor around this time. At some point between 150 and 200 CE, riots in Ephesus's agora, allegedly instigated by a group of bakers, inspired the proconsular governor to promulgate an edict in response. A copy, etched in stone, has been found at Magnesia, about ten miles from Ephesus.[24] In it, the Roman proconsul states that, while the bakers should be rounded up and brought to trial, he must first consider the welfare of the city. Such language harkens back to the belief in the early Principate that certain associations were needed for their utility to or for the welfare of the state—and thus should be allowed to exist. The proconsul bans the bakers from meeting as a political club called a *hetairia*, asks the leaders not to act in an impudent manner, and tells them to supply the city with bread without interruption, according to regulations that had been established for the well-being of the city's inhabitants. If any baker was caught meeting in secret, his foot would be branded and the people of the city forbidden to give him shelter. The bakers' association of Ephesus was a necessary evil, it seems, since, unlike other associations, it could not be disbanded without inflicting a significant negative impact on the populace. Therefore, it had leverage. In theory, the good of the many was supposed to trump the benefit to a single individual.

Bread was a staple in the diet of the people of Ephesus and of all ancient cities. Between 50 and 75 percent of the calories in the Roman diet were grain-based, composed largely of bread made from wheat, barley, spelt, and other grains.[25] Although bread could be baked at home, this would have posed a fire hazard in the myriad apartments, made predominantly of wood, that filled many Roman cities. Additionally, the firewood required for baking in home ovens could be expensive.[26] In cities, flour could be ground by groups of millers and then made into bread by associations of bakers. Rome had acquired its own associations of bakers, called *pistores*, after the Third Macedonian War against Perseus (171–168 BCE). In the East, associations of bakers were most often known by the Greek term "*artokopoi*," although there were specialty bread-makers of various types as well. Bakers provided an important service, but with great responsibility came great power, and the bakers were potent associations in many cities. As Peter Kruschwitz has remarked, "The edict is not only testament to the effectiveness of collective industrial action in causing disruption and public attention to pressing matters, especially when the disruption affects central aspects of provisions in the public interest."[27] Because the bakers provided a critical service, they could not simply be expelled in the same manner that the Jews and the Isis worshippers of Rome had been.[28]

Around the beginning of the second century, other occupational groups in Asia Minor, such as the linen-workers of Tarsus, were singled out for causing upheavals. Even if some considered them an upstanding civic association, it appears that they could be troublesome to citizen council members, of Tarsus in particular. In his speech to the assembly of the polis, the Greek orator Dio Chrysostom commented that, if the linen-workers were so disruptive, the assembly could just throw them out; exile helped the body politic heal from infection. Chrysostom's speech also gives us insight into the status of this seemingly large and tumultuous group of linen-workers; he notes that even though these men did not have citizenship, they were occasionally allowed to attend the civic assembly meetings.[29] Tarsiot citizenship cost 500 drachmas (around 2,000 sesterces, about two-thirds of a year's salary for a regular Praetorian Guardsman in Rome). This meant that, while the linen-workers could afford membership in an occupational association, it appears they could not pay the high price required to become a citizen of the city. This anecdote is a good reminder that, while some occupational associations were indeed high status and quite costly to join, as evidenced by glittering statue dedications, inscribed membership lists, and pricey clubhouses, many others served regular workers of a foreign status who lacked money and the many civic and legal perks that came with citizenship.

Associations, Fears, and Christians under Trajan

Prefects and governors had great power to act, to build, to ban, and to adjudicate within their provinces. Flaccus's actions in Egypt are a prime example of this. But sometimes, one simply needed to check in with the emperor on certain hazy issues. Under Trajan (r. 98–117 CE), the Roman Empire reached its largest geographic extent, and a sizable portion of its administrative functioning relied on provincial administration and support staff headed by a governor called a proconsul or propraetor. A man named Gaius Plinius Caecilius Secundus—we just call him Pliny the Younger today—was appointed the governor of Pontus-Bithynia around 109 or 110 and likely served as governor from around 111 until 112 CE. The younger Pliny was quite a prolific letter writer, and the first nine books of his *Letters* were published while he was still alive. However, the tenth book, containing letters he sent to the emperor Trajan from his provincial post, was published posthumously. It documents many of the issues and travails he faced while serving as governor.

It is in this last book of letters that we find a missive discussing a devastating fire that broke out in the capital, Nicomedia, while Pliny was traveling on his gubernatorial circuit through his province.[30] As evidenced by the formation of a public fire brigade under Augustus, fires were a common and devastating occurrence in most ancient cities. In Petronius's *Satyricon*, a satire reflecting the age of Nero, one passage depicts the local *vigiles* carrying firefighting supplies and using their axes to break into the house of the wealthy freedman wine merchant Trimalchio, on the Bay of Naples. The brigade, which regularly patrols the district at night, arrives because the horn-blowers hired for Trimalchio's fake funeral set off a false alarm.[31] Although Petronius's text is a satire, it does illustrate the intense dread of fire entrenched in many Mediterranean cities. This fear was not limited to Rome, Ostia, and the Bay of Naples. Fire was a problem that plagued almost every ancient city.

State paranoia over the potential abuses and turmoil that might be caused by a new group of night watchmen had to be balanced against the threat posed by urban fires that could quickly wipe out grain, buildings, and people. As usual with associations, risk and reward had to be factored into the calculations constantly being made by civic leaders. Amid the seditious activities of Sejanus (the prefect of the Praetorian Guard), in 31 CE (during the reign of Tiberius), the *vigiles* had been deployed in Rome to fight against his Praetorian Guards. And during the upheavals of the year of the four emperors in 69 CE, these night watchmen took the side of the Flavians, at the behest of Vespasian's brother, in order to battle the opposing forces of the Vitellians in the city of Rome and help secure Flavian rule.[32]

We must keep such instances in mind in considering Trajan's mindset when Pliny the Younger informed him that the fire in Nicomedia had spread because, with no public fire spigots or buckets to aid them, the people stood idly by as the wind fanned the flames. The governor wanted to form an association of *fabri* (builders) to act as a fire brigade. He notes that he would like about 150, which was a small number compared to those at Rome and Ostia. He states that no one who is not a true fireman will be allowed in. Finally, he tries to mitigate Trajan's fears by saying that these men would be closely overseen and that the privileges given to them would not be abused. In remarks that illustrate persistent imperial anxieties at the top, Trajan responds that Pliny must remember that such associations have caused trouble in his province before and, no matter the underlying reason for their formation, many turn into *"hetaeriae"*—yet another word and variant spelling for political clubs.[33] Trajan suggests that, instead of forming a fire brigade, public buckets and water supplies for firefighting be made available to property owners and the populace. To Trajan's mind, Asia Minor was too great a hotbed of sedition to be allowed an association that could go rogue or be weaponized.

The history of upheavals in the provinces of Asia and Bithynia, combined with long-held state fears of associations mutating into political clubs in the region, informs our reading of the most famous letter Pliny ever wrote to Trajan, concerning the predawn meetings, trials, and execution of Christians in Pontus-Bithynia. This exchange of letters occurred around 111 CE.[34] Pliny describes the early-morning meetings of Christians and says that these seem rather harmless. He also remarks that they stopped their meetings altogether following an edict he promulgated: "They had ceased this practice after the edict in which, in accordance with your orders, I had forbidden all political clubs (*hetaeriae*)."[35] While it is true that Pliny does not call the Christians themselves a "political club," the Christians halted their predawn meetings as a result of this edict. This cessation suggests that they must have realized that they fell under its purview. Like the earlier municipal charters, legislation is more about stopping illegal assembly that could result in sedition than completely disbanding all associations.[36] Unlike artisans such as those in the leather-workers' association at Thyatira, who courted the market overseer for the city, or the elite unions of performers of Dionysus favored by Trajan and Hadrian, the Christians did not serve a public utility, did not have the protection or advocacy of market magistrates, and did not have the justification of "antiquity" to prop up their argument for the right to assemble. Whether or not a group was directly labeled as a *collegium* or a *hetaeria,* to Romans, a rose by any other name still had sharp thorns.

Fears from above still had to be tempered by a general policy of tolerance and respect for the rights of individual cities. In a different pair of letters, when Pliny asks Trajan whether to grant special dispensations to the free city of Amisus on the Black Sea, we see the emperor taking this into account.

Amisus was a port city that had rights to make its own policies and a privileged civic status. Trajan is quick to note that the requested associations should be formed explicitly for the benefit and support of the poor, rather than for any illegal assembly.[37] The emperor agrees to this allowance due to the city's special status: the Amisians can do as they like in this case because of their status. And some bans did not last long.[38] Just after Trajan's reign, under Hadrian, a group of builders did exist in Bithynia.[39] Once again, certain problematic groups fell under the watchful eye of a governor or civic councils, while others were allowed loopholes or tolerated.

Christians were among those who incurred imperial suspicion due to their newness and to their religion being characterized by many—as Pliny did—as a *superstitio* (illegitimate superstition) that ran counter to traditional Roman religion. Christians themselves were quite aware of this reputation. A defense of Christianity written in the form of a philosophical dialogue by a man named Minucius Felix in the second or third century CE references the allegation against Christians of nocturnal meetings and superstitious behavior.[40] Because they were not perceived as having the same level of loyalty to the emperor as other associations and refused to engage in sacrifice to show piety to the imperial cult, they were eyed with distrust. Trust was an incredibly important part of imperial toleration.

The elite Roman allegation of superstition was also more commonly made against groups of enslaved and foreign worshippers. Pliny mentions the torture of two enslaved domestic maids (called *ancillae*) who likely were also deaconesses.[41] The evidence of enslaved persons was made admissible in court if given through torture. But, as with the objections of the silversmiths against Paul's followers, there may have been a slight economic component alongside the religious distrust of Bithynian Christians. Pliny is upset by their failure to attend festivals, as well as the inability of local butchers to sell the meat of sacrificed animals to them. To Pliny, this mix of religious and economic dissent meant that Christians questioned by him who would not recant their Christianity were then held criminally responsible for their actions and executed. Even though there would not be persecution across the Roman Empire of groups of Christians until Valerian in 257–8 CE, they were still seen as a bothersome countercultural faction in some provinces.[42]

Well after Pliny, we find evidence of civic disruptions tied to associations—albeit sporadically—in Asia Minor. Governors continued to intervene and play key roles when a problem arose, particularly when there were building and construction holdups.[43] An edict from one proconsular governor, likely dating to the time of Hadrian, notes that he went to inspect a building site in Pergamon due to significant delays to the project caused by the artisans and contractors.[44] The fragmentary text suggests that there may have been interruptions to the project's progress due to worker strikes. The proconsul expresses compassion for those workers who had continued to show up, but then threatens those who were absent or persisted in such behavior with fines and repercussions.

In the later empire, legal contracts provide us with additional clues as to the fears (whether real or imagined) of magistrates, patrons, and employers. This may have been especially true when they were contracting with building associations, which were notorious for falling behind schedule on jobs. Although associations of builders had long been perceived as benefitting the public good, that does not mean there were not still problems in the sector with labor and the punctual finishing of projects. An inscription from Sardis in Asia Minor dated to 459 CE addresses many of these concerns. Inscribed on a marble block, it records the contract of a mixed association of Christian builders and craftspeople, in the form of a statement and oath, which bound the workers to finish the job while following certain professional guidelines.[45] The association states that a member who provides a valid excuse for missing work will be replaced by another association member; that workers will continue their responsibilities even if there are stoppages of seven days; that sick artisans have up to twenty days off but could then be replaced on the worksite by another association member as a substitute specialist; and that fines are to be paid by both workers and the association in the event of a breach of contract, among many other stipulations.

Much as contracts and oaths were used in Egypt to ensure completion of work, it seems as though the building association made these promises to the overseeing magistrate of Sardis, named Aurelianus, because there had been previous reports from private employers that association members were not completing their work. Some scholars have seen this inscription as being analogous to modern union contracts and collective insurance schemes. In the 1950s—a time in America when one-third of the private workforce were members of unions, as opposed to the 6 percent in the United States today—the Sardis inscription was cast as a "trade union pact."[46]

Although many currently shy away from such terms as anachronistic and criticize attempts to view this inscription in a more modern context, the promises made by the builders' association at Sardis bear a striking resemblance to union contracts today and sound as if they might have functioned in a similar way.

Associations and Collective Action in the Late Second and Early Third Centuries

Not all associations were created or treated equally by the Roman state. As noted prior, many non-Christian Roman magistrates such as Pliny regarded Christianity as a *superstitio*—a term often applied to a dangerous religious sect, and especially given to ones that were also seen as a political threat to the state.[47] This fear of illegitimate religious sects among the Roman populace was not unique to the early Roman Empire. Over three centuries prior, in 186 BCE, the Senate had told the people of Rome that it was a *superstitio* to oppose the senatorial and legislative actions taken against the Bacchic cults in response to alleged "nefarious" and "debauched" nocturnal meetings in Rome.[48] In 59 BCE, Cicero similarly cast riotous Jews as a "barbarous superstition" that caused disorder during public speeches, and noted that opposing them in the interests of the Republic was of the highest dignity.[49] In strong contrast to early Christ groups and others cast negatively as a superstition, we see an alternate treatment of the agonistic associations responsible for putting on athletic competitions in the cities of the Mediterranean. While Christians faced strong opposition in some cases, the performers of Dionysus and associations of athletes were instead elevated to new heights under the emperors Trajan and Hadrian. Whether an association was banned or elevated would once again come down to issues of trust, the imperial loyalty of the association, and its public utility.[50]

The literary record, which often does not address such subjects, is here largely silent. However, surviving petitions to the emperor tell the story of how and why certain favored associations of athletes and entertainers came to prominence, while less "useful" associations were actively extinguished. An Ephesian athlete named Marcus Ulpius Domesticus, a Roman citizen and professional who specialized in a vicious type of wrestling competition called the pankration, lobbied the emperor Hadrian in support of his athletic union.

As the representative for a synod of athletes dedicated to Hercules, he asked that they be granted their own clubhouse and an accompanying archive.[51] This special building would eventually be constructed under the next emperor, Antoninus Pius, near the Baths of Trajan. During this pivotal period for the systematization of games and athletic competitions in Rome and across the Mediterranean, reorganization in Rome and direct imperial patronage brought certain unions of athletes, musicians, singers, and actors even closer into the fold of the emperor—professionals who acted as instruments or symbols of his will. They were public examples of beneficence, and players featured in a ritual calendar meant to promote the worship of the emperor.

The importance of the games and of the unions that enabled them to happen would be further confirmed with the ascent of a man named Septimius Severus to the position of emperor in 193 CE. This began what we call the Severan Age, which would last until 235 CE. The Severan men were Punic in origin, and Septimius's father was a wealthy equestrian. Severus was born in Leptis Magna, in what is modern-day Libya. He later married a Syrian woman named Julia Domna. During his reign, he continued the policies of his predecessors when it came to the treatment of agonistic associations and the special privileges given to them. Upon his accession as emperor, one of the worldwide synods of *technitai* wrote to congratulate him.[52] He responded with what they wanted to hear: reconfirmation of their special privileges and praise for their pious ties to Dionysus. Here the old Latin maxim noted by the Stoic philosopher Seneca holds true, and might serve as a fitting mantra for imperial Roman attitudes toward the role of associations: "*Manus manum lavat*" (One hand washes another).[53] There is no denying that the Romans were a quid pro quo society. This went for the proverbial circuses that provided entertainment, but also for those who cultivated and shipped the grains for the bread.

A pivotal question in the Severan period is whether associations had the power to protest their treatment and to use a strike as leverage. There is some evidence to suggest they did. Sometime between 198 and 203, during the reign of Septimius Severus, a group of local shipowners living in the Roman town of Arelate (now Arles in southern France) who supplied grain to Rome for the grain dole inscribed a copy of an imperial letter on a bronze plaque.[54] Arelate had a vibrant harbor economy of artisans and tradespeople.

Likewise, it was filled with wealthy associations of businessmen, merchants, textile dealers, and shipowners. Many of these businessmen were also wealthy freedmen with memberships in multiple associations; they belonged to occupational associations, but many also served as priests in a religious group called the *seviri augustales*. In many Roman cities, such associations were composed of freedmen (with a few freeborn men sometimes allowed in) who served the imperial cult in addition to performing other civic and religious duties.

The shipowners addressed their letter to the prefect of the grain supply and, in it, they complained of mistreatment by Roman officials. They apparently threatened to stop the grain shipments unless these abuses were rectified. The prefect, Claudius Julianus, was quick to write back and try to appease this important group. He assured them that the abuses would be addressed and, by doing so, carefully diffused the shipowners' threat to go on strike. The food supply was far too important: Arles's shipowners could not be allowed to use their powerful corporations to disrupt service to Rome. Even if it was just a threat, Julianus did not take it as an idle one. From the Egyptian textile workers to the bakers of Ephesus, the power of collective action remained visible and viable during the imperial period, as used by a variety of different types of associations.

In the transition to the later Roman Empire, a fundamental question that emperors and the state appear to have grappled with was whether there were more intensive, assured ways to make associations, corporations, unions, and errant religious groups fall into line. It was not only formal unions of performers and athletes or associations of wealthy shipowners in places like Arles who possessed the socioeconomic capital and agency to bargain collectively, to petition the emperor for his aid, or then to receive his protection at this time. Inscribed petitions and their imperial responses from the emperor, erected on stone by more modest collectives in the late second century, illustrate that there were legal rights and a degree of agency granted to certain other workers—particularly those integral to certain supply chains.

The power to write to the emperor included tenant farmers tied to the land called *coloni*. These farmers could be tied to both imperial estates and private farmlands. The power of these workers was potent when they banded together and threatened to abandon their imperial work by using the long-known tactics of *anachoresis*—work desertion or flight from one's duties—

that were long known in places like Egypt for many centuries.⁵⁵ Bands of *coloni* in North Africa could work and petition en masse from the estate they worked upon, even if they did not refer to themselves formally as a synod or association. At certain times, groups of these sharecroppers even threatened work stoppages or secessions on imperial and private estates in the region, in areas vital to the Roman food supply.

Roman tenant farmers were able to voice their displeasure at certain junctures that point to their collectivity and ability. During the early reign of the emperor Commodus (180–192 CE), maltreatment of *coloni* by rent collectors and abuse at the hands of administrators called procurators was rife. It was an issue recorded on petitions particularly in the area of the Bagradas Valley in North Africa.⁵⁶ As Dennis Kehoe has pivotally shown, these *coloni* were not feeble peasants, but rather a well-organized group that included Roman citizens and those with enough money to help finance the process of imperial petitioning. These tenant farmers also had "considerable leverage" to pressure the state.⁵⁷ Sometimes their threats to leave their positions were implicit, while at other junctures, they were more explicit about the repercussions of ignoring their pleas. Around 181 CE, one recorded petition and imperial response indicates an unambiguous threat by the African *coloni* at Gazr-Mezuar to leave the imperial estates for a private one if the maltreatment was not rectified.⁵⁸ We should not imagine that *coloni* were mere serfs bound to work the land and be commanded from above.⁵⁹

The abandoning of agricultural duties by workers in North Africa and Egypt was a looming fear harbored by the emperor and wealthy landowners during the imperial period into late antiquity. This went for private estates as well. In a letter in the early fifth century CE, Augustine recounted an act of collective resistance and bargaining by *coloni* working on the North African estate of a wealthy Roman woman at Thogonoetensis. These tenants threatened to leave together, unless their landlady and the bishop removed an abusive local cleric named Antoninus of Fussala.⁶⁰ But North Africa was not the only place to have farmers threaten desertion if wrongs such as extortion and overwork were not righted. There is evidence that at Aga Bey Köyü in Lydia, within modern Turkey, hereditary tenant farmers similarly threatened to leave their jobs due to abuses from imperial tax officials, who even used soldiers to put the farmers in chains.⁶¹ This occurred either in the reign of Septimius Severus and Caracalla in the early third century CE or, more likely, under Philip I (244–249 CE), and ended with the emperor yielding to many of their demands. As the early Republican plebeians of Rome had exemplified hundreds of years prior, using the threat of a boycott or a secession as a bargaining chip to protect against corruption and abuse was not a new approach to negotiating work conditions—and it remained an effective one.

The End of the Golden Age

The golden age of association formation in the Roman Mediterranean occurred from the first to the second centuries CE. Some of these associations created formal charters and membership rules, while others were more informal and loosely based, without leaving much of a written record. In the case of powerful occupational groups such as the silversmiths and the bakers in places like Asia Minor, they were capable of causing public disorder and economic disruption. Some even went on strike or mobilized their group into actions that benefitted their membership. Although many of these associations were tolerated by the Roman state and various provincial governors, still others were banned or kept from forming altogether, due to fears that they could turn into political clubs or paramilitary groups. But not all associations were treated with the same level of suspicion. In the second to early third centuries CE, in particular, respected associations of entertainers and athletes enjoyed patronage ties with the emperor that grew ever closer and more intimate. Such ties blurred the always-hazy lines between public and private spheres in the ancient world. As per usual, entertainment and athletic associations had leverage in their popularity and public profile in a way many other associations did not.

In the late second century CE, this increase in imperial patronage and state oversight of certain pivotal associations remained a tool used to signify the emperor's magnanimity and care for the Roman people. But this increase in state control also allowed the emperor to more tightly regulate key lines of communication with the populace within the public spaces of the theater, amphitheater, and hippodrome. Intensifying patronage of key associations could also function as a method for securing supply chains crucial to the provision of food, coinage, military arms, and other products needed by the people, the state, and the Roman military. This was a slow process of forming state corporations that continued and expanded into the late Roman Empire. Governmental creep and deliberate expansion into certain economic areas with already-strong associative networks underpinning them may have been attempts to reduce corruption and mismanagement within the private sector. This was the thinking behind safeguarding the grain ration and contracting with associations of shipowners to transport the grain to the city of Rome. But even in this case, the threat of a strike or desertion loomed.

6

Castes, Law, and Compulsory Labor in Late Antiquity

IN THE SPRING OF 271 CE, a group of mint workers barricaded themselves on Rome's Caelian Hill. Together with the city's chief financial officer and their supervisor, a man named Felicissimus, they waited for the soldiers of Rome's current emperor, Aurelian, to arrive.[1] Later sources allege that the mint workers had tampered with the monetary supply. This likely means committing fraud, such as counterfeiting coins.[2] Although the list of their demands does not survive, their strike and resulting uprising, dubbed the *bellum monetariorum* (war of the mint workers), created a dire situation. The widespread rioting in the city that followed the civil insurrection left perhaps thousands dead in the streets of Rome. One report noted that seven thousand of Aurelian's soldiers were killed during it.[3] Felicissimus died in the commotion as well. Today, the mint workers' rebellion is instructive in terms of how organized workshops might mobilize against the Roman state. Their revolt may also reveal the ways in which emperors and the Roman state increased their control, surveillance, and legal subjugation of certain associations and their workers into the late Roman Empire as anti-corruption tactics and for supply-chain security.

The mint workers whom Felicissimus oversaw, known collectively as *monetarii*, were not independent artisans. They were state employees who chose to strike and to riot. Those from among the artisans who were enslaved were legally viewed as state property and were therefore more vulnerable to physical censure than freeborn, citizen workers. Within the mint, the minters were organized into individual, assigned workshops called *officinae*, the source of the modern word "office." Their chosen refuge during the insurrection, Rome's Caelian Hill, was a sector of the city familiar to these artisans. The mint of Rome had been moved there, close to the Flavian amphitheater (known today as the Colosseum), sometime after 70 CE. This likely occurred after the fire of 80 CE, which had caused the emperor Domitian to undertake extensive rebuilding of the city. The mint workers' revolt demonstrates that, in addition to the more distant "barbarian" and provincial challenges to his power in places like Dalmatia, Gaul, and Palmyra, Aurelian had internal animosities to quash. It also indicates that, at certain times, Roman workers could and did use the power inherent in their labor organizations to withhold services and advocate for their needs.

Those who labored in the Aurelian-era mint were likely a mix of enslaved and freed workers. They may have numbered around two hundred or more, as had been the case over a century prior, under Trajan.[4] Although the rather unreliable *Historia Augusta* includes a likely fictional letter from Aurelian to his adopted father that refers to Felicissimus as a *servus* (enslaved man), it seems more probable that he was a man of equestrian rank, as were most of the administrators of the mint at the time.[5] However, other types of enslaved persons did support the functioning of the Roman state in cities and in the military. Enslaved men who maintained city infrastructure such as aqueducts and performed other services for Roman cities (known as *servi publici*, or public enslaved persons) were legally classified as chattel property of the state or city itself under Roman property law and were organized into associations called *familiae*. There is also evidence that the Roman army employed state-owned enslaved persons called *calones*. In addition to using these public enslaved persons to provide services to the populace, the state depended on a network of skilled associations to perform contracted services for the state, particularly in regard to the food supply.

As was explored in the previous chapter, there is some evidence that the workers in the *collegia* tied to the late Roman supply chain (known as the *corporati* system) had held at least the threat of a strike or disruption to services as a trump card in case of mistreatment or in reaction to abuse by the system or its agents. Like the shipping *corpora* active in Arles, the state mint workers in Rome provided a similarly important service to the state. They were in charge of molding, hammering, and generating the coinage produced at Rome's mint. The coins were then circulated in the monetary supply used to pay soldiers or to purchase goods. Like diamond miners or oil rig engineers, these state workers had direct access to valuable resources on a daily basis. This made them both a necessity and a threat to the Roman state's function. The inherent threat that the mint workers posed to the Roman government stemmed in part from the fact that the economy of the Roman Empire relied on precious metal coinage. In antiquity, the coin was the commodity. The weight of the pure gold, silver, copper, or bronze allegedly contained in a coin in proportion to the alloy or filler metal was an important numismatic metric, later termed its fineness. A coin's fineness helped to determine its value on the market. However, when the weight or percentage of precious metal in a commodity coin is decreased while its face value remains unchanged, it is said to be debased. Coin debasement and inflation, both hallmarks of the mid-third century CE, were issues that Aurelian needed to address.

The economy inherited by Aurelian in 270 CE from Claudius II Gothicus, who had died of plague, was already struggling with consumer confidence in the monetary supply. The news of the mint workers' rebellion did not help matters, and Aurelian had to act fast to reassure the populace. The imperial government and the many emperors of the third century continued to rely on the quarrying of imperial mines and the minting of precious metals in their names. They often used enslaved or penal labor for these mining efforts in imperially owned mines. Safeguarding state resources is not a novel concept; the Romans also stationed guards and some soldiers on watches to surveil and protect their mining operations. Because money had to be hammered rather than printed, the minting of coinage took much more physical effort and strength than it does in the current era. Like the hired gladiators employed by Clodius as a personal militia, mint workers were skilled and likely rather buff men similar in strength to blacksmiths. As was the case in the involuntary gladiatorial unions called *familiae* discussed in relation to Spartacus, mint workers also seem to have been organized into *familiae* that made religious dedications as associations. In his assessment of the civil uprising, late Roman historian Michael Kulikowski casts the mint workers as a testament to "how militarized the Roman civil service was becoming that skilled craftsmen like the mint workers should be able to organise rioting just as effectively as a mutinous army unit."[6] In actuality, the internal organization of involuntary workshops and *familiae* is what allowed this type of agile, coordinated rioting to occur—just as it had with Spartacus many centuries prior.

At that moment in time, opportunity was as plentiful as dissatisfaction among both the elites and non-elites. The support of wealthy, meddling senators—who could often manipulate artisans and the populace to work in their interests—is also evident in the mint workers' rebellion. In the city, there was a notable decrease in direct supervision by the emperor. Rome's current emperor, Aurelian, was in the provinces, fighting the Iuthungi in Raetia and Noricum; thus, his attention was focused on threats far outside the Eternal City—until the riot occurred. Many were dissatisfied with his absenteeism. After all, while the Augustan-era poet Propertius originally coined the adage that absence makes the heart grow fonder, the elegist was referring to lovers, not emperors.[7] Rome's senators and many in the capital saw Aurelian's absence as occasion for upheaval, and the senators seem to have encouraged the mint workers' revolt, along with the urban population of Rome. Rioting then broke out in the city, which had to be put down with force by Aurelian's soldiers.

The rebellion was a jolt that spurred the emperor to close the mint at Rome for two years. He executed most of the rebellious minters and ordered a decrease in the number of workshops within it. Closing mints and encouraging a more mobile minting process that could accompany the enormous traveling clique that followed the emperor across the empire—and thus be closely supervised—was a surveillance strategy. Aurelian would later close mints in Trier and Cologne in order to regain control within the Gallic Empire. He also undertook major changes in the monetary supply and coinage reforms that would inspire Diocletian over a decade later. When the mint at Rome reopened in 273 CE, he ordered the minting of a new silver coin called the *aurelianus* there, as well as at the mint in Milan. Aurelian's anxiety over both internal and external threats did not stop there. The uprising may have also prompted the emperor to create Rome's largest and most symbolically charged monument: the Aurelian Wall. Like other civic and frontier walls throughout history, the Aurelian Wall was meant to be a material testimony to the power and the paternal concern of the leader who constructed it. The emperor's new fortifications for the city of Rome were about twelve miles long and would take five to ten years to build. Aurelian would be long dead before his walls were finished, but for hundreds of years, they were as functional as they were allegorical.

The famed walls became the symbol of Rome and were likely erected by teams of construction workers called *fabri*, who were highly organized into labor associations in the city. Building associations and construction specialists often worked in tandem. In his analysis of the building of the Aurelian Wall, Hendrik Dey noted that, even with the army predominantly in Palmyra on campaign, there were still enough associated specialists at Rome to handle this mammoth undertaking ordered by the emperor and likely designed by military architects: "In addition to the principal *collegium* of builders, the *fabri tignuarii*, which alone counted 1,300 members in Hadrian's time, there were also the bronzeworkers, ironworkers, pavers, stonecutters, demolitions experts, and possibly an additional college of builders, the *structores*, all of which would have had their part to play."[8] Although building activities in the city of Rome had plummeted in the mid-third century prior to Aurelian, the men who belonged to building associations and the subordinates in their workshops would have been sufficient to staff the teams needed to build the massive wall. However, there was not always consistency in the workforce committed to a project over time, from start to completion. Modern analysis of the brickwork that makes up the Aurelian Wall suggests that, while more experienced *collegia* of bricklayers and construction workers began the monumental project, more haphazard building techniques were adopted toward the end and in later repairs to the fortifications under Maxentius.[9]

In September or October of 275 CE, Aurelian was killed by his own soldiers at Caenophrurium, near the Black Sea, in modern-day Turkey. These assassins had been falsely told by his administrative assistant, perhaps using forged documents, that the emperor planned to kill them.[10] Aurelian and his troops were en route to Byzantium, a city later refounded by Constantine as Constantinople, in order to begin a campaign against the Sassanids. His assassination at the hands of his soldiers may have triggered the election of an elder senator named Marcus Claudius Tacitus, rather than a soldier, to the role of imperator. Although Tacitus swiftly traveled to Thrace to take over Aurelian's army and execute the assassins, he too would die only a few months later, either from a fever or also by assassination. As had occurred in many of the years prior to the reign of Aurelian and immediately after, a number of claimants to the purple, such as Tacitus's half-brother Florianus, reigned briefly before meeting bitter ends. Other successors, such as Marcus Aurelius Probus, who ruled from 276 to 282 CE, lasted a few years longer than most.

Like his predecessor, Aurelian, Probus appears to have viewed infrastructure and building as means of appearing to restore the Roman Empire. But it was perhaps his use of soldiers as compulsory construction workers and manual laborers that caused discontent among his troops and ultimately led to his death. The *Historia Augusta*, although notoriously untrustworthy, notes their use as compulsory laborers to carry out Probus's building program: "There are still to be seen in many cities in Egypt public works of his, which [Probus] caused to be built by the soldiers. On the Nile, moreover, he did so much that his sole efforts added greatly to the tithes of grain. He constructed bridges and temples, porticos and basilicas, all by the labor of the soldiers, he opened up many river-mouths, and drained many marshes, and put in their place grain-fields and farms."[11] The same source notes that when the emperor then arrived at his hometown of Sirmium, in modern Serbia, he aimed to beautify it by once again using soldiers' labor.[12] He set soldiers to the task of draining the nearby marshes, so that a canal connecting to the Sava River could be constructed.

The troops mutinied against this job and chased Probus, forcing him to seek refuge in an iron-clad tower. Why such a negative reaction? As Sara Elise Phang has shown, Roman soldiers commonly engaged in building activities, particularly when not on campaign. Such projects were a means of reinforcing the existing military hierarchy and instilling obedience in troops. However, it seems that soldiers were always aware when their overuse as compulsory builders shifted into the territory of servile manual labor.[13] Roman soldiers were highly sensitive about being used like enslaved laborers doing menial work, rather than receiving the deference owed to freeborn legionaries: "Soldiers resisted work that seemed servile, seeking slaves to perform this work.... Resenting excessively degrading labor, soldiers might mutiny."[14] That is exactly what happened in the case of the soldiers forced to drain the marshlands of Sirmium at Probus's behest. After five years, Probus was killed by soldiers, and a former head of the Praetorian Guard named Carus was heralded as emperor either just prior to or immediately upon Probus's death.

It would not be until Diocletian's ascension to the purple in 284 that a modicum of political stability would be achieved in the Roman Empire. At this point, we must pause and distinguish a new era for workers and of imperial labor organization moving forward. The period between the murders of Severus Alexander and Julia Mamaea in 235 CE and Diocletian's accession in 284 would later be referred to as the Crisis of the Third Century due to the social, political, and economic disorder experienced in certain Roman provinces and the relative breakdown in imperial succession during this time.[15] To counteract this turmoil, many of the policies of the late third century CE espoused by Diocletian and his form of imperial rule, called the Tetrarchy (Rule of Four), were aimed at reorganizing, restructuring, or creating more enduring institutions. During his reign, the rather autocratic Diocletian also attempted to improve imperial recordkeeping, to modify the succession so that rulership passed from two Augusti to two Caesars, to enlarge the army, to reform provincial governance, and to halt rampant inflation through monetary reforms. In addition to these changes, he was also responsible for the inception of the largest persecution of Christians in antiquity, the Great Persecution, begun in 303 CE. He went into voluntary retirement in May of 305, along with his fellow Augustus, Maximian; however, the persecution continued intermittently until 311, when the emperor Galerius at last formally ended it with the Edict of Toleration.

Due to the new regime's domineering approach to rule, it is often referred to by modern scholars as the Dominate.[16] Diocletian was a seasoned soldier who fashioned himself as a *dominus et deus* (master and god). He distanced himself from the populace and used systematic governance, bureaucracy, and the law as aggressive tools—in particular, to address corruption. While contemporary critics viewed these tactics as stemming from "insatiable avarice," Diocletian and the Tetrarchs cast them as means of establishing efficient governance.[17] Anti-corruption and supply-chain security were foci of many emperors in the period of late antiquity, to varying degrees of success. And, as this chapter argues, labor associations played a pivotal part in anti-corruption efforts.

Any attempt to analyze the reforms of Diocletian and his successors from the vantage point of such tactics must first define "corruption" and, consequently, "anti-corruption"—both terms are open to broad interpretation and do not make for an altogether feasible analytic category.[18] Within the context of this brief survey of the use of associations and labor associations as late antique anti-corruption strategies, corruption is any attempt to abuse, circumvent, undermine, or debase the laws, systems, or institutions that underpinned the intended functioning of the *res publica* (state). Anti-corruption tactics are attempts to address these impairments. Anti-corruption methods in late antiquity often emphasized the use of stringent laws to address corrupting practices such as *peculatus* (embezzlement of state money), venality, *repetundae* (extortion), *vis* (violence), and the maladministration of the *annona* (interfering with the grain supply). They could also encompass efforts to guarantee funding or supplies to the state and military through the requisitioning of resources or people and the restriction of movement: geographically, professionally, or even in respect to social class. Rome began to increase its imposition of what we today might call professional castes as a means of securing goods and services. To many subsequent emperors, what happened with the mint workers in 271 CE was merely a lesson in how and why certain artisans had to be kept more legally controlled and under the imperial thumb.

Diocletian's imperial ideology was one of efficiency through the creation of quasi-static financial and labor models. To be effective, these articulated models relied upon the capabilities of the state and the military to prescribe, enforce, and maintain such a system in the Roman Empire; however, there was always some degree of disconnect between the word of law and its imposition in the empire. There is always a gap between ideal and execution. But many of the fiscal and documentary changes made in the late third century did have an impact on labor for many centuries to come. Although tenant farmers called *coloni* had existed for over a century, under Diocletian they were secured and counted by the Roman state through financial registration in his property census (formulated in 296 CE) for a five-year cycle. He taxed the property of landowners by a notional unit of land output called a *iugum* and by another unit of output for living beings called the *caput* (head). A *caput* could include various impoverished men, women (who were half a *caput*), children, tenant farmers, and livestock. In the fourth century, under Constantine, the *coloni* were bound to the land on which they were registered.[19] As Noel Lenski has recently argued, Diocletian's system of tying *coloni* to estates influenced the creation of a new legal status: it "had the unintended consequence of locking them into a position between free and slave articulated over the course of the fourth and fifth centuries."[20] Freedom existed on a continuum in antiquity, rather than as a binary of enslaved and freeborn. And in the late Roman Empire, tenant farmers became increasingly tied to the property they worked.

It is important to consider the limitations of the legal sources available to us today when evaluating the disconnect between intent and praxis in Roman law during the later Roman Empire, especially in relation to labor and compulsory corporatization. Most of our legal evidence for this period is derived from normative sources, particularly those in the *Codex Theodosianus* (438 CE), compiled during the reign of Theodosius II. From the mid-sixth century, we also have the *Digesta* (or *Pandecta*, in Greek), which consists of fragments from classical jurists (533); the *Institutiones*, predominantly for law students (promulgated in 533); the *Codex Justinianus* (534); and then the *Novellae* of Justinian, a compilation of new laws published between 535 and 548. Much of this legal evidence, prima facie, seems to suggest pervasive corruption through bribery and venality, but looks can be deceiving. As legal historian Jill Harries warns, "Emperors in their laws resorted to a language of power designed to hold their officials to account; this has been, wrongly in my view, interpreted as evidence of extensive wrongdoing on the part of officials, and especially of judges."[21] The cultivated language of anti-corruption tactics employed in law, literature, and oratory was particular to this time, and was itself part of a broader "rhetoric of execration" that was intricate and understood in the moment—but often difficult to penetrate today.[22] We should attempt to understand these laws as often addressing specific instances while simultaneously expressing consistent imperial efforts at transparency and accountability through law.

One allegation it is crucial to evaluate is whether corruption caused the decline of Rome, as many a historian and modern political pundit has claimed. The shift in Roman law texts to increasingly emphasize oversight and protections against corruption has led many to see an extreme escalation in corruptive practices from the third century on. Such legislation influenced Edward Gibbon, who proposed that a mix of luxury, Christianity, bureaucrats, and internal corruption collectively brought about the decline and fall of Rome. Since 1776, Gibbon's Enlightenment-era views have continued to have an impact on modern assessments of the late empire and have unjustifiably severed the period prior to Diocletian from that of the later empire.

The perception of an inefficient and characteristically different late antique administration was later furthered by Ramsay MacMullen's influential work on late Roman corruption, in which he argued that corruptive practices were endemic.[23] However, recent legal scholars have begun to temper allegations of widespread and deleterious corruption by looking at how the rhetoric of law may have contributed to a rather more fictive "fall" due to corruption than actually occurred in reality.[24]

A way to test scholars' assumptions is by examining the Diocletianic changes to tax assessment and collection, the establishment of associations of imperial agents for the oversight of certain essential state organizations such as the *cursus publicus* (Rome's courier service for transporting communications), and the state's increased emphasis on the creation of compulsory trade associations in the later empire. These moves collectively reveal that major Roman statesmen did view corruption as a pervasive problem, even if there was often little they could do to enforce sweeping anti-corruption legislation outside of a few city centers—but perception must be separated from reality. It is also admittedly difficult to assess the efficacy of these measures from legal and literary sources alone. The constraints imposed by the evidence, which is primarily in the form of legislation, mean that Roman anti-corruption tactics must be explored largely through the "top-down" language employed in legal rescripts, decrees, and edicts that note labor and the use of compulsory associations, rather than through the thoughts of the workers themselves. Ideally, we would have more feedback and insights from the workers. Legal texts instead record threats of personal violence, attempts to order society through the law, and the creation of a late antique system of compulsory professions that made some occupations and civic positions both hereditary and inescapable—a move that elevated state security above the free will and civic rights of workers to choose their jobs and their spouses.

Before we can examine attempts to control these labor associations, we must first understand the organization and deployment of groups of state bureaucrats such as land surveyors and tax collectors. A pivotal area of Diocletian's reorganization addressed taxes and the officials who assessed them. These taxes secured income essential to funding the state and to his expansion of the military. Diocletian and the Tetrarchy implemented a change to the administration of tax assessment and collection aimed at increasing tax revenue and decreasing tax evasion. In order to notify the public of the new system, Diocletian sent out written indictions that announced regionally variant tax revenues to be collected for a certain period through both the *iugatio* (a land tax) and the *capitatio* (a poll tax).[25] A census was then supposed to progress methodically through the provinces in order to assess what each could afford to pay, recurring every five years. In part, Diocletian's policies tackled issues of tax evasion and administrative corruption (for example, through extortion) in the tax collection process by instituting a culture of documentation, routine, and law—what we might today call a paper trail.

The state's focus on a paper trail meant a massive increase in the use of ink, papyrus, maps, and cadastral archives within a complex recordkeeping system. The worth of land, livestock, and people was collected by groups of town councilors (called *decuriones*), local officials, imperial bureaucrats, and associations of land surveyors (called *censitores*) who traveled from village to village, leaving behind a number of inscriptions and boundary stones.[26] The notably biased early Christian author Lactantius lamented the heavy taxes and number of tax collectors under Diocletian; however, the mid-fourth-century historian Aurelius Victor viewed that same tax plan as one of *modestia tolerabilis* (tolerable moderation) compared to Constantius II's later tax reforms.[27] It is difficult to judge from these conflicting literary sources alone whether the late Roman tax system from Diocletian onward was in fact as oppressive and violent as it was sometimes accused of being.[28]

As Diocletian soon discovered, assessing a fluctuating labor force in an economy dependent on a debased monetary supply was akin to trying to step in the same river twice. Attempts at stabilization brought the imposition of greater restrictions on movement, particularly for tenant farmers.[29] Despite Diocletian's efforts, petitions committed to papyrus and other contemporary sources indicate that corruption—especially in terms of illegal exactions by the tax collectors—continued well after his reign.[30] At this time, the language of law certainly became more recognizably caustic. Whereas the legal sources emphasize the fairness and objectivity of Diocletian's revamping of Rome's tax assessments, the literary sources were not as kind. Lactantius notes the proliferation of professionalized associations of land surveyors throughout the provinces at this time—groups of men who often treated locals more like enemy hostages than fellow Romans.[31] Later writers suggest there may also have been an amplified use of fear and threats of violence in imperial approaches to policy enforcement and tax collection from the late third century onward by these tax collectors. However, these writers may not reflect empire-wide practices.

The degree of severity of the emerging culture of state and religious violence in the later empire is still hotly debated by scholars; regardless, it is possible to identify an increasing ethos of documentation aided by state-organized administrative associations. It is also likely that this imperial focus on the compiling, archiving, organization, and accumulation of records under the direction of the Tetrarchic era's rulers helped to develop a wider habit of encyclopedism both within the state and among individuals.[32] The effects can be seen publicly in the growing emphasis on systematic assessment, the use of law, and procedures for recordkeeping, but it can also be seen in private initiatives. The collection and codification of imperial rescripts and constitutions in the privately compiled *Codex Gregorianus* and *Codex Hermogenianus* assembled during the reign of Diocletian (dated to around 291 and 295, respectively) represent, quite tellingly, the first efforts at systematic law since the reign of the emperor Hadrian.[33] The state, and hence legislation, was shifting, and thus the practitioners of law were trying to catch up. These codes are part of a broader movement in the late empire toward the organization of both knowledge and people into tightly classified groups. As Ramsay MacMullen noted, "Certainly the ambition to plan their world possessed the Tetrarchs."[34] Material creations such as the Peutinger map, likely dating to the early fourth century CE and perhaps displayed in a throne room, demonstrate that, from new archives to land surveys to maps, the Tetrarchs planned their world.[35] The problem was that not everyone was on board with their stringent blueprint. This is especially true in regards to controlling what businessmen, artisans, and merchants could charge for goods and services.

Besides tax reforms and recordkeeping, another technique used as an attempt to secure funding and prevent its misuse was to organize, oversee, and regulate both coinage and commerce at the state level. Could this have been in part to block collective actions? An earlier papyrus from 260 CE in the reign of Gallienus remains instructive on why this might have been necessary and also may demonstrate how financial associations during the mid-third century banded together to address coin debasement and other problems with the monetary supply.[36] The document records the pronouncement of a *strategos* for the Oxyrhynchite nome in Egypt, regarding a group of local bankers or money changers called *trapezeitai*. It appears the bankers had, perhaps in an act of collective action, closed their banks and refused coinage. The *strategos* then demands they reopen the banks and accept the "sacred coinage of the Augusti." Only counterfeit and suspect coins could be refused.

Were the Oxyrhynchus bankers a formal association working in coordination? We know that there were bankers operating out of the Serapeum—that is, the Temple of Serapis—within the town during the Roman era, but their organizational structure is murky during the third century CE. Ancient association specialist Koenraad Verboven has argued that there is no indication of an official association of bankers together choosing to close the banks there in 260 CE.[37] Other papyri indicate that there were public bankers connected to the nome and contracted by the state who made payments and could issue receipts as one body. A small archive dated to 154 CE and later papyri from the mid-third century show these "public bankers" working as a group.[38] But the order of the *strategos* in 260 CE does not specify precisely public or private bankers, just bankers generally. But even here, there is precedent. As we saw with the silversmiths of Ephesus, groups could and did simply refer to their associations in the collective plural, simply saying "bakers," "bankers," or perhaps "tanners" as shorthand. In fact, this is exactly what the association of *trapezeitai* of Ephesus, who had their own stalls in the latrines of the gymnasium of Vedius, did in the mid-second or third century.[39] It remains difficult to discern for sure what the level of cohesion of the bankers chastised in 260 was, but it does seem as though it took a degree of state interference to get them to annul their protests of the debased coinage and again accept it for exchange.

Diocletian tried to address the rampant inflation and problems with the monetary supply through coinage reforms that re-standardized the weight of gold coins and reintroduced the minting of a pure silver coin.[40] He was unsuccessful. In addition to these coinage reforms, he again turned to legislation, this time as a mechanism for setting the maximum amounts that could be charged for goods and services. This produced the famous—though largely ineffective—Edict of Maximum Prices, or Price Edict. Dating to November or December of 301, the edict provided over one thousand prices for goods and standard wages for several occupations and artisans. While the language of law became more ferocious, there often remained a message of paternal concern in much of the legislation aimed at quashing corruptive practices. In the preamble, the Tetrarchs carefully outlined the reasoning be-

CASTES, LAW, AND COMPULSORY LABOR 145

Fig. 9. Plaster cast of the Price Edict of Diocletian, first and second columns of orthostat 8 of the left part of the rotunda in Aizanoi, Turkey, 301 CE. Münzkabinett, Staatliche Museen, Berlin. (Photo: bpk Bildagentur/ Münzkabinett, Staatliche Museen, Berlin, Germany/Art Resource, NY.)

hind their decision to fix the prices of certain goods and services throughout the empire: "For who has so unfeeling a heart or has removed himself so far from human feeling that he is ignorant that he has not indeed felt in commercial affairs, whether done in merchandise or dealt with in the daily hustle and bustle of the cities—to such an extent that it has been allowed for shameless prices to rise? Neither abundance of goods nor the fruitfulness over the years mitigates this unbridled lust for plundering."[41] The rulers of both the East and the West—Diocletian, Maximian, Constantius Chlorus, and Galerius—cast themselves collectively as the protectors of the entire human race. They portrayed themselves as men who had to protect the people against avaricious merchants for the public good. Although the edict would prove unenforceable without the appointment of hundreds of additional officials and market overseers, the public presentation of the law did communicate a concern for the common people through a visible record sent out to the provinces, written in Greek and Latin, and displayed visibly throughout the Mediterranean.

The Price Edict is not all that different from a modern politician addressing the people to reassure them that they are aware of and actively combating high gas prices or inflated prices at the supermarket. When running for office, empathy for the common person is encapsulated in such gestures as being able to correctly recite the price of bread or a gallon of milk. Even if the law was beyond the bounds of feasible enforcement, the dozens of pieces of the Price Edict inscription, found predominantly in cities of the eastern empire, do at least provide insight into the Roman labor market in the early fourth century and, once again, expose a regime attempting to assess, archive, and impose organization on an empire that did not fall into line.[42] But while Diocletian's monetary reforms and his use of legislation to address extortionate prices have long been noted by modern scholarship, his formation of state associations of tradesmen (for example, *collegia, corpora*) can also be seen as an imperial endeavor, in the same vein as the Price Edict, to secure goods and services essential to the functioning of the state. By circumventing private suppliers for certain goods and increasing the bureaucracy used for oversight through highly regulated state trade associations, price gouging could be addressed and mitigated.[43] These *corpora* may have been a tactic of anti-corruption in late antiquity. This is not meant in any way to defend their use or the attempted subjugation of such professionals within them, but simply to conceptualize how they were viewed by the state.

Although private craftsmen continued to operate and be of use to the military, the establishment of imperial arms factories guaranteed a necessary supply for the army and dodged concerns such as extortionate prices. Legions could more confidently rely on supply chains, and budget accordingly. It is likely that during Diocletian's time in the late third century, state factories called *fabricae* began to operate in order to directly supply the army with clothing and armor.[44] The workers in these state-owned factories, who were called *fabricenses*, were organized into an association called the *corpus fabricensium* overseen by the *magister officiorum* (master of offices).[45] This *magister* oversaw various other components of the palace administration, too: the *agentes in rebus*, the *cursus publicus*, and certain state clerks. Close to forty *fabricae* were spread throughout the provinces of the eastern Mediterranean and, in the West, were located in Gaul, Illyria, and Italy. In addition to establishing state-owned *fabricae,* Diocletian (like Aurelian) also sought to control the workers within the *monetae* (mints) who created the gold, silver, and bronze coinage that circulated in the empire. In order to provide on-the-spot coinage, a mobile *moneta comitatensis* still followed the emperors, and could thus be more closely overseen, while a limited number of static imperial mints were allowed within the empire. Diocletian's reforms of local minting and control over the minters who worked in them were partially inspired by Aurelian. The increasing focus on the organization, oversight, and control of both the *fabricenses* who worked in the *fabricae* to supply the army and the *monetarii* who labored in the mints perhaps demonstrates a valid concern with securing supply chains at the lowest possible cost. Preoccupation with the internal administration and control of *corpora* then continued into the reign of Constantine.

Anticorruption Tactics and Associations under Constantine

Following his triumph at the Battle of the Milvian Bridge on October 28, 312 CE, Constantine became emperor of the western half of the Roman Empire, while Licinius remained in power in the East. The late antique law codes from this time show a keen interest in associations of staff members that governors and other magistrates and judges used to act as their guards, record documents or take dictation, make announcements, deliver letters, and perform any number of tasks they needed to help them govern. These bureaucrats, called *apparitores* or *officiales,* were organized into recognized associative *ordines* (ranks) attached to various bureaucratic magistracies. A number of laws from the fourth and early fifth centuries address avaricious *officiales* and *apparitores* who needed to be checked.

In 331, Constantine even noted that the "rapacious hands" of these men would be cut off if they did not desist.[46] Bodily mutilation of citizens was uncommon, even frowned upon, under earlier Roman law; thus, Constantine's law is remarkable in that it is introduced here in the context of abuse of power.[47] And yet, as was often the case in Roman law, status determined the punishment. Constantine had earlier ruled that since some imperial minters were still engaged in counterfeiting money, they could be tortured for information. And while counterfeiters from the decurial class and their sons would suffer exile and property confiscation for their crimes, enslaved persons convicted of counterfeiting—the likely status of many of the *monetarii*—would receive the "supreme penalty" for such an offense: in other words, the death penalty.[48]

In addition to using the law to discourage corruption and cast the emperor as a *dominus,* there was also another imperial approach: creating or expanding bureaucratic associations that encouraged a culture (and fear) of popular surveillance. In the late Roman world, imperial officials and soldiers were often employed as spies and informants, ostensibly as a check on corruptive practices. Earlier in the third century, certain men were already being reviled and mocked as *curiosi* (snoopers), who are cited by Tertullian as agents collecting the vectigal tax from disreputable professionals operating in Africa.[49] Similarly, groups of men beholden to the praetorian prefect, called *frumentarii,* had been employed as couriers and envoys during the Principate, along with military *speculatores* attached to the legions, to snoop while they performed courier services and report back their findings.[50] It appears that the infamous *frumentarii* were disbanded under the Tetrarchy in order to improve the imperial approach to gathering information from the provinces. In 361, the fourth-century historian and imperial bureaucrat Aurelius Victor reported on this development in his treatise on the virtues of the Caesars. In it, he remarks on Diocletian's use of law and discloses Tetrarchic attempts at reform and reorganization.[51] By the early fourth century, these intelligence agents formed a more standard corps within an official *schola* (clubhouse).

Under Constantine and Licinius, these associations of intelligence agents were called the *agentes in rebus* (persons active in affairs) by at least the year 319. They exemplify the aspiration to employ imperial agents to root out and report on tax evasion, corruption, treason, or any number of further offenses. The *agentes* may have had antecedents in the Tetrarchic era; however, they were now under the supervision of Constantine's newly formed *magister officiorum,* formalized after 312.[52] In part, these men were connected to the oversight of the *cursus publicus,* the supply and communications network of horses, mules, and wagons used to transport imperial letters, tax money (though not taxes paid in kind), and the products of state-owned factories, as previously noted, called *fabricae.*[53] By law, much of the cost of this imperial network was subsidized on a local level; locals provided wagons, animals, and even housing as part of imposed duties called *munera* or liturgies. The extensive legislation the compilers chose to include in the *Theodosian Code* reveals that, while there were abuses of the *cursus publicus* system, emperors such as Constantine tried to safeguard locals from the overuse of commandeered animals and to protect the system from misuse for private rather than state-sanctioned travel.

Items that needed to be sent securely and at high speed could be dispatched with the *cursus velox*, the quick post, with special agents charged to defend valuable items (for example, gold or silver) as added security against bandits or corrupt officials. In addition to the highly regulated *cursus publicus*, the *agentes in rebus* were also engaged in the oversight of ports, another key hub for the information and income that ran the empire. In a crucial centralizing move, the *agentes* were connected to the imperial court rather than under the supervision or judicial jurisdiction of the provincial governor or the praetorian prefect, thus creating more direct lines of information to the central executive through the *magister officiorum*.[54] By the time of Theodosius I in 386, these men could stand for election to the Senate after completing their service as *principes* within the corps.[55] Although an imperfect system that was vulnerable to abuse, ideally, the *agentes in rebus* provided a secure route for information.[56] Compulsory associations were an important part of the function of the state, but so were growing corps of bureaucrats.

In addition to making changes to the associations that supplied and maintained communication networks, the state began to accelerate the shift toward compulsory trades in the fourth century. This is a movement that came to include weavers, purple-dye makers, and muleteers, to name a few professions organized within this *corporati* system. We can see this trend particularly among the tradesmen who contributed to the food supply that fed the army and to the imperial grain dole known as the *annona*. Several trades that contributed to the food supply became compulsory or state-controlled in the later empire, including the *suarii* (pork suppliers), *pistores* (bakers), *piscatores* (fishermen), and *navicularii* (shippers). By the mid-fourth century and into the early fifth century, freeborn women who married weavers became bound to the lowly condition of their husbands, and purple-dye makers were denied civic honors and confined to a lowly status.[57]

In regard to the pork suppliers, this change was chiefly due to modifications in the pork ration. The state had in the early empire bought its pork from private dealers, but it developed closer ties with corporations of pork dealers under the Severans during the later second and early third centuries.

Pork was already a regular part of *annona* by the time of Aurelian in the late third century. By the reign of Constantine in 324 or 326, service in the *corpus* was a *munus*—meaning it was compulsory service.[58] Many pork farmers and bakers were, like many of the individuals tied to the *annona* system, also large landowners. These landowners were compelled to serve and fulfill their various quotas, as set by the state.[59]

Is it an occupational caste if it is not enforceable? Many of the laws later included in the codes of Theodosius II and Justinian emphasize that individuals within this *corporati* system had a legal ceiling that prevented them from climbing higher or rejecting service. They were not permitted to escape service by attaining higher honors, joining the clergy, or engaging in trickery in order to elude their obligation to the state. Such laws even allowed for individuals to be dragged back to their positions by force if need be—although it is difficult to say how often this threat of violence was exercised.[60] Some modern scholars have termed the system of compulsory and often hereditary trades in the late Roman Empire a "caste-system"; however, we must still consider the disconnect between legal ideal and enforceable reality.[61] It was a limited caste system in name but perhaps not in social practice. There simply was neither a large enough urban police force nor sufficient soldiers to oversee every tradesman who had fled from their *corpus* or *collegium* into a Mediterranean world without drivers' licenses or identity databases with which to positively identify people. This means that, while legislation may have intimidated some compulsory tradespeople and created a culture of fear and oversight, there were surely many loopholes and cracks in the system that people could slip through if they wished to escape.

In 337 CE, in a villa outside Nicomedia, not long after his baptism, Constantine died. Surveillance of and corruption by bureaucratic associations appear to have continued well after his demise. The legal evidence hints at corruption problems with the *agentes de rebus*, particularly during the reign of Constantine's son and successor, Constantius II (r. 337–361), in the mid-fourth century. Constantius warned these men that they were to report crimes to judges and not devise false accusations that might unjustly land people in prison.[62] In his *Funeral Oration over Julian*, likely not finished until 365 CE, the Antiochene rhetorician Libanius even launched an invective attack against these bands of men, whom he calls "the King's eyes." To Libanius, these were unwatched watchmen: "Thus the very people there to prevent crime were the protectors of the criminal, like sheepdogs hunting with the wolf pack, and it was like coming across hidden treasure to have a share in this goldmine—rags to riches in no time!"[63]

The oration notes Constantius II's successor, Julian, and his attempt to suppress the corps. But while the "apostate" emperor soon died, state spies lived on. Nevertheless, for all the ire directed at them in the law and by provincials such as Libanius, the number of surveillance associations was relatively small compared to the vast population of the empire, which was likely around fifty million at the time.[64] Their numbers fluctuated in the later empire, but a law of 430 CE fixed their maximum at 1,174, with a precise *cursus honorum* (that is, a set path for rank and promotion) for advancement.[65] Many curials may have used the post to escape their own civic obligations at home, and many passed down the position in their families. Keeping this in mind, we see in the *agentes in rebus* and the infrastructure of the public post dubbed the *cursus publicus* two legal ideals that—while clearly themselves vulnerable to corruption—were tactics of creating state associations ideally meant to protect the income of the imperial fiscus, allow secure transport, and provide a reliable network for the passing of information and goods in the late empire. It was this same aspiration for financial security through knowledge organization and increased administrative protection that would also influence the system of imposed trade corporations.

Even as some cities such as Rome and Constantinople increasingly relied on certain compulsory associations for staples like bread or for shipping, magistrates elsewhere continued to grow exasperated with the non-compulsory associations that they did not feel fulfilled their positions, and that they believed caused social unrest. This was particularly true in regard to private associations of bakers that were still relied upon in cities across the Mediterranean. The compulsory corporations of *pistores* that fed Rome and Constantinople get the most citation and imperial threats in legal codices, but private associations of bakers also continued to feed the cities of the empire as well and to have interruptions in service. As with the bread strike in Ephesus, balancing the need for bread and pacifying the associations of bakers remained a delicate dance in diplomacy.

Upheavals in the city of Antioch in Roman Syria (in what is modern Turkey) and the provision of the grain dole there in the late fourth century are telling. There were allegations waged against bakers by the people saying that they were being bribed to inflate the price of bread sold to the populace. In 382 CE, tensions came to a head. Philagrius, the count of the eastern diocese based in the city, had a number of these bakers publicly flogged to coerce them into falling in line and show the people he was taking actions against the corruption.[66] Libanius steps in as a defender of the bakers' associations and mediator with the count. He remarks that the bakers had already begun to decamp in order to save their skins by going into hiding. The rhetorician also notes that the bakers were afraid to come out of hiding lest they be arrested—that is, until he coaxed them back to their shops. The next day, Libanius claims there were not lines for bread because the bakers had returned to work from their collective stoppage, and now provided a surplus of bread to the city.[67]

Should we consider this an organized strike? It certainly was a desertion of services that Libanius notes would have, in turn, caused widespread famine if the bakers had not returned to their bakeries. We cannot say with any confidence whether the members of the Antiochene bakers' associations met and called for a formal, citywide strike or all chose individually, bakery-by-bakery, to close their shops and flee from the wrath of Philagrius. We are again in the dark about the internal logistics and at the mercy of a spotty literary record. And yet? It is a marvel to even have this account of daily life. Areas such as Asia Minor, Egypt, Rome, and Constantinople had strong literary traditions into the late Roman Empire. This record overrepresents these areas and tells us much about popular issues that often go unremarked on in other cities. Even if such strikes among bakers in other cities regularly occurred, they may not have been remarked on by aristocratic writers—or their accounts simply did not survive. But it remains evident that strike tactics were known and, at times, employed either to force collective bargaining or perhaps just to save the literal hides of the artisans themselves.

The lack of success in trying to tie various occupations to service can perhaps be detected in a law of July 398 CE from Arcadius and Honorius. In it, the emperors direct the praetorian prefect Eutychianus on what to do if certain groups of people, such as slaves, maidservants, decurions, public debtors, procurators, collectors of purple-dye fish, or those involved in public or private accounts, attempted to take refuge in a church: they would be subject to forcible seizure and returned.[68] As with the Ptolemaic kings in Egypt many centuries prior, revoking asylum was a tactic for stopping strikes or work shortages. It seems that many (perhaps most) in the state corporations lived up to their obligations—whether in the production of arms or clothing, the cultivation of grain, or perhaps the provision of pork. However, there were assuredly still those who fled from their assigned *munera*, despite the violently punitive legal prohibitions. Compulsory *collegia* were one way in which the late Roman state sought to prevent price gouging and to secure crucial goods and services for the state, the recipients of the *annona*, and the military. But the creation of the *corporati* system came at the expense of free will and individuals' ability to choose their occupation. Many, like the *navicularii* and the heads of the baking corporations called the *corpus pistorum*, were usually wealthy landowners assigned to compulsory service, but others, like the weavers and the purple-dye workers, were impoverished artisans.

The corporal protections that had previously served as a kind of legal armor for many higher-status individuals began to erode in late antiquity, leaving more people vulnerable to physical punishment than ever before. This included tradespeople. And yet certain tradespeople were also now under the protection of the emperor. Later laws from the early fifth century attributed to Honorius and Theodosius again attempted to halt the fleecing of provincials, *curiales* (town councilors), and, specifically, trade associations: "We wish to protect the *curiales, navicularii,* and all *corpora,* so that no *apparitores* [office staff] of any magistrate shall be permitted to do anything, which helps loot the provinces."[69] These laws may suggest an endemic problem in the empire. Or the problem may have only been pervasive in certain provincial areas, such as Africa. Regardless, such pronouncements were one way for emperors to express concern over the welfare of their people and underscore that the proverbial watchmen should be watched. The laws also helped encourage citizens to trust the court system, while calling on magistrates and judges to protect their people. An articulated culture of accountability was developing, which is certainly evident in these laws. Corruptive practices and anticorruption tactics were not a development unique to the later empire. The abuse of power for personal profit had long been an acknowledged and systemic part of Roman government as well as a topic of legislation in the Republic and the empire. As historians have noted, power had always been for sale.[70] However, direct accusations of corruptive judicial, administrative, decurial, and occupational practices became a more frequent theme in the legal texts from late antiquity than they had been in the earlier legislation that survives.

Anti-corruption tactics in late antiquity are largely revealed through laws pertaining to tax collection, bureaucrats in the imperial administration, and the creation of compulsory trade associations. However, this chapter has argued for a disconnect between legal texts and the social reality experienced in the empire, just as there is today between the letter of the law and the experience of it. The leading expert on judicial malpractice in late antiquity, Jill Harries, perhaps put it best when she noted that the "rhetoric of imperial laws about *iudices* expresses a concern about accountability, present from Augustus onwards, but now more emphatically expressed, in accordance with the linguistic conventions of the time, and stringently enforced."[71] The emphatic vocabulary of obligation, along with the language of liability, were woven into the legislation that governed the later Roman Empire and even mixed into the literary prose of writers such as Lactantius, Libanius, and Salvian. As we have seen, texts contain numerous allegations of bureaucrats stealing money, provincial governors abandoning their duties on town councils, and mint workers absconding with gold from the imperial mint. However, it is altogether unclear whether these examples mean that corruption truly increased in the late empire—or whether emperors were simply more likely to address it through written laws that then survived at a high rate through the Middle Ages and into the present.

From Gibbon onward, many have focused on Roman emperors disseminating threats of land confiscation, corporal violence, and fines in an attempt to curb corruption. It is less sensational, but still quite notable, however, that they also turned to other methods: knowledge organization and archives, supply-chain security, and more direct oversight of compulsory associations. These aspects are not usually harped upon in the op-eds that compare Rome's corruption to that of today. Despite this, improved recordkeeping, new associative corps of bureaucratic agents, state associations of land surveyors, new information-gathering corps, an improved postal system, and the increased use of compulsory trade associations were part of an expansion in public versus private associations in the late empire. These attested methods for countering perceived abuses of power—including embezzlement of state money, venality, extortion, bribery, excessive violence, and maladministration—help us form a more well-rounded impression of the roles of the emperor, the state, and certain associations in the late Roman economy. They also reveal that imperial anti-corruption tactics became more varied, violent, documented, and dependent upon compulsory labor. Workers seen as essential to the state were organized and controlled to a higher degree than ever before in the late Roman Mediterranean, after Aurelian. And yet many other workers still continued to create their own private associations, collectives, and organized workshops for providing goods and services outside the state *corporati* system as well. Rome was and would remain dependent on both public and private associations of workers for food, coinage, infrastructure, purple textiles, and the maintenance of certain supply chains that kept the empire and the army afloat.

7
Athletic Factions and Popular Rebellion

ARRESTING A CHARIOTEER IN THE LATE ROMAN WORLD was a perilous act. A large portion of the Roman populace felt great affinity for members of one of the four *factiones* (factions) that dominated the chariot-racing scene in the dozens of Roman cities with a hippodrome or circus. The arrest of a charioteer put the success of these factions at risk. Roman emperors knew the popular position of power occupied by such athletes, while also acknowledging that games were a necessary way to interact with the people. But there was a risky balance to maintain. Imperial patronage and building programs during the early fourth century, under the Tetrarchy, signal this tension between the lure of the circus and the need for emperors to protect themselves while in them. It was a moment of peak importance for creating civic structures such as the hippodrome; however, emperors also recognized how quickly hippodrome crowds could mobilize and direct their ire at them, particularly if marshaled by a faction leader.

The circus was as much a political space as an athletic one. Consequently, there often needed to be secure routes in and out of these venues for emperors.[1] Construction or revamping of circuses in cities such as Nicomedia (304), Rome (306–312), Trier (c. 310), Sirmium (c. 312), Thessaloniki (under Galerius), and Constantinople (324–330) were financed by the state—often with a palace adjacent to the hippodrome to allow secure access and exit for officials.[2] Emperors patronized but also feared the sway of circus factions—associations that in late antiquity included far more than just charioteers. The urban factions employed in the hippodrome economy were large athletic and entertainment unions that included overseers, trainers, doctors, veterinarians, and a network of other individuals who worked collectively to put on games in a circus. By the late Roman Empire, control of these factions had been transferred from private elites wishing to put on games to state-backed and -controlled events. Professional charioteers, often called *aurigae,* or drivers of four-horse chariots, called *agitatores* or *quadrigarii,* were the star athletes of the main factions: the Blues, the Greens, the Reds, and the Whites. As previously noted, like gladiators, most charioteers were either enslaved persons or freedmen from previously enslaved families, although some charioteers were freeborn. Due to the hazards of their profession, they only rarely lived beyond the age of thirty.[3] Recent studies have revealed that while charioteers likely did not suffer the legal infamy called *infamia*—a stigma experienced by actors, gladiators, sex workers, and other infamous professionals— they did live with a social stigma that could affect their standing in institutions such as the church.[4] At the Council of Arles in 314, the bishops declared that charioteers and theatrical participants were excluded from Christian fellowship.[5] But even if they did not belong to a church, they found fellowship in their athletic unions.

Similar to gladiators, cohorts of charioteers were organized into *familiae quadrigariae* (families of charioteers) from the mid-Republic on. An inscription likely from the reign of Domitian in the late first century CE notes one such *familia* owned by Titus Ateius Capito, possibly associated with the Reds.[6] Within the *familia,* there were twenty-four or twenty-five professionals. A financial administrator called a *quaestor* distributed olive oil to these members, who were given the title of decurion and included an overseer, a trainer called a *conditor,* a *sellarius* (either a male sex worker or, more likely, the inscriber actually meant a *cellarius* tasked with supervising storerooms), a doctor, a blacksmith, numerous starting-gate operators referred to as *tentores,* a horse prepper called a *morator,* a *sparsor* who kept the horses watered and cool, and even a messenger.[7] Study of these charioteers indicates that, while there were never again uprisings of enslaved persons on the scale of the three late Republican Servile Wars during the remainder of Roman antiquity, enslaved and manumitted leaders did continue to incite popular rebellions, drive collective action, and act as a focal point for resistance to the state—particularly by using the podium offered by the hippodrome in late antiquity.

In Rome and elsewhere, the *ludi circenses* (circus races) were a regular part of life, well into the later Roman imperial period. The calendar of 354 CE notes sixty-six such games in Rome per year in the mid-fourth century, meaning that, on average, Romans had the chance to go to a race in the circus about every five and a half days. The earliest factions likely formed in Rome around the fourth century BCE, and then elsewhere in the Roman Mediterranean in the centuries to come.[8] Although Domitian attempted to add factions called the Purples and the Golds, these two expansion teams seem to have faded sometime after the emperor's assassination in 96 CE.[9] In major cities like Rome, Thessaloniki, Antioch, Alexandria, and Constantinople, charioteers—and their ability to compete on race day—were a vested popular interest akin to today's professional athletes. Their arrest was an affront to the people and also challenged the chances of their faction winning in the circus races.

Circus charioteers were public figures who sat betwixt and between: they held informal political and social sway, but were still part of the disreputable ludic industrial complex of paid fighters, entertainers, dancers, actors, musicians, and mimes.[10] While enslaved charioteers stayed tied to their faction unless sold, manumitted and freeborn charioteers appear to have moved more freely between factions, especially if highly sought after and renowned. But the creeping shadow of imperial oversight in late antiquity also included these entertainment associations. First at Constantinople and Alexandria from the fourth century on, circus factions increasingly organized games, with the imperial administration exerting more and more financial control in terms of the stables and purse strings. State financing and oversight heavily expanded into the fifth century.[11] Factions were often overseen by men called *factionarii* who could be former charioteers themselves, rather than by private *domini*. The size of these factions varied, but a later membership album of 601 CE listed nine hundred Blues and sixteen hundred Greens in Constantinople, which would have included performers, personnel, and four hundred to six hundred young men.[12] The associations of rowdy and often aristocratic youth of the early empire still continued to gather, well into late antiquity. Now, many were in the circus factions themselves.

It was a magistrate called the urban prefect who often had to deal with rowdy factions and their fans. Ammianus Marcellinus, a late Roman historian of the mid-fourth century CE, discusses the urban prefect in 355 to 356 CE, Flavius Leontius.[13] During the reign of the emperor Constantius II, a riot broke out in Rome over the arrest of a charioteer named Philoromus. Ammianus praises Leontius's swiftness in addressing the melee. He quickly interceded and had his officers seize, torture, and then banish many of the rioters. A few days later, the populace rioted again, this time due to the scarcity of wine in the city. Leontius again interceded, made arrests, and punished the ringleader, Petrus Valvomeres, with banishment to Picenum.[14] Corporal punishment, coupled with banishment or exile, came to be seen as the proper penalty for many public disturbances in late antiquity.[15] Historian of late Roman exile Daniel Washburn has characterized it as "a spatial punishment [that] fit the crime" and also reflected Greco-Roman beliefs that agents of social miasma should simply be removed in order to restore the health of the body politic.[16] Removal of the pollutant meant the traditional hierarchy could then be restored. Whether the contaminant had been a bishop, a magistrate, a corrupt bureaucrat, or the leader of a popular riot, his removal (rather than execution) could help assuage discord and reestablish the status quo. Elites tended to be exiled, while many of lower status were executed. However, how to deal with charioteers, their factions, and their passionate fan base was a much more complex, delicate problem, as we will see.

In his descriptions of Rome during the reign of Valentinian I (r. 364–375 CE), Ammianus also exposes the connections between senatorial elites and charioteers. In 368 CE, a future prefect of the city named Tarratius Bassus and his esteemed friends were prosecuted for allegedly aiding a charioteer named Auchenius in carrying out a poisoning.[17] Legislation, literature, and curse tablets reveal that charioteers were often seen as agents at the center of a matrix of magic. Members of opposing teams were known to curse one another, and they aided in cursing others. Ammianus even alleges that men fearful of debt collectors would gain the assistance of a charioteer when threatened.[18] Fears of prognostication, magic, and poisoning would continue to be attached to other occupational groups as well: soothsayers, astrologers, augurs, and magicians. All were outlawed by Constantius II in 357 CE.[19] The punishment for these crimes of divination was now death. And yet, despite laws attempting to halt its use, charioteers remained embedded within the matrix of magic; they were blamed for using it to win matches and were often cursed by spectators in an effort to make them lose. But it has been suggested that the angst expressed in literature over their use of magic may simply represent a signifier of anxiety at their increasing social power and disregard for social boundaries.[20]

Charioteers competed in the circus or hippodrome, but it seems they could also be used as personal militias and bodyguards. In the 360s, intense religious rivalries led to the employment of associations of both charioteers and gladiators, as competing religious groups used them as hired muscle to enact their will. Just as we saw with Clodius, factions and *familiae* of both charioteers and gladiators could be wielded as personal militias and instruments of violence. This was particularly the case in Rome in 366 CE, after the death of the bishop of Rome, Liberius, in late September. In the wake of Liberius's death, two rivals named Ursinus and Damasus competed for control of the bishopric. Ursinus's followers consecrated him and protected a number of priests who served as his supporters within the city of Rome. In the early morning hours a few weeks later, Damasus led groups of *arenarii* (arena workers), *quadrigarii* (charioteers), and *fossores* (gravediggers) who ultimately killed 137 Ursinan supporters in the city's Basilica of Sicininus (later called the Basilica of Santa Maria Maggiore).[21] Ursinus was then exiled to Gaul. He returned to the outskirts of Rome briefly, before being exiled yet again in a back-and-forth that ended with many of his adherents moving to Milan and Ursinus continuing to fight from Cologne for almost twenty years. Unlike Clodius's case, Damasus's apparent connection to and deployment of entertainment associations and groups of gravediggers paid off. He also put many of them to work on ecclesiastical projects in the city. It is likely that the associations of *fossores* (gravediggers) helped Damasus completely revamp the physical spaces for the Cult of the Martyrs in the catacombs of Rome, until his death in 384.[22] A number of their inscriptions and graffiti still survive in the catacombs today.

Labor, Military Levies, and "Barbarians"

Outside of the circus, other areas of labor organization were also shifting and transforming within the late Roman Empire. Into the 370s, this was particularly true along the empire's frontiers. Moving in from the Eurasian steppes, the Huns had begun to conflict more with the Goths and to displace and push them to the west. Roman authorities attempted to squelch Roman traders' commercial interactions and social intermingling with these alleged barbarians. A law of 370 to 375 CE banned the selling of wine, olive oil, and fish sauce to barbarians, even for commercial purposes.[23] And yet, these barbarians were also viewed as a labor resource. In 376 CE, during the reigns of the emperors Valentinian and Valens, the Roman military was in desperate need of more soldiers. The Romans saw the migrating groups of Goths, now under the leadership of men named Fritigern and Alavivus, as a solution to their emptying ranks and the growing military labor deficit.

The Goths were settled in camps across the Danube in Thrace in exchange for the military service of many of their men in the East. The remaining Goths in Thrace, called the Tervingi, were at the mercy of corrupt Roman commanders in charge of the resettlement to provide them with sustenance. The Roman officers Lupicinus and Maximus withheld food, and thus a black market developed, eventually forcing the Goths, according to one tale, to sell their children into slavery in exchange for dog meat.[24] The Goths honored their end of the levy labor agreement to supply soldiers, but the Romans did not keep up their end of the quid pro quo. The Goths were not treated as equals nor as the refugees that they were, but rather as expendable bodies to be raped and abused for pleasure. The sixth-century historian Zosimus later noted that Roman officers "occupied themselves solely in the gratification of their brutal appetites, or in procuring slaves, neglecting everything that related to public affairs."[25]

Why this treatment of the Gothic people? Historian Noel Lenski points out that the Romans saw Goths and Scythians—an ethnic group often enslaved in the Roman Empire—as being interchangeable, and thus treated both as little more than chattel.[26] Starved and unnerved, in August of 378, the Goths rebelled against their tormenters in what would be one of the most devastating Roman military conflicts in history: the Battle of Adrianople (modern Edirne, Turkey). Unlike the plebeians who in the early Republic resisted the levy through withdrawals, the Goths did not see themselves as Romans, and now resisted Rome and its policies. The battle was a retaliation. Valens returned from the East for this fight and hastened headlong into battle without waiting for backup from Gratian, the western emperor, who had taken over from Valentinian in 375. The crushing defeat wiped out about two-thirds of the eastern Roman troops, including the emperor. The body of Valens was never recovered.

Replacing Valens in the East was a new emperor named Theodosius I. Theodosius is perhaps best known for the so-called Edict of Thessalonica, or *Cunctos populos,* promulgated on February 27, 380, which was technically also in the name of Gratian and the nine-year-old child emperor, Valentinian II.[27] This edict addressing the people of Constantinople condemned Arian Christianity as heresy while proclaiming Nicene Christianity as orthodox and supreme. It authenticated the ecclesiastical power of Nicene bishops in the Mediterranean, particularly the bishop of Rome, Damasus, in the West, and Peter II, the patriarch of Alexandria, in the East. In addition to his religious proclamations, there were also concessions made by the new emperor to fill the military ranks once again.

In 382, Theodosius resettled the Goths as formal *foederati* (those with whom there is a treaty), and they were given arable land in what is modern-day Bulgaria. The resistance at the Battle of Adrianople and the heavy loss of troops had shown Theodosius that it was time for some diplomacy. And yet, even as turmoil plagued the army and the peoples along the Danube, day-to-day trade, commerce, and the use of associations carried on elsewhere in the Roman Empire. A late fourth-century papyrus from Oxyrhynchus in Roman Egypt mentions a labor collective of canvas and carpet workers addressing issues surrounding the payment of the *anabolikon* tax.[28] Adrianople and its aftermath were indeed devastating for Rome's political and military institutions, but for many artisans, professionals, and occupational associations working elsewhere in the Mediterranean, daily life and labor continued on.

Social Discord and the Late Roman Circus

In terms of civic discord and sports, tensions between the people and imperial power continued to come to a head near hippodromes and circuses. This is similar to the violence in the earlier empire that had bunched topographically near the amphitheater at places like Pompeii during the riots of 59 CE. In 390, a charioteer was arrested in the port city of Thessalonica (modern Thessaloniki) along the busy trade route that cut east to west through what is now the Balkans. The charioteer had allegedly made sexual gestures toward a Roman commander of Gothic descent named Buthericus. The people needed their charioteer for the upcoming races, so they seized the reins of the situation, with rioters electing to kill Buthericus.

The homicide led Theodosius to take drastic action. He gathered the people into the hippodrome on the pretense of games and then had them slaughtered. Under Theodosius's orders, his Gothic soldiers may have killed as many as seven thousand civilians. The fifth-century historian and Syrian bishop Theodoret would later comment: "Multitudes were mowed down like grain in harvest time."[29] The ecclesiastical historian Sozomen even tells a moving story of a merchant begging for the lives of his sons, to no avail.[30] The bishop of Milan, Ambrose, excommunicated Theodosius for his violent reaction and required the emperor to do penance. Theodosius's actions in locking civilians in the hippodrome (fundamentally converting it into a prison) would not be that far off from those of Justinian and Theodora during the famed Nika riots of Constantinople in 532 CE.

Again and again, the amphitheater and the hippodrome were mediating spaces where the people could speak to the emperor or a magistrate. But like any social media technology, this was not without its risks. Ancient historians David Potter, Alan Cameron, and Charlotte Roueché have done a great deal to anatomize the violence in the late Roman Empire through the eyes and actions of the circus factions, particularly those in late antique Constantinople.[31] As Potter has pointed out, in the Republic and early Principate, it was the equestrian order that oversaw factions privately. But in the third century and into the fourth, there was a shift in who managed the circus factions and an increase in state subsidies to support them.[32] By the fifth century, senatorial roles in and imperial management of the factions were enshrined in law, and factions of the same color operated in an extended entertainment network that also now included dancers, mimes, and other types of athletes.[33] Outside the formal faction, associations based upon occupational, ethnic, or religious identities could also cluster together with a faction section in the stands. Roueché notes that at Aphrodisias (in modern Turkey), Jews, butchers, workers of gold, and members of another neighborhood association hailing from the same sector of the city all customarily sat together in the section usually reserved for fans of the Blues.[34]

Many centuries prior, Augustus had already recognized that people who sit together (all the while seeing and being seen) at spectacles often form strong connections. Inscribed seats that survive today communicate where many associations sat in theaters and in the circus. Ancient historian Garrett Fagan recognized these seating patterns as a means of strengthening associative identity as well: "The social psychology of crowd dynamics suggests that the presence and mutual visibility of subgroups in a crowd strengthens the social identities of both the crowd and the subgroups within it, increases sensations of solidarity that stem from those identities, and amplifies the expression of identities that lends crowd members feelings of empowerment."[35] It meant something to convene together as an association in sports seats, and it had a galvanizing effect on both associations and their members to sit in a particular section. As they always had, social, political, and economic connections between groups occurred during spectacles. And many groups in the crowd also had direct links to those working in the circus itself. The gymnasium groups of young men known as *neoi*, the corps of beast fighters known as *venatores*, and the gladiatorial superfans called *philoploi* all had strong links to those competing.[36]

Within the factions themselves, there were also many internal changes. The decline of gymnasium culture in the late Roman period merged unions of athletes and theatrical artists into the factions of the circus games.[37] Even though legislation in 391 to 392 banned sacrifices and incense burning, games of various types, including the Olympic Games, continued into the fifth century CE, since athletics had already been separated from religious sacrifice about fifty years previously.[38] While the Olympics held at the ancient Greek site of Olympia probably died out around 426 CE, Antioch's Olympic Games in Syria lasted until 520 CE. Even then, as Sofie Remijsen has pointed out, this was not a reaction to the expansive imperial bans on paganism, but rather to the local and more temporary bans on performances and games often imposed as a punishment for popular riots—most recently, those incited by the Blues faction.[39]

Law continued to be a political tool used to isolate social and political threats under the guise of dishonor. Marriage restrictions limited the connubial options of certain artists, craftspeople, and *corporati* workers even further in the fourth century—particularly those in the entertainment industry. In 336, Constantine had expanded the earlier Augustan ban on senators marrying actresses and other lowborn women by prohibiting marriage between local Roman male elites and the daughters of formerly enslaved women, tavern keepers and their daughters, women who sold public wares, and more ambiguously categorized "humble and lowly" women.[40] In the mid-fifth century, the emperor Marcian (r. 450–457 CE) would clarify, in response to a petition, that the aforementioned "humble and lowly" persons cited by Constantine were in actuality actresses and sex workers.[41]

Families connected to the *corporati* system that formed the basis of the *annona* system were often kept from marrying outside their corporate network of families and landed elites too. Laws continued to attempt to separate the families of the compulsory associations called *corporati* out from other groups of entertainers and athletes. A law of March 403 CE addressed to the prefect of the Annona in Rome named Vitalis kept *pistores* (bakers) and their children from marrying a private person, a person belonging to the theater (for example, connected with acting, music, or the stage), or a charioteer.[42] All rogue bakers who married outside their order were also threatened with the humiliation of being beaten and sent into exile, and having their property revoked and maintained by the remaining members of the *corpus* of the bakers. And what if a charioteer or person of the stage dared to marry a breadmaker's daughter? Well, he was assigned the onus of service within the bakers' corporation as well. The policing of dignity and social orders through the application of marriage laws was, on the face of it, an old-fashioned attempt at maintaining and structuring Roman honor through the separation of social groups. But make no mistake: in many instances, it was another means of ensuring that the late Roman supply chain would continue into perpetuity, inherited from family to family, with less disruption.[43]

Into the late fourth century, hippodrome races continued to provide a space where the crowd could interact with the emperor. This was particularly true at Mediolanum (later called Milan), where there was a late third-century palace with an adjoining circus.[44] On January 17, 395 CE, after falling ill and quickly leaving the circus, Theodosius died.[45] Before exiting, he had asked his ten-year-old son, Honorius, to oversee the races. At that point, Theodosius had been on a victory tour of sorts throughout Italy. Only months before, he had enlisted the military service of the allied *foederati* troops of Goths, Alans, and other "barbarian" soldiers. These included a man named Alaric, who, along with another general named Stilicho, helped Theodosius to defeat a usurper to the purple named Eugenius at the Battle of the Frigidus in northwestern Italy in 394.[46] Stilicho, a trusted soldier as well as the husband of Theodosius's niece, was the son of a Vandal father and a Roman mother. He had served Theodosius and even witnessed his death, claiming that the emperor's last act was to appoint him guardian to guide the emperor's young sons. The empire was now to be run by Theodosius's younger son, Honorius, in the West, while Honorius's older brother, Arcadius, continued to rule in the East.

Although the chariot factions were more popular, we do still hear of the gladiatorial associations that had long been used and abused by politicians in Rome. In the fourth century, emperors, senators, and other elites had begun to turn more to the hippodrome as a place for presenting honor and status; however, the famed lure of the arena was not yet totally gone in terms of providing private muscle for ambitious politicians. A law posted in Rome in 399 warns senators to stop using gladiators from gladiatorial schools and threatens gladiators with exile for serving them.[47] The old habits of the Republic died hard, and conspicuously hired paramilitary troupes, staffed by the men of the arena, were constantly instrumentalized in order to carry out the dirty work of elite men, it seems.

At the dawn of the fifth century CE, other occupational associations similarly relied on patronage from the emperor and wealthy citizens. Some associations still celebrated patrons with statues as they had in the earlier empire; however, the custom of commemorative inscriptions, which we call the epigraphic habit, waned considerably in the western Roman Empire in particular.[48] In Rome, the influential association of *caudicarii seu piscatores* (the associations of barge-owners and fishermen) still honored Flavius Stilicho, then the master of the soldiery and a consul in the year 400 CE—but such expensive gifts were on the decline.[49] New preferences for certain goods and materials did, however, have an impact on trade associations. The court poet Claudian remarks on commemorative painted ivory diptychs given out as souvenirs during Stilicho's consular games that year. Such ivory diptychs soon became more common as consular gifts in the late fourth century CE.[50]

Shifts in luxury tastes among Roman elites, such as ivory from India used for these diptychs and other wares, had an impact on long-distance trade and the associations that facilitated it. The Roman ivory workers in early imperial Italy, often referred to as *eborarii*, were a close-knit group predominantly made up of freedmen who had multiple familial connections to each other.[51] Much earlier, a Hadrianic-era (117–138 CE) association charter for the union, the law of the *collegium* of businessmen of ivory workers and citrus wood traders, was found across the Tiber in what is now Rome's Trastevere region.[52] The rules restricted membership, set festival days and dues to be paid, defined a hierarchy with a president, and established a clubhouse. Since ivory was often used in furniture at the time, it makes sense that these two groups came together as occupational associations.

The ivory supply and the citrus wood supply, both originally sourced from North Africa, were severely depleted by the late first century CE.[53] Pliny the Elder notes that, at this time, an alternative to North African ivory came in the form of ivory from India, and, in fact, associations of Indian artisans called *shrenis* had already been at work for centuries creating ivory figurines and pieces of furniture.[54] Coins, ceramics, and even graffiti attest to Rome's continuing trade links with the Indian Ocean well into late antiquity, even if the ivory was preferred for boxes, covers of books, and—albeit briefly—consular diptychs. Kasper Grønlund Evers has convincingly argued that trade in the Indian Ocean from the first to sixth centuries CE was predicated on hundreds of tradesmen (and their associations) of Roman, Nabataean, Palmyrene, Arabian, Axumite, and Indian backgrounds, and that "no single group or empire dominated the trade."[55] Associations of tradespeople formed a vital part of long-distance trade at this time, and were of particular significance to organizing commerce in spaces where there was no centralized state power to oversee it.

Slavery, Goths, and Rebellion

In a geographically strategic move, Honorius moved the court from Milan to Ravenna in 402 CE. Ravenna had an advantageous position near the sea, within its own marshy protective layer. At this time of migration, movement, and warfare, human trafficking was also extremely high. Groups of Roman traders in enslaved people, called *mangones,* were busily selling "barbarian" bodies. The Gothic invasions of Italy had inflated the supply of enslaved persons even further. In 405 to 406, a Gothic king named Radagaisus led more than two hundred thousand men in an invasion of Italy.[56] Orosius, the presbyter, historian, and protégé of Augustine, called him a Scythian—a common late antique way of labeling a Goth as a barbarian—and a pagan.[57] As Radagaisus and his troops moved into and down through the Apennines, Stilicho, along with Gothic troops led by Sarus and Hunnish troops led by a man named Uldin, hemmed him in among the mountains not far from what is modern-day Florence.

Surviving Christian sources point to a belief in God's hand in these events. Orosius records that while the Christian, Roman soldiers drank and ate their fill, the Gothic, "pagan" troops were starved out. Radagaisus eventually deserted and was killed by the Romans, but his soldiers were taken as captives. Around twelve thousand of these Goths were forced to fight in the Roman army, while the rest were sold "like the cheapest cattle for an *aureus* apiece."[58] Most died not long thereafter, likely of malnutrition and poor health. We are told that the money saved by the enslavers on the purchase price was then spent on the burial expenses. Historians of late Roman slavery have long recognized that the market for enslaved people was flooded with captives after a battle and that the Romans did not hesitate to enslave "barbarian" peoples. As Maijastina Kahlos noted, intense warfare escalated the flow of enslaved persons into Italy and, as Augustine attests, to places like North Africa.[59] This glutted market, filled with groups of people depended upon by Romans for military service or sold as chattel, drove the breakup of "barbarian" families, destroyed attempts at integration, and increased Gothic animosity toward Romans. Neither slavery nor rebellion dissipated in the late Roman Empire with the ascent of Christianity.

In May of 408, the emperor of the East, Arcadius, died, and was succeeded by a seven-year-old named Theodosius II, who would rule until 450 CE. Amid all the turmoil, intrigue, and even a mutiny, Stilicho, who had allied with Alaric, took refuge in a church and was eventually beheaded. Thousands of Stilicho's loyal troops, along with their wives and children, were murdered, and their property was taken by Honorius and the state. Many of the remaining soldiers and enslaved persons at work in the fields transferred their allegiance to Alaric. In the manner that Spartacus had raised rebel troops in the first century BCE, he gained many recruits as he marched through the Italian countryside. In addition to troops joining Alaric's march against Rome, the insensitivity of the Romans and the increase in human trafficking had, in turn, fostered the growth of a ransom market. Romans were often taken and ransomed to their families for coin and goods as a way of making extra money.

We must hold both the luxury market and this burgeoning ransom market in our mind when evaluating the events in and around Rome in the early fifth century. Alaric's occupation of the Italian peninsula and his dealings with the senators in the city of Rome in 408 are economically telling. The historian Zosimus remarked on senatorial negotiations to keep Alaric from sacking the city. These parleys involved a large quantity of prestige items, including vast amounts of pepper: "After long discussions on both sides, it was at length agreed, that the city should give five thousand pounds of gold, and thirty thousand of silver, four thousand silk robes, three thousand scarlet fleeces, and three thousand pounds of pepper. As the city possessed no public stock, it was necessary for the senators who had property, to undertake the collection by an assessment."[60] Following this payoff, Alaric marched his troops back to the area of Ravenna, likely carrying a lot of pepper to resell to wholesalers and traders near the port city. In 410, he and his troops then returned to blockade Rome and cut it off from its important port, Ostia. Goods and trade played an important part in Alaric's famed sacking of the city, even if his military movements have garnered more attention.

The actions of Alaric and his troops were their own, but they do gesture to animosity toward Roman troops and the long-standing abuse of Gothic soldiers. This all went back to the 370s, and was in part responsible for the hostility that led to the city's first sacking since the fourth century BCE. Spartacus had never sacked the city of Rome, but Alaric and many of his formerly enslaved troops successfully did so, for the first time in nearly eight hundred years. We can see this hostility at play if we ask ourselves just how the Goths gained entry into the walled city. Reports vary, but enslaved persons played a key role. A dubious but revealing story from the sixth-century historian Procopius later noted that it was undercover Gothic enslaved persons who had opened Rome's northern Salarian Gate to allow the waiting Goths into the city in August of 410. Earlier, Alaric had allegedly chosen three hundred of them to be given as gifts to Rome's elite families, where they could serve as double agents.[61] Procopius also reported another more likely story: that the blockade's cutting off of the harbor, food, and supplies upset a senatorial woman named Anicia Faltonia Proba, who sent her enslaved domestic servants (called *oiketai*) to open the gate for the Goths.[62] Meanwhile, in Ravenna to Rome's north, the emperor Honorius found out about the fires and devastation in Rome from a eunuch poultry-keeper. As the story goes, the potentate was upset and confused, since, at first, he believed the eunuch was breaking the news of the death of his favorite rooster, which he had named Rome. True or not, the story was meant to show that Rome was no longer the great political and social center it had once been.

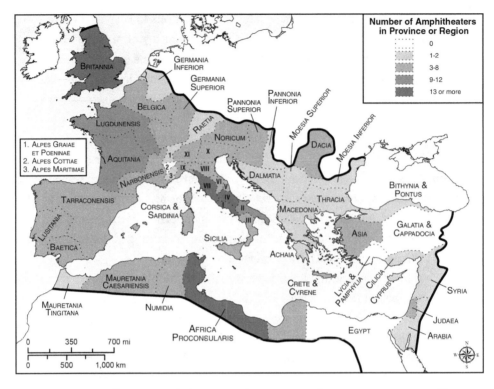

Fig. 10. Map of known amphitheaters in the Roman Mediterranean. (Map created by Gabriel Moss, with amphitheater distribution based on data collected by S. Heath, available at https://github.com/roman-amphitheaters/roman-amphitheaters.)

Across the eastern Mediterranean at this time, independent evidence for the unions of entertainers called the *technitai* of Dionysus, who had been active on the Greek theater circuit since the third century BCE, plummets.[63] However, absence of inscribed evidence does not mean they had disappeared. These groups of poets, singers, actors, performers, musicians, costume seamstresses, and stagehands did not vanish altogether; many simply became a part of the larger, more diverse circus factions in late antiquity.[64] Other ludic endeavors, such as gladiatorial games, were waning under the pressure of heavy expenses and some Christian attitudes. In the West, the building and funding of amphitheaters were already in steep decline, even while circus races continued to grow in popularity. The emperor Honorius had banned gladiatorial games in 404 CE (although many continued to hold them elsewhere), and the costs and regularity of earlier exhibitions could no longer be sustained by many cities, nor by the wealthy men who lived in them.

Other cultural practices were also evolving that, in turn, may affect our understanding of associations at the time. By the end of the fifth century, the erection of statues and their attendant bases—a major source of our surviving evidence for associations, especially in the city of Rome—had almost ceased, as Carlos Machado has recognized.[65] Some workshops for statuary continued elsewhere, particularly in the East, in places like Constantinople and Aphrodisias. But even the latter city's famed sculpture workshop dated from the second to only the fifth century CE.[66] Although the inscriptional testaments relied on to identify occupational *collegia* in the Roman Empire decreased at this time, we cannot definitively state that the associations themselves dwindled. Just because habits of writing shifted does not necessarily mean that there was a general decline in occupational associations. If we look elsewhere, at places such as Roman Egypt, papyri continue to alert us to the strong presence of such occupational associations in the East. In 426 CE, an *ergasia* (association) of bankers or goldsmiths at Oxyrhynchus in Upper Egypt laid out their membership regulations, the existence of a president for the association, and noted required meetings that had to be attended unless a member was sick or out of town. They also set an amount and date for payment of the monthly membership fee and detailed many other parameters of the group.[67]

In terms of the authority of groups focused on trade in the economy of the late antique Mediterranean, historian of the late Roman economy Jairus Banaji and others have posited that, into the fifth century, trade associations and groups of wholesalers gained more "considerable autonomy" than they had possessed in the fourth century CE.[68] Wholesale traders, businessmen, and bankers—many of whom originally hailed from the East and brought products back for resale there—maintained long-distance trade between the East and the West, becoming a kind of powerful "middling class" in many eastern Mediterranean cities. Even in the sixth century, Caesarius, the bishop of Arles in southern France, still talked about the robust presence of businessmen in his congregation, alongside many other types of workers that had long been important to Roman cities: doctors, builders, artisans, salespeople, goldsmiths, and professionals in various trades practiced by the mélange of Romans, Goths, Franks, Syrians, Greeks, and Jews that populated late antique Gaul.[69]

Occupational organizations, group loyalties, and patronage also came in more varied forms at this time, oftentimes overseen by bishops, clerics, and abbots. In 415 CE, three years into Cyril of Alexandria's controversial term as patriarch of the city, monks from the monastery at Nitria came to protest against the Roman prefect Orestes and his feud with Cyril. Much like Damasus, Cyril mobilized and depended upon occupational associations as his personal gang and bodyguard—specifically, a group of lower-level, clerical funeral workers and stretcher-bearers of Alexandria called the *parabolani* (or *parabalani*), an association that had likely been formed in the late fourth century to cater to the sick and the deceased.[70] Cyril deeply disliked and targeted Jews in the city, as well as members of a heretical sect called Novatianism. Insulated by his fanatical Nitrian monks and burly funeral workers, Cyril grew emboldened. When a monk named Ammonius threw a rock at Orestes that same year, the monk was arrested and killed. Cyril declared him a martyr and used the event to further whip up his supporters. Not long thereafter, in 415 or 416, a mob, likely populated with Cyril's *parabolani* and monastic supporters, attacked the Neoplatonist philosopher Hypatia.[71] Since Hypatia was a public supporter of Orestes, the crowd (which may or may not have had *parabolani* among it), without the consent of the magistrate, pulled her from her chariot and took her to a converted church along the Great Harbor called the Caesareum, where they stripped her naked and killed her with roof tiles.[72] Bishops may have often physically stayed out of the fray, but could use the associations they supported to fight their battles.

Soon after Hypatia's death, Theodosius II tried to use legislation to limit the number of *parabolani* to five hundred members in 416 CE. The law stipulated that these men be recruited from among the poor of the city—an indirect consequence of which was that they would assuredly need money and patronage, which a bishop could provide.[73] They increased in number and again reemerged as a bishop's militia to support Cyril at the third ecumenical council, the Council of Ephesus, in 431. They worked with another powerful occupational group in the city of Alexandria: sailors. For his part, the patriarch of Constantinople, Nestorius, was later alleged to have arrived at the council with his own gang. His militia was perhaps composed of men termed *Zeuxippitai*—enslaved bath workers from Constantinople's popular Baths of

Zeuxippus. This was an establishment near the city's hippodrome.[74] The bishops knew the utility of having certain associations of men armed and weaponized for their own ends, and lowly funeral workers were often their preferred choice.

Even after Cyril, the Alexandrian *parabolani* continued to be used as a personal militia under a new patriarch of Alexandria, Dioscorus, who presided over the Second Council of Ephesus in 449 CE. The notorious dispute between a powerful abbot in Constantinople named Eutyches and the patriarch of Constantinople, Flavian, ended in violence and Flavian's death. After a legate of Leo I, the bishop of Rome, protested the proceedings, Dioscorus is alleged to have mobilized his group of *parabolani,* along with other groups, to lock the doors and force the bishops to cast their votes under duress. The ecclesiastical events of the fifth century demonstrate that monks and clerics were not always the kind, quiet, bookish types glimpsed copying manuscripts in medieval depictions of monastic *scriptoria*. Many were manual laborers and craftspeople who felt a strong allegiance to their ecclesiastical leaders for their patronage—much as late Republican occupational groups had felt for Clodius as their populist supporter and *patronus*. It is also a good reminder that monks and other artisans tied to the churches were a part of the underlying labor organization and economic engines within certain late Roman cities. As we saw with the Temple of Artemis in Ephesus, these economies often relied on the money of pilgrims.

Monastic Economies and the Organization of Labor

The economic exchange between pilgrims and monasteries is exemplified at Nitria, an early monastic center thirty miles southeast of Alexandria. It was first settled by a hermetic monk named Amoun around 330 CE in the western Nile Delta, and the name likely came from a valuable local resource, natron, used for cleaning and in the embalming process for mummification. In his letters, Jerome, the translator of the Vulgate Bible, mentions his close friend Paula, a wealthy Roman senatorial woman who later became a saint and desert mother, in a letter to her daughter, Eustochium. Jerome tells her that Paula went to Egypt and visited Nitria, as did many other wealthy male and female pilgrims, with increasing frequency, often giving gifts and buying religious souvenirs.[75] In his *Lausiac History,* the bishop Palladius wrote that there were fifty-six hundred permanent monastic residents in the desert there, many of whom supported themselves by linen working from flax, and seven bakeries existed to serve them.[76] Near the main church on the mountain, there was also a feature common on pilgrim routes and in monasteries, a *xenodocheion*—a hostel or guesthouse—that allowed visitors to stay one week for free before having to pay with their labor in the garden, bakery, or kitchens. By the early fifth century CE, Nitria, like many monastic centers in late Roman Egypt, was a flourishing community. Palladius says that there were many doctors, wine-sellers (and thus much wine), merchants, bankers, and cenobitic monks serving the tourist economy generated by these visitors and creating goods to be sold elsewhere, such as in Alexandria.[77]

Monasteries in Egypt could have robust maker economies, with dozens (if not hundreds) laboring in workshops for pottery, weaving, and textile production. These artisans resembled what we might today call fine artists (such as painters and sculptors). For building projects focused on churches and other ecclesiastical structures, it was good to have in-house artists. On larger building projects, however, there could be a mix of clerical, monastic, and lay labor working side by side to plaster, put in window glass, or install mosaics. The male and female monks working as craftspeople in the urban and suburban monasteries that grew in the fourth century bear some resemblances to the earlier Roman occupational *collegia* in terms of religious cohesion, established hierarchy, communal eating, welfare services, and the organized selling of their wares.

Painted graffiti known as dipinti left by monastic workers are one way to reconstruct the voices of these monastic laborers. At the Red Monastery (modern Deir al-Ahmar) in Upper Egypt, for instance, ubiquitous graffiti covered cell walls. Historian of eastern monasticism Paul Dilley has, by studying the dipinti from the Red Monastery near modern Souhag and other monasteries in the Egyptian desert, recognized a number of artisans recording their thoughts.[78] In these scribblings, there was an occupational pride expressed by artisans, particularly by painters often termed *zographoi*. At the monastery of Apa Jeremiah, two monks named Markos and Abraham served as painters, while at another monastery, Apa Apollo, a painter, wrote: "I, John the Painter, was worthy to paint this vault and I gave it a whitewash. Pray that God might have mercy on me."[79] They also likely produced saintly icons and aided in the painting (and repainting) of basilica interiors. Such *zographoi* were important for reflecting the majesty of God in earthly spaces.[80] But elsewhere, private painters also continued to paint and decorate secular spaces as well.

Late Roman Labor and the Entertainment Economy

Growing pilgrimage routes and monastic communities underpinned the economies of some locations, particularly in the areas of the Levant and Egypt. Entertainment also continued to be an important socioeconomic sector, with performance associations and charioteer factions now largely being funded and overseen by the state. The sixth-century statesman and administrator Cassiodorus would later sneeringly refer to this sector as the *artes lubricae* (slippery arts) due to their disrepute, and note that the local magistrate, the tribune of spectacles, had, in the fifth century, replaced earlier types of magistrates to supervise games in various cities.[81] To Cassiodorus's mind, these tribunes oversaw ignoble persons who had erred by diverging from the correct moral path. Imperial movement to solidify and keep the performers in their roles is also evident in legislation of the time. These laws indicate that, when there was a dearth of mimes or actors, even those who no longer practiced such occupations could be recalled to their disgraced social order.

In 413 CE, Honorius wrote to a tribune in Carthage ordering that female mimes who had previously been freed from service should be called back to provide pleasure to the people on festival days.[82] Just as those compulsory corporations that served the state by supplying the grain supply and the military were of great importance to the emperor, so were the entertainer associations that facilitated wildly popular public spectacles. As we have seen, these performers served as a proxy for the imperial family by expressing care and concern for the Roman people. In his *De gubernatione Dei* (The Government of God), Salvian, a Christian writer in Roman Gaul, noted that when the Vandals captured Carthage in 439 CE, the voices of those dying outside the city walls intermingled with the cheers of the Carthaginians attending games in the circus as the troops approached.[83] For Salvian, this was a hyperbolized, cautionary tale for residents of Gallic cities like Trier. It illustrated that popular obsession with the games could bring destruction to the people.

Meanwhile, migrating groups continued to be a threat to the Roman Empire. Attila and his Huns swept into Gaul in 451 CE, before eventually being rebuffed by the Romans. The Roman military drew heavily on the aid of Gothic troops and another "barbarian" group, called the Burgundians, at the Battle of the Catalaunian Plains. After sacking a few more cities, Attila died in the night in 453, but the impact of migrating groups was not over. The Vandals later sacked the city of Rome in 455 CE, carrying away many spoils that would only later be partially repatriated by Belisarius in the sixth century. Just prior to its sacking, Rome likely had a population of only 320,000 to 340,000—about a third of the one million it had supported in the early Principate.[84] And yet? Rome and many other cities of the western empire were populated with highly resilient peoples, who continued to rebuild and to live.[85] Gregory of Tours acknowledged Rome's ability to restore and remodel itself year after year, always rising once again from the ground.[86]

In the West, changes were also afoot in terms of Roman political leadership and oversight. In 476 CE, a usurper to the western throne—a child named Romulus Augustulus—was deposed by the Scirian officer Odoacer (who also eliminated his father, Orestes). Odoacer then ruled as a king and a "patrician" with support from the eastern Roman emperor, Zeno. Despite this political shift, the former western provinces maintained many Roman cultural elements. In 488 to 489, a king of the Ostrogoths named Theodoric, with the support of the eastern emperor Zeno, pursued power in Italy. In 493, Theodoric and his troops finally defeated Odoacer. The final scene of their rivalry was an alleged dinner of reconciliation and joint rule on March 15, to which Theodoric had invited Odoacer and then assassinated him. One must beware the Ides of March (and Roman dinner invites) even in the late empire, it seems.

This move established the Ostrogothic kingdom of Italy under Theodoric until 526. As was common, the new ruler sided with one circus faction. The letters of Cassiodorus indicate that he particularly supported the Greens in Rome. He also continued to pay the salary of certain famous charioteers, such as one named Thomas.[87] Around 509 CE, Theodoric wrote to two senators in Rome asking them to be patrons for the Greens faction there, which was perhaps a response to an earlier petition from the Greens regarding abusive senators.[88] Such letters suggest the complicated role of pantomimes, who now often held leadership positions within these circus factions as fused entertainment, theatrical, and ludic associations. The same letter mentions two pantomime actors, Helladius and Thorodon, who had been selected by the king to compete for this leadership position in the Greens. Later letters reveal that, in 509 CE, a riot in the circus broke out over which pantomime was to lead.[89] Theodoric was quick to point out that senators had been implicated in inciting violence among the factions and sheltering people from oversight by the prefect of the city, who enforced order and put down many of the disturbances connected to the pantomime shows that were a part of circus games.[90] Senatorial collusion with charioteers, it seems, was a continued concern.

In smaller Egyptian cities at the beginning of the sixth century, charioteers still attained prominence and gained the admiration of the populace. A well-known sixth-century illustration called the Charioteer Papyrus, from the Egyptian city of Antinoopolis, provides a colorful glimpse of charioteers similar to the dozens of mosaics depicting the Blues, Greens, Whites, and Reds in cities with a hippodrome.[91] In Egypt, Palestine, and Syria, in particular, a mix of privately and publicly funded circus factions remained popular.[92] But such factions were also still closely tied to violence, disorder, and prejudice. In 507, a riot of the Greens in Antioch resulted in the burning of a synagogue and the killing of numerous people, before the leader of the Greens was finally killed in a church. This caused even more rioting that led, eventually, to the deaths of many of the Blues who had supported the forces assigned to put down the riot. There was little doubt that the charioteer factions held great sociopolitical sway in these cities and could mobilize their own labor and supporters quickly, particularly the leaders of the factions of the Blues and Greens.

In Constantinople, circus factions created the model that was then often imitated and replicated elsewhere in the East. Upon Zeno's death in 491 CE, a man named Anastasius ascended to the purple as the eastern Roman emperor. While he disliked spectacles and their disruptive presence in Constantinople, Zeno's brother, Longinus, had the support of the Blues and Greens. Consequently, Anastasius, a fan of the Reds, exiled Longinus, as well as many of his supporters. He also outlawed pantomimes in 502, after much upheaval and rioting connected with these theatrical power players. Upon Anastasius's death in the summer of 518, however, there was renewed upheaval over who would replace him. In the debate over succession, a young Thracian in the imperial bodyguard named Justinian aided his uncle, Justin, by whipping up the Greens and the Blues. The new emperor, Justin, was finally carried to Constantinople's hippodrome, which could hold one hundred thousand spectators, to be acclaimed by the soldiers, the senators, and—most importantly—

the factions. And yet Justin knew that the popularity of these factions could be either a blessing or threat to his own power. This likely led him to eventually ban dancers (and thus also pantomime) everywhere in the East except the city of Alexandria, although he allowed circus factions to continue.[93] Despite these bans, the art of pantomime continued until the seventh century at least.

As it happens, Justinian's relationship with the circus factions was important both personally and professionally from an early age. Soon after 523 or 524 CE, he married a former actress named Theodora, who, we are told by the historian Procopius, was the daughter of a father who was a bear-keeper for the Greens and a mother who was an actress and dancer.[94] After the death of Justin I's wife, Euphemia, who had objected to Justinian marrying a lowly daughter of a circus faction worker (although she had herself been enslaved and come from a background seen as humble), the emperor was persuaded by his nephew to lift the earlier marriage legislation that had long prevented senators and legally stigmatized actresses from marrying.[95] Justinian married Theodora, but her connection to the factions and her association, as an actress, with sex work were never forgotten by sneering historians like Procopius.

On April 1, 527 CE, Justinian, with Theodora as his empress, became co-emperor with Justin and then took sole power upon Justin's death a few months later, in August. Together, Justinian and Theodora were supporters of the Blues faction; however, less than five years into his rule, their power and patronage were tested by the Nika riots. In January of 532 CE, a fan from the Blues and another from the Greens survived a bungled execution of rioters who had been arrested by Justinian. The Blues and Greens joined forces to lobby the emperor to free their faction member, to no avail. The resulting riot and subsequent imperial massacre of thirty thousand participants by soldiers stationed within the hippodrome likely went far beyond anything Theodosius could ever have imagined. It was the most devastating circus riot and mass execution of the Roman populace by an emperor in ancient Mediterranean history. It demonstrated the state fear of these unions and their fans, as well as the emperor's might to combat them.

In the hippodrome of Constantinople in the early sixth century CE, a bronze statue commemorated a deceased charioteer named Constantinus.[96] The statue had an accompanying epigram inscribed on its base that spoke to the charioteer's connection with the crowd during his racing career in the circus. It cites his role in civil strife on the streets of the city. Both aspects defined his popularity and influenced the memory of him among the people. Constantinus the charioteer is but one example of how circus factions and their leaders took to the late antique streets of cities such as Antioch, Thessalonica, Alexandria, and Constantinople. While this violence sometimes came from rivalries between competing factions—what Alan Cameron termed "hooliganism" akin to modern soccer riots—at other times, they could also use their numbers and their following for effective economic, political, religious, and populist ends.[97] The cultural currency of spectacles and popular support for the circus factions imbued them with power in late antiquity, but it was their internal organization and capacity to mobilize quickly—albeit not always successfully or with full control over the actions of their followers—that endowed the circus *factiones* with the collective ability to use their groups to lobby and to resist as one body formed out of many.

Glimpses of charioteers' civic activism and role as popular leaders occur particularly in the fifth to early seventh centuries within the eastern Mediterranean. At Alexandria, factions united with the people and each other to protest an oil shortage in 515/516 CE; during the Nika riots of 532, the leading factions of Constantinople came together to petition for the release of prisoners; and in Constantinople yet again, there were protests against bread shortages in 556 CE, as well as a bread run on the bakeries led in part by factions in 559.[98] Into the early seventh century, these factions continued to play an active role in early Byzantine politics. Such upheavals provide us with new insights into the collective mobilization incited by factions and their leaders for economic and political ends. Factional politicking supports the conclusion that while the elite political infrastructure transformed, various ancient associations continued to influence and to change the course of Roman history through small but still important acts of collective resistance in many late antique cities. Rome's last recorded chariot race was held in 549 CE, but the hippodrome continued to be a focus and locus of civic life, political movements, and popular turbulence in many eastern cities until the seventh century CE.[99] Thereafter, these racetracks were largely abandoned, but in Constantinople, the popular practice endured until the twelfth century.

Reviewing the historical leadership undertaken by charioteers and reassessing the power of factions is a restorative undertaking. Doing so illustrates a higher degree of agency exemplified by certain enslaved (or likely enslaved) and manumitted persons than is often granted by historians today to those of servile status in the past. Enslaved persons were largely excluded from participation in most Greek athletics and their festivals in the Republic and early empire. By extension, they were only rarely allowed to be members of the prestigious athletic associations and synods of the earlier periods.[100] However, through circus factions, enslaved and manumitted persons often led the way rather than being marginalized. Servile and low-status charioteers were the norm and could become popular leaders who, in certain instances, incited and steered acts of resistance and protest within their cities. This fact perhaps allows us to provide more nuance to one of the most commonly reiterated notions about ancient slave revolts, namely, that they were "exceedingly rare" and largely a product of the late Republic in the Roman Mediterranean.[101] While it is true that large-scale slave revolts constituted entirely by enslaved resistors attempting to escape servitude were indeed highly atypical after the Servile Wars of the late Republic, if we expand to include revolts led by, involving, and also empowering groups of enslaved persons, they were not as infrequent as we might think. The history of the factions in late antiquity reminds us that sports and spectacle were and are a form of labor. Their history also underscores that Roman history is filled with myriad acts of "everyday resistance" to the Roman state that, while oftentimes overlooked, frequently involved enslaved or formerly enslaved persons, and depended upon organized associations that could assemble quickly and effectively in order to work toward a shared goal.[102]

Conclusion: Uniting Ancient and Modern Laborers

BY NOVEMBER OF 562 CE, the silversmiths of Constantinople, an association known as the *argyropratai,* had had quite enough of Justinian. The powerful group functioned as jewelers who crafted items of gold and silver, gem dealers, occasional creditors, and bankers. They had their own workshops in the city and were a wealthy commercial circle. In the tenth century and likely long before, their workshops were located on the Mese, Constantinople's main thoroughfare. Into the Middle Ages, this was a street where artisans belonging to their own occupational associations sold glass, pottery, leather, candles, bread, and many other products. At the time, the silversmiths were likely exasperated with the emperor due to the forced loans they were compelled to give him. Ancient sources suggest that the silversmith association may have then backed a group of assassins—a musician named Ablabius (likely a performance member of one of the circus factions); a silversmith named Marcellus (perhaps with two other silversmiths); and a relative of a high-ranking official named Sergius. Their mission was to kill the emperor.[1]

The plot was foiled by loose lips before Justinian could be assassinated. Ablabius blabbed about the so-called bankers' conspiracy to kill Justinian in his dining room. It was stopped before it could be executed. However, the general Belisarius, along with his own personal banker, were implicated in the plot. Belisarius had a short period of disgrace before ultimately having his name cleared. Although it was not successful, the alleged scheme of the bankers' association throws into relief the influence and political interests of certain associations well into the early Middle Ages in the eastern Mediterranean. Just a few years later, in 565 CE, Justinian—the great lawmaker, emperor, and temporary reunifier of the East and West—died in bed at the imperial palace. This momentous event is where our formal investigation into Roman labor organization, unions, and collective resistance to the state ends. But even after Justinian's death, the existence of important and influential occupational associations in the eastern Mediterranean—often termed *systemata* or *somateia* in the sources—continued on into the Byzantine Empire until the sack of Constantinople in 1453.

The persons whom we today call Byzantines were in fact people who identified as Romans. The Roman Empire, to their minds, continued on with them for many more centuries. Likewise, their artisans, craftspeople, and professional associations persisted in the long tradition of associative formation and collective activity for centuries after the Roman Empire in the West declined. Those associations in the city of Constantinople itself seem to have experienced stronger state oversight and more legal limits. The impacts of the earlier Roman associative mold and the constant state anxiety over these groups are still clear. Byzantine occupational associations are particularly visible within the most extensive source that we have for them, the tenth-century *Book of the Eparch*. This book of ordinances was likely published under the emperor Leo VI around 911 or 912 CE.

The regulations governed twenty-one occupations in Constantinople, each with its own associations overseen by the civil official known as the eparch. The rule book speaks to the continued attempts by the state to control certain important associations from above within the city. Attempts to command, extinguish, or regulate associations and assemblies are a tale as old as their existence, after all. Some had membership fees for entrance, while others did not. Other portions dictate rules for the buying and selling of goods. For instance, there was an ordinance that said that raw silk merchants were forbidden to sell raw silk to Jews or to tradesfolk who would resell it outside the city. The persons who contravened this law were to be flogged and shaved.[2] As a whole, the *Book of the Eparch* gestures to the persisting significance of occupational associations to the city's economy and to the Byzantine political system. It also indicates that state control was extensive and invasive at times—perhaps a pivotal reason why there is an absence of evidence for Byzantine strikes.

Historians of the Byzantine economy have done far-reaching research into the influence and regulation of these associations in the East, showing that there was some political activism on their part and participation in state functions such as imperial processions. However, state interference was much higher than in the western areas of the former Roman Empire.[3] In the western Mediterranean, there is also much less evidence for either cohesive associations or centralized state intervention into their functioning and oversight, except in special cases such as the Carolingian Empire. But there were still some cities in the West where occupational associations were relied upon. At the highly trade-centered city of Ravenna in the sixth century, for example, we find strong evidence for earlier Roman associations continuing. In this important northern Italian city, written and archaeological evidence indicate there continued to be powerful banker groups called *argentarii,* as well as distinct associations that were part of an organized labor market. Occupational associations at Ravenna included everyone from wax-makers to bakers to physicians to marble merchants.[4]

Elsewhere in the West, we have only scraps of evidence for other such associations at work in the early medieval period. A letter from Pope Gregory I in 599 CE notes abuses visited on the powerful soap-makers' association in Naples by an official, and discloses that associations could petition powerful clerics in the Church in the face of abuse such as the pocketing of entrance fees.[5] But the character of many trade associations changed into the early Middle Ages. As economic historian Rory Naismith has argued, many early medieval associations of northwest Europe simply were not economically focused.[6] They were more religiously based collectives, focusing on faith, and on "feasting and mutual protection," over trade. But even then, they could provoke fear from above. Familiarly worded ordinances under Charlemagne attempted to malign these groups by dubbing them *coniurationes* (conspiracies) that were counter to the state. Associations were still known by a litany of Latin and Germanic names and titles at the time, but the use of oaths in secret societies to bind everyone from serfs to aristocrats into a collective was, in that moment, looked at with extreme unease by the Carolingians ruling in medieval Francia. To the mind of Carolingian kings (and many Roman emperors prior), oaths should be given to the crown and not a confraternity.

This book does not focus on the extensive histories of the later associations of craftsmen and merchants dubbed "guilds" that formed in western Europe during the high to late Middle Ages. But parallels abound between these groups and earlier Roman associations. Like Roman *collegia* prior, these guilds played essential roles in organizing feasts, could be used as drinking clubs, often played a spiritual function during religious festivals, and provided community to members. And yet equity was not a common characteristic of these groups. Guilds could be highly exclusionary to those persons viewed as outside the bounds of honorable society. Oftentimes, they took on and replicated the same biases, chauvinisms, and prejudices of medieval society at large. While a pivotal part of many cities in the Middle Ages, they—to an even greater extent than in ancient Rome—oftentimes served to reinforce the exclusionary policies embedded within the overall Christian social structure of these towns. Especially in the thirteenth and fourteenth centuries, many guilds excluded Jews explicitly in the articles governing the guild. In regard to gender, while there were women within certain guilds tied to things such as the silk industry in Paris, they were often allowed only a limited participation within them.[7] The enslaved were almost completely excluded from medieval guilds; however, some allowed for enslaved persons to aid masters who were guild members. We also know that, at times, certain guilds engaged in strikes. In the thirteenth century in France, in particular, the refusal to work by scholars within *collegia* of teachers was called a *cessatio*—a cessation of teaching. But as we have seen, they were neither the first nor the last to withhold their labor as a way of renegotiating their work terms.

These guilds and their occasional strikes allow us to piece together the long social, economic, and political impact of associations and cross-compare with associations in Roman cities. While the economic value of medieval trade guilds in western Europe is debated, their social value is much more evident and accepted today. Renaissance historian Konrad Eisenbichler remarks that "confraternities became important venues not only for the acquisition and distribution of social capital, but also wealth, be that spiritual or material."[8] The guilds and social clubs that are typically studied during the Middle Ages are those that reemerged amid urban renewal in the eleventh century to twelfth century onward in Europe, during the period of the high Middle Ages. And while the overarching impact of these medieval guilds on innovation and technology is still a source of some debate among economic historians, their overall influence in many cities and towns is undeniable.[9] Sheilagh Ogilvie and many other scholars have long contended that such guilds in fact manipulated markets, excluded large swaths of the population from participation, and could block both apprentices and technological innovation.[10] Ancient associations and, later, the medieval guilds, were not, then, an intrinsically positive force in the lives of all premodern peoples. They had the capacity for good; they had the capacity for ill. Creation of an association alone is not a virtuous act. It is what you do with your collective might that matters and defines it.

Medieval Europe was not alone or exceptional in its use of collective labor or in the existence of voluntary associations. Within certain Islamic cultures, medieval and early modern guilds were often referred to as *akhis*. These guilds were much more inclusive than medieval Christian guilds and could include Jewish, Christian, and Muslim members. There were also guilds in China and India, many with kinship-based models of apprenticeship, in contrast to the European models, which had broader policies for apprenticeship training.[11] While neither Rome nor Europe was remarkable in its dependence on occupational or merchant associations at various times, these groups remain, and their nuances are an important prism for examining almost any society—including America. As the current new labor movement develops and pushes for workers' rights, pay protection, and representation, it might behoove us to look at the successes, failures, and impact of those who came before. One thing that is on the horizon is a backlash to the renewal of collective action, strikes, and unions. In fact, the counterattack from above is already gaining steam.

Looking Back While Moving Forward

In late 2023, the 160,000 members of the Screen Actors Guild and American Federation of Television and Radio Artists (SAG-AFTRA) concluded an epic 118-day strike. Membership in this entertainment labor union runs the social and economic gamut from major actors like Harrison Ford all the way down to actors who earn only a base day rate for their work speaking just a few lines. Among other requests, the union demanded improved royalties from streaming services sharing their work, higher wages, and regulations against studios using artificial intelligence (AI). Big studios pushed back against these demands, but protesting writers and actors banded together and persevered. Like many ancient and modern entertainment unions, they benefitted from solidarity with another, similar labor union: the Writers Guild of America (WGA). They also did something many ancient unions did: leverage their high public profiles by appealing to the people with social media. These strikes are only the latest and most publicized examples of how workers are unionizing and joining the picket line to halt work in the name of improving their working conditions and wages.

Nonetheless, if Roman history teaches us anything, it is that with every collective action, there is often an equal and opposite reaction—from above. Corporate leaders are seeing the union writing on the wall and already trying to halt it. Starbucks' former chief executive, Howard Schultz, has been accused of allegedly union busting by firing baristas who have joined new Starbucks unions. There are allegations of spying on these unions and offering special incentives such as education benefits to those workers who choose not to join union efforts. And such tactics are not relegated to the United States. In 2005, in the United Kingdom, more than six hundred workers at Heathrow Airport were fired, allegedly after speaking with a transport union and having one shift refuse to attend work. Rather than fire workers, some corporations simply shut down a portion of the business entirely. A Chipotle restaurant in Maine under threat of unionization recently closed the store altogether. CEOs and corporate executives are already taking action to stop the tide of unionizing that has followed in the wake of a global pandemic and a renewed focus on social justice in 2020. What remains to be seen is whether this new push to form unions will be sustained into the future or recede.[12]

Labor movements are not only stymied by corporate bigwigs. As Roman history demonstrates, legislation and judicial policy have a huge impact as well. In Florida, a law called Senate Bill 256 (SB 256) has put new limits on unions for many public sector employees. And if experts are correct, anti-labor sentiments among wealthy elites in corporate America will likely also be supported by the U.S. judiciary branch, as well as the many conservative lawmakers who now stand against union rights. As one reporter put it, there is "an increasingly aggressive anti-labor Supreme Court" in the United States that echoes many of the anti-labor laws passed in the twentieth century.[13] But what can be done to parse this public back-and-forth? Why should we venture to look backward to understand the present moment?

The overarching history of occupational associations from antiquity to today accentuates the power of collective action and strikes as a tactic. However, the most essential reasons for studying them is not just assessing this tactic, but understanding how those in power recast actions from below and reframed them as actions against the state and the public good, rather than as actions that affected their own personal fortunes. Roman labor history is not simply about making analogies with the past, but rather about identifying how wealthy elites and politicians (groups that heavily overlap) have, depressingly often, used well-worn oratory to recast collective action and worker strikes in a negative light. This reframing has often tried to put them at odds with the civic interest, rather than seeing them as achieving social justice. In the wake of the widely publicized strikes and public protests happening today, we can then be more vigilant about engaging with the historical precedents for the ways that corporations and even governments have long slandered unions or cast collective action as the work of mobs. Defaming and then marginalizing groups and movements as antipatriotic, conspiratorial, self-serving, and even violent threats to public order has always been a way of justifying the extreme actions taken to disband and disempower them.

Time and time again, Roman antiquity offers up historical examples of the ways in which two groups that heavily overlap, the wealthy and political leaders, weaponize legislation. They also often move to use state intervention in the form of police forces or soldiers to stymie the efforts of workers to attain their objectives—whether they be higher wages or a better work environment. And yet studying Roman history does not mean that we suddenly acquire sacred answers to the unknowable problems of the future, or that we save ourselves from being doomed to repeat the mistakes of the past. That is not the deeper purpose of history from below, and it is an impossible ask. Studying the labor organization, unions, and state tactics taken against associations or informal groups in the Roman Mediterranean allows the people of the present to apprehend the longue durée politics behind the freedom to assemble. In the process, workers may also identify with the complexity, emotions, and actions of the myriad laborers, artisans, and tradespeople of the past. Compassion is one benefit of rewriting the way we tell the story of Rome, but it is not the only one.

Writing and reading histories from below can create empathy for the millions of regular Romans who lived and died in the Roman Empire. Such histories also have restorative powers. By reporting on the humanity, the choices, the triumphs, and even the failures of associations of regular workers, professionals, and businesspeople, we provide them the textual space, visibility, and dignity often denied to them by men like Tacitus. Acknowledging the many ways that informal and formal associations influenced Roman history can also confer the less visible persons of the past with a degree of agency by exploring their participation, membership, and status within larger collectives. Rather than viewing these individuals as "primitive" workers only interested in social clubs for feasting, or poor laborers who needed collectives only to help to bury their loved ones, we can instead begin to acknowledge that many associations were vibrant and complex entities whose capabilities and impact still need further study.

Roman associations had a substantial role in shaping both the familiar and unfamiliar events, people, and places of the Roman Mediterranean. Beyond that, they provided ancient peoples with important group identities in the face of a vast empire, extended insurance to those living in a world with few welfare programs or social safety nets, allowed risk mitigation within precarious ancient economic networks, and offered a host of other benefits that could be social, religious, and economic. These associations were themselves dynamic organisms that were a regular part of everyday life in the Roman world, just like the people within them. They offered community to many living across the Mediterranean and some, at opportune times, even provided ancient workers the collective strength to resist, to rebel, and to make their voices heard.

NOTES

Introduction

1. Sheldon, "London Sailors' Strike," 12–17; Phan, *Bonds of Citizenship*, 174–75.
2. The following definition for "strike," given by the U.S. Bureau of Labor Statistics, provides the starting point for my own applied definition: a "temporary stoppage of work by a group of employees to express a grievance, enforce a demand, or protest the terms, conditions, or provisions of a contract." United States Bureau of Labor Statistics, "Work Stoppages."
3. Cordery, *British Friendly Societies*, 40.
4. Morris, "Criminal Conspiracy." Morris notes that since the mid-fourteenth century (1349), English laborers working together to raise wages or limit hours had been seen as engaging in "criminal" and "seditious" behavior, but that the eighteenth century brought changes to the common law. He states: "The inclusion by the later courts of labor combinations as conspiracies at common law can be traced to an ambiguous statement of Hawkins, in his *Pleas of the Crown*, published in 1716" (55). This precedent was copied and applied in numerous cases, particularly in wage disputes with the journeyman tailors in 1721. In the early nineteenth century, the legal precedent then made the leap from English common law to American labor law.
5. Rule, *Labouring Classes*, 259–60. Trade unions were not legalized in Britain until 1824. The British Parliament's earlier passing of the Combination Acts of 1799 and 1800 indicates how strongly they worked against attempts at the forcing of wage hikes and the use of strikes by labor collectives.
6. *Corpus Inscriptionum Latinarum* (hereafter *CIL*) IV, 710.
7. The tent-makers' association at Rome: *CIL* VI, 9053 = *Inscriptiones Latinae Selectae* (hereafter *ILS*) 1777 = Ascough, Harland, and Kloppenborg, Associations in the Greco-Roman World (hereafter AGRW) ID# 24410 (70–200 CE); Association of purple sellers in Thessalonica: *Inscriptiones Graecae* (hereafter *IG*) X.2.1 291 =

AGRW ID# 2465 = Inventory of Ancient Associations Database (hereafter CAP-Inv.) 786 (second century CE).
8. Diosono, *Professiones Gentiliciae*, 251. For her remark on their elision in elite literature in antiquity, see 254.
9. Tacitus, *Annals* (hereafter Tac. Ann.) 13.31.1.
10. Sancinito, *Reputation of the Roman Merchant*.
11. Suetonius, *Life of Nero* (hereafter Suet. Nero) 12.1.
12. Engels and Marx, *Communist Manifesto*, 62. The so-called Struggle of the Orders was still on the mind of Karl Marx in June 1865, when he delivered a lecture to the First International Working Men's Association (IWA), a mixture of worker groups and unions formed in London the previous year. At the time, Marx was working on the draft of his book, *Das Kapital: Volume I*, and he harangued the group about the need to abolish class rule: "When the Roman plebeians went on strike against the Roman patricians, the patrician Agrippa told them that the patrician belly provided the proletarian limbs of the body of the state with nourishment. Agrippa failed to show how someone could feed the limbs of one man by filling the belly of another" (Marx, *Value, Price and Profit*, 10).
13. Further study has shown that the plebeians did not constitute what might be called a monolithic or homogeneous social class in the way Marx understood them. However, as Chapter One will explore, large numbers of plebeians did indeed engage in secessions that withdrew their labor from the urban economy and, more crucially, withheld their military service.
14. In his chapter within *Handbook: The Global History of Work*, social and economic historian Sjaak van der Velden argues the secessions of the plebs cannot be termed a strike in the modern sense because it included soldiers who owned land; he sees the "early stages of modern Capitalism" as the point at which strikes become regularized (van der Velden, "8.3. Strikes, Lockouts, and Informal Resistance," 525). It is unclear and unexplained why that is a disqualifying status, since owning property does not keep one from participating in a strike. Frank, *Economic History of Rome*, 284, noted that "we never hear of labor strikes in Italy" and stated, overconfidently, that in the face of slave competition, *collegia* could not be used to better wages or achieve collective bargaining. A summary of this prior work is provided in a short but important article by Ramsay MacMullen ("Note on Roman Strikes," 269), whose evaluation is spot on: "Strikes did occur in the Roman Empire and they are quite often mentioned in modern works, where they are described as being extremely rare due to the existence of servile labor and due more especially to the highly organized and eventually compulsory form into which the state dragooned the labor force." Also note Frank's contemporary, Rostovtzeff, *Social and Economic History*, 303, and his assessment of strikes as due to a "low standard of industry."
15. Cicero, *Letters to Atticus* (hereafter Cic. Att.) 1.16.11: "*misera ac ieiuna plebecula.*"
16. Drury, "'When the Mobs Are Looking,'" 42.
17. MacMullen, *Roman Social Relations*, 74; Perry, "Organized Societies," 504. Here, Perry boldly states, "Nothing in the ancient documents suggests that *collegia* ever called for a strike to secure their interests." This is not the case.

18. Brice, "Second Chance for Valor," 106–7, has made the case for applying the word "mutiny" to certain incidents of Roman unrest and indiscipline in the Roman army.
19. On the concept of "strategic anachronism" and argument for its use, see Gray, "Appendix C."
20. Patterson, *Slavery and Social Death*.
21. For the terms applied to these various associations, see the pivotal work by Waltzing, *Étude historique*, 236–42.
22. In terms of digital nomenclatures, Verboven has chosen to call them guilds and occupation-based communities in his Verboven et al., Ghent Database of Roman Guilds. Philip Harland labels them as "occupational guilds" in the metadata category in his AGRW.
23. See Kloppenborg, "Collegia and Thiasoi."
24. Ogilvie, *Institutions and European Trade*, 19.
25. A popular textbook with three editions by Howard M. Wachtel summarizes the narrative most succinctly, noting that following the American Civil War, the United States "went through a period of capital accumulation and industrialization that has not occurred since," which caused new industries to arise, eventually culminating in the creation of the American Federation of Labor (AFL) in 1886 (Watchtel, *Labor and the Economy*, 386).
26. Brentano, *History and Development of Gilds*.
27. Perry, *Roman Collegia*; and "Organized Societies"; Waltzing, *Étude historique*.
28. Finley, *Ancient Economy*, 138.
29. MacMullen, *Roman Social Relations*, 78. On the absence of strikes or evidence for associations pursuing benefits connected to work, see 75. Walker-Ramisch, "Graeco-Roman Voluntary Associations," 133.
30. The work of association scholars such as Jinyu Liu, Koen Verboven, John Kloppenborg, Nicolas Tran, and many others will be cited and drawn on extensively in this book. Other association scholars, such as Philip Venticinque, are important for their focus on how associations created trust in the economy of Roman Egypt, while economic historians such as Miriam J. Groen-Vallinga, in her study of labor in Roman Italy, have uncovered their essential role in the development of Roman Italy. See Venticinque, *Honor among Thieves*; Groen-Vallinga, *Work and Labour*, 254.
31. Romans were indeed not the only ones to create associations that could be economically beneficial. See Thaplyal, *Guilds in Ancient India*. This "sense of belonging" would be an important aspect of medieval guilds as well. Note Hoogenboom, Kissane, Prak et al., "Guilds in the Transition to Modernity," 258.
32. Varro, *De Re Rustica* (hereafter Var. *Rust.*) 2.1.9. The most readily accepted dating system and date for the founding of Rome were devised by Marcus Terentius Varro in the first century BCE. However, Cicero, *Brutus* (hereafter Cic. *Brut.*) 18.72, and later Censorinus (*De die natali* 21.4 [238 CE]) recognize that, into the late Republic, debates continued over this founding date, although Varro's came to be preferred. Dionysus of Halicarnassus (hereafter Dion. Hal.) 1.74.1–4, lists a number of people with differing calculations, from Timaeus (813 BCE) who, like many, used the Olympiads as benchmarks, to Marcus Porcius Cato, who thought it was

751 BCE. By the time of Plutarch in the second century CE (*Life of Romulus* 12), Varro's dating seems to have become the accepted one. See Samuel, *Greek and Roman Chronology*, 249–50. Even then, there were still literary quarrels over the exact year and day of the month.

33. Plutarch, *Life of Numa* 17: "But of all [Numa's] administrative acts, the one most marveled at was his distribution of the populace into groups according to their artisan skills. . . . He distributed them, according to their artisan skills, into musicians, goldsmiths, carpenters, dyers, leather-workers, leather curriers, coppersmiths, and potters. The remaining arts, he gathered together into one corps out of all who belonged to this group. He also dictated associations and assemblies and rites of worship rendered to each association."
34. For a similarly cynical view of the Numa story, see Benton, *Bread Makers*, 149–50.
35. Gabba, "*Collegia* of Numa," 85. See Suetonius, *Life of Julius Caesar* (hereafter Suet. *Iul.*) 42.3: "*Cuncta collegia praeter antiquitus constituta distraxit*" ("He disbanded all the *collegia*, except the ancient ones"); Suetonius, *Life of the Divine Augustus* (hereafter Suet. *Aug.*) 32.1: "*collegia praeter antiqua et legitima dissolvit*" ("he dissolved the *collegia* except the ancient and legally allowed ones").
36. In the words of ancient historian Brent Shaw, "The Roman state, as most other central states in antiquity, had an almost morbid fear of any unofficial assembly or association" (Shaw, "Rural Markets in North Africa," 47).
37. Pliny, *Naturalis historia* (hereafter Plin. *HN*) 34.1, 35.159.
38. L. Annaeus Florus (hereafter Flor.) 1.6.3. In describing Tullius's separation of Rome's populace into census classes and other kinds of divisions, Florus remarked that the Roman people were "distributed into *decuriae* and *collegia*." See Richard, "Sur les prétendues corporations numaïques," 423–28; Flor. 1.6.3: "*decuriis atque collegiis distributus*"; Liu, *Collegia Centonariorum*, 100.
39. *CIL* XIV, 2112 (136 CE).
40. For Athens, see Ismard, *Cité des réseaux*. For Hellenistic associations beyond Athens, Delos, and Rhodes, see Fröhlich and Hamon, *Groupes et associations*. For their continuity into the Roman era in the eastern Mediterranean, see van Nijf, *Civic World of Professional Associations*.
41. Ismard, *Cité des reseaux*, 1: "La cité apparaît comme un faisceau d'entités composites, un ensemble de réseaux de multiples dimensions, loin de l'image stéréotypée de la cité une et indivisible promue par l'idéologie civique."
42. Aristotle, *Ethica Nicomachea* (hereafter Arist. *Eth. Nic.*) 8.9.4 (Bekker 1160a): "αἱ δὲ κοινωνίαι πᾶσαι μορίοις ἐοίκασι τῆς πολιτικῆς."
43. Monson, "Ethics and Economics."
44. Arist. *Eth. Nic.* 8.9.4–5 (Bekker 1160a).
45. On the overlapping economic and social networks connected to political associations in the Greek world of the fourth century BCE, see Gabrielsen, "Naval and Grain Networks," 203–5.
46. Plutarch, *Aristides* 2.4: "ὁ μὲν οὖν Θεμιστοκλῆς εἰς ἑταιρείαν ἐμβαλὼν ἑαυτὸν εἶχε." See Calhoun, *Athenian Clubs*, 1.
47. Dowse and Blackburn, "Improving Supply Chain Resilience."

Chapter 1. The Plebs

1. According to legend, Romulus had established an advisory body called the Senate, made up of one hundred men from a total population that then numbered perhaps around eighteen thousand. The exact population number estimated by Carandini (*Rome: Day One*, 109) is 17,837, based on calculations by Capogrossi Colognesi, "Curie, centurie e 'heredia,'" 41–49.
2. Livy (hereafter Liv.) 4.9.11. Special levies for pacifying the plebs were likely set up in 508 and 495. In 406 BCE, pay was given in the form of a stipend funded by a *tributum* tax meant to take the place of the labor lost on their farms. The tax was paid by propertied Romans as well as indemnities gained from warfare. This *tributum* was paid by Roman citizens only until 167 BCE.
3. Mignone, *Republican Aventine*, 39; von Ungern-Sternberg, "Formation of the 'Annalistic Tradition,'" 83–84.
4. Meunier, "Decemvirate," 155.
5. Dion. Hal. 6.1–22.
6. Dion. Hal. 6.26.
7. Dion., Hal. 6.26.3.
8. Dion., Hal. 6.26.2.
9. Liv. 2.27.5. Originally, these were a college of priests, it seems, formulated explicitly to take care of the temple. Only later did this *collegium* become an association for merchants, many of whom, in the later evidence, are also well-off freedmen. See Verboven, "Guilds and God," 282.
10. Ovid, *Fasti* (hereafter Ov. *Fast.*) 5.663–92; Macrobius, *Saturnalia* 1.12.19.
11. Dion. Hal. 6.29.
12. Liv. 2.28.1: Specifically note the language of "*coetus nocturnes*" given by Livy.
13. Liv. 2.27, 2.32: "*rursus coetus occulti coniurationesque*" ("[there would] again be secret gatherings and conspiracies"). Livy notes that it was the Sacred Mount, rather than the Aventine Hill.
14. Cornell, *Beginnings of Rome*, 263; Lintott, *Constitution*, 129–31. The aediles perhaps originally cared for a temple on the Aventine dedicated to the gods Ceres, Liber, and Libera.
15. Riggsby, *Roman Law*, 205.
16. Festus 372L.
17. For patrician power maintained through collegial co-option, see Beard, North, and Price, *Religions of Rome*, 64.
18. There does not appear to have been a plebeian Vestal until Oppia in 483 BCE.
19. Liv. 2.42.11 (the Vestal is called Oppia); Dion. Hal. 8.89.4–5 (the Vestal is called Opimia).
20. Liv. 2.31. Livy notes how the moneylenders' precautions rendered the people and the Dictator powerless.
21. Ste. Croix, *Class Struggle*, 336.
22. Perhaps originally established around 509 and then again by a law in 449 BCE, the right did not become legally sanctioned until the waning years of the Struggle of the Orders, in 300 BCE, with the passing of a law called the *lex Valeria*. Cicero

saw this as an important popular or civil right established at the earliest beginnings of the Republic, citing it again and again. Cicero, *De republica* (hereafter Cic. *Rep.*) 2.53–54, notes that the books of the pontiffs record that the right existed even earlier, during the regal period as well. Also note his *De legibus* 3.6.2. In the second century BCE, as Rome's empire expanded, the law was extended to apply outside the city's sacred boundary zone called the *pomerium*, so that Roman citizens elsewhere could appeal against abuse. See Martin, "Provokation," 72–96.

23. Cornell, "Tyranny of the Evidence," 8–9. Greek writing was discovered on a ceramic in the nearby town of Gabii dating to 770 BCE, and similarly dated Greek ceramics were discovered in the excavation of Rome's port along the Tiber and its cattle market, called the Forum Boarium.
24. Daniels, "Annexing a Shared Past," 240.
25. Cifani, *Origins of the Roman Economy*, 143–45.
26. There were also two older popular assemblies for male citizens: the Curiate Assembly, made up of the thirty early Roman units of the population called *curiae*, and the Tribal Assembly, which voted across the tribes, of which after 241 BCE there numbered thirty-five.
27. Armstrong, *War and Society*, 78. Legend said that the Centuriate Assembly was reformed under the sixth king of Rome, Servius Tullius (c. 578–535 BCE).
28. Pomponius, *Digesta* (hereafter Pomp. *Dig.*) 1.2.2.4: "*ut possint leges apertius percipi.*"
29. In Greek a "ἑταιρεία." Gaius, *Digesta* 47.22.4: "*sodales sunt, qui eiusdem collegii sunt; quam Graeci vocant* ἑταιρείαν" ("members are those who are of the same *collegium*, which the Greeks call a *hetaireia*"). See Liu, "Professional Associations," 99, 352.
30. Gaius, *Dig.* 47.22.4 (Fr. 76a).
31. I have here followed the suggestion of Michael H. Crawford, *Roman Statutes*, vol. 2 (London: Institute of Classical Studies, 1996), Tabula VIII, 14–15, 694–95, that this should not be seen as explicitly nocturnal gatherings, as reported by the suspect mention in Latro (*Decl. in Cat.* 65 [Kristoferson]), but rather as *coetus* generally. No reconstruction in full is suggested, but what is to be understood here is, Crawford says, <<<*coetum ne facito.*>>>. This is borne out in the later municipal laws from Urso and then from Irni. See Frolov, "'Wrong' Meetings?," 236–51.
32. Liv. 3.44.5.
33. In addition to Livy's account (3.44), see Cic. *Rep.* 2.61–3; Diodorus Siculus (hereafter Diod. Sic.) 12.24. 2–4.
34. At the time, Rome had no formal public-school systems paid for by the state. Instead, it had many privately commissioned classrooms that could be set up by teachers in tents, in open air spaces such as stoas, and, as classicist Lisa Maurice has explored, under pergolas, in shops, in houses, and particularly at busy street crossroads. Verginia's story signals that while literacy rates were likely low at the time, nothing barred elite plebeian men and women from attending schools, learning to read, and practicing their grammar—just as patricians did. See Maurice, *Teacher in Ancient Rome*, 29–31.
35. Liv. 3.50.13; Dion. Hal. 11.43.5–6. See Mignone, *Republican Aventine*, 28.
36. Mignone, *Republican Aventine*, 30.

37. Polybius (hereafter Polyb.) 3.22.3–14; see Serrati, "Neptune's Altars," 133.
38. Plin. *HN* 35.154.
39. See Cifani, *Origins of the Roman Economy*, Table 7, 179–80.
40. From the Greek "βάναυσος." Aristotle, *Politica* 8.2.1, 1337b; Xenophon, *Oeconomicus* 4.2–3. In a bit of a twist, Plato (*Leges* 644a, 743d) saw everyone as banausic—that is, beholden to either wages or people—except for the philosopher, who was the only truly free individual.
41. Herodotus (hereafter Herod.) 2.167.1. The comment about Corinth follows directly afterward (2.167.2).
42. Liv. 8.20.4: "Indeed, it is said that a common group of workers and sedentary artisans was enlisted in the army, a group least suited for military service."
43. Liv. 21.63.3–4.
44. Isayev, *Migration, Mobility, and Place*.
45. In providing an origin story for the Celtic presence in northern Italy, for instance, Livy (5.33) pointed specifically to the Etruscans introducing the Celts, lovers of beer, to the civilized production of wine and the lure of the vineyards. For the use of wine being associated with Celtic "feebleness" and as an ethnic marker, see Almagor, "Health as a Criterion," 79–82.
46. Pope, "Re-Approaching Celts," 1–67; Isayev, *Migration, Mobility, and Place*, 122–23.
47. Liv. 2.9.6. This was during the Etruscan invasion under Porsinna. The Senate did this to pacify the plebs.
48. Liv. 6.1.11–12. Livy notes that this battle date, July 18, also coincided with the date of the Roman loss to the Etruscans at the Battle of Cremera in 477 BCE. Ovid says this battle actually occurred on February 13 (Ov. *Fast.* 2.195).
49. Woolf, *Rome*, 39–40. It encompassed 988 acres within central Rome's hills, including the Roman Forum and Circus Maximus.
50. Armstrong, *War and Society*, 233–89.
51. Bodel, "Slave Labour," 311.
52. Bernard, *Building Mid-Republican Rome*, 75–117.
53. Cicero, *Pro Murena* 25: "*inventus est scriba quidam, Cn. Flavius, qui cornicum oculos confixerit et singulis diebus ediscendis fastos populo proposuerit et ab ipsis his cautis iuris consultis eorum sapientiam compilarit.*"
54. Plin. *HN* 16.37; Liv. *Periochae* 11.11; Mignone, *Republican Aventine*, 32–34.
55. As Cornell ("Conquest of Italy," 400) correctly states, to see the Struggle (or Conflict) of the Orders as a fight for democratic rights is to perhaps "submit to a whiggish fallacy." The tug-of-war did not end in the creation of a democratic government in Rome.

Chapter 2. We Are Spartacus

1. Although she calls them associations, this is the argument of Aneziri, "Artists of Dionysus," 293–312. For the epigraphic evidence for the *technitai*, see Le Guen, *Associations de Technites dionysiaques*. Also note Csapo and Slater, *Context of Ancient Drama*, 239–55; and Jory, "Associations of Actors in Rome," 224–53. A rider

is a document created by an entertainment act prior to the performance to set further terms and demands in addition to the legal contract. Perhaps the most famous rider in history was the one used by Van Halen in the 1980s.

2. Rehm, "Festivals and Audiences," 191–92; Fountoulakis, "When Dionysus Goes to the East," 85. Alexander the Great had also been a patron of the *technitai*. Plutarch, *Life of Alexander* 72.1, notes that three thousand such performers from Greece met him at the Persian city of Ecbatana to celebrate and perform.
3. See, for instance, *Sylloge Inscriptionum Graecarum*³ 399 and 460, concerning the Athenian as well as the Isthmean and Nemean performers given special privileges and protections from 279 to 278 BCE. Also note the Euboean decree (*IG* XII, 9, 207), redated to 280 to 240 BCE by Kent Rigsby, which indicates the already strong organization of labor unions of *technitai*. See Rigsby, "On the Early Technitai," 283–86.
4. Skotheim, "Association and Archive."
5. Liv. 7.2.
6. Festus 446–8, L; Mignone, *Republican Aventine*, 97. As Festus notes and Gruen points out, in the middle Republic, the term "*scribae*" could apply to both clerks, called *librarii*, and poets, called *poetae*. See Gruen, "Poetry and Politics," 90.
7. The details of Andronicus's early life, debated both in antiquity and today, were discussed by Cicero (Cic. *Brut.* 72) and Livy (27.37.7). See Conte, *Latin Literature*, 39–40.
8. As Flora R. Levin discusses (*Greek Reflections*, 91), according to Iamblichus, Pythagoras allegedly lived in Tarentum for a spell. As she notes, other famed Pythagoreans, such as Lysis and Archytas, also came from that city. For commercial products from Tarentum, see Marzano, *Harvesting the Sea*, 154.
9. In his work on grammarians, Suetonius described the first two known to him in the Republic, Saevius Nicanor and Aurelius Opilius, as freedmen. Suetonius, *De grammaticis et rhetoribus* 5–6. A *grammaticus* was a professional teacher.
10. Valerius Maximus (hereafter Val. Max.) 2.4.7; Ausonius, *Griphus ternarii numeri* 36–37. Ausonius locates it by the tomb.
11. Futrell, *Blood in the Arena*, 22. Futrell has remarked on the fact that the Thracian gladiatorial type was likely not introduced to Rome until about a century or more later, and thus Ausonius's claim is perhaps a projection onto the past.
12. Plin. *HN* 8.16.
13. Polyb. 1.20.9, 14; for the training of ship crews, see 1.21.1–3.
14. Serrati, "Garrisons and Grain," 115–33.
15. Liv. 25.12.
16. Flower, *Dancing Lares*, 205–6; Lott, *Neighborhoods of Augustan Rome*, 40–41.
17. Polyb. 10.17.9; Liv. 26.47.2.
18. Varro, *De lingua Latina* 8.82–3.
19. Liv. 22.57.9–12, 24.11.7–9.
20. Appian, Λιβυκή (hereafter App. *Pun.*) 2.9. See Lenski, "Framing the Question," 26–27. Lenski appears to believe the enslaved persons came from Carthage, but the artisans sent to Rome follow the capture of New Carthage, in Spain.

21. See Roselaar, "Roman State Prisoners," 189–200; Walker, "Hostages in Republican Rome," 133.
22. Liv. 32.26.4–18.
23. Var. *Rust.* 1.17.5.
24. We can see this approach in the laws of the Republic, where killing enslaved persons was generally prosecuted as a civil rather than a criminal matter until 82 BCE. Under Sulla, the *lex Cornelia de sicariis et veneficis* (Cornelian law regarding murderers and poisoners) created penalties for the killing of an enslaved person, such as deportation. Under Claudius and then Antoninus Pius, the unjustified killing of enslaved persons was further prohibited. See Pomp. *Dig.* 48.8.1.2.
25. Murders were capital crimes—that is, those that could carry the penalty of death—and were investigated by the *quaestores parricidii*, since at least the creation of the Twelve Tables (450–451 BCE), according to the second-century CE jurist Pomponius (Pomp. *Dig.* 1.2.2.23), and perhaps even since the reign of Numa Pompilius.
26. Paulus, *Digesta* (hereafter *Dig.* preceded by the name of the jurist) 32.99.
27. Clinton, *Plantation Mistress*, 203. This was a reversal of English Common Law, which had given the children their father's status.
28. Ulpian, *Dig.* 48.5.24; Macer, *Dig.* 48.5.25.
29. *CIL* I², 364 (in flawed Saturnian verse). They are called, in Archaic Latin, a *gonlegium* (which should be the archaic Latin "*conlegium*," which is analogous to the later spelling of "*collegium*") of "*ququei*" (an Archaic Latin spelling for "cooks"). See Taylor, *Local Cults in Etruria*, 79; Linderski, "Notes on *CIL* I² 364," 362–65, who believes that there are two different "guilds" dedicating each side of the votive plaque (side a, side b); Tran, *Membres des Associations Romaines*, 1–2.
30. These were called μάγειροι in Greek and often called *coci* or *coqui* in Latin.
31. Bernard, *Building Mid-Republican Rome*, 182.
32. See *CIL* VI, 7458, 8750, and 9262. (The last is Aelius Epaphroditus, a scribe among the cooks who were part of the *familia Caesaris*.)
33. Zanda, *Fighting Hydra-Like Luxury*, 50.
34. Liv. 39.6.9.
35. Gruen, "Poetry and Politics," 89.
36. Dion. Hal. 2.19.3–5; Val. Max. 7.6; Jensen, *Barbarians*, 125. The processions of the priests of Cybele, their begging, and their castration were viewed with apprehension by the Roman elites for many centuries thereafter, as has been pointed out by Hartnett, *Roman Street*, 278–79.
37. Liv. 39.8.1–4.
38. *CIL* I² 581 = *ILS* 18 = *Inscriptiones Latinae Liberae Rei Publicae* 511.
39. Pailler, "Dionysos against Rome?," 67.
40. Polyb. 30.15; Strabo (hereafter Strab.) 7.7.3; Scheidel, "Roman Slave Supply," 294.
41. Trümper, "Das Sanktuarium," 265–330; and "Where the Non-Delians Met in Delos," 49–100.
42. *Inscriptions de Délos* (hereafter *IDelos*) 1519.
43. *CIL* X, 3773 (112/111 BCE); *CIL* I, 2947 (930); Verboven, "Guilds and Organisation," 175–76; and "Structure of Mercantile Communities," 342.

44. AGRW ID# 224 = *IDelos* 1520.
45. For associations of Italian merchants selling olive oil and wine on the island, see *IDelos* 1711–1714; Kay, *Rome's Economic Revolution*, 201.
46. Strab. 14.5.2. See Roselaar, *Italy's Economic Revolution*, 69, for the impact of Delos's designation as a tax-free port on commercial integration in the Mediterranean.
47. Kay, *Rome's Economic Revolution*, 199–201; Rauh, *Sacred Bonds of Commerce*, 30–32.
48. Scheidel, "Roman Slave Supply," 295.
49. Orosius (hereafter Oros.) 4.23.3–6. The fifty-five thousand from Carthage allegedly consisted of twenty-five thousand women and thirty thousand men, with only a few leading men not sold into slavery. Appian (App. *Pun.* 130) says it was fifty thousand.
50. Diod. Sic. 34/35.2.1–2.
51. Stewart, *Plautus and Roman Slavery*, 160.
52. Oros. 5.9 calls it the "contagion of the slave war" (*belli seruilis contagio*) and Diodorus Siculus (34/35.24) refers to Eunus's followers as a πλῆθος (mob) whom the leader called Syrians.
53. Diod. Sic. 36.3.
54. Diod. Sic. 34/35.15. Richardson, "Early Synagogues as Collegia," 90–109. Group self-designation as an *ekklēsia* does not seem to appear in the epigraphic sources until the first century CE, as is argued by Korner, *Origin and Meaning of Ekklēsia*, 22–68.
55. Diod. Sic. 36.7.4.
56. Beek, "Pirate Connection."
57. The best collection of translated primary sources for each of the Servile Wars, and particularly the ancient and modern reactions to Spartacus, is Shaw, *Spartacus and the Slave Wars*. For slave revolts in general, the best resource remains Urbainczyk, *Slave Revolts in Antiquity*.
58. Plutarch, *Life of Crassus* (hereafter Plut. *Crass.*) 8. Also see Pailler, "Dionysos against Rome?," 76.
59. Welch, *Roman Amphitheatre*, 91.
60. Liv. *Periochae* 95.2; Plut. *Crass.* 8.1. calls him Lentulus Batiatus, but "Batiatus" is likely a corruption of "Vatia."
61. Cic. *Att.* 7.14.2. I have here preferred Shackleton Bailey's reading of one thousand over five thousand, although I disagree with him that the use of "*scutorum*" (shields) is not necessarily indicative of armed gladiators. See David Roy Shackleton Bailey, *Cicero's Letters to Atticus*, vol. 4, 49 B.C. [*Letters*] 133–210 (*Books Vii. 10–X*) (Cambridge: Cambridge University Press, 1968), 19, 309.
62. A number of initiates who were arena performers, gladiators, and staff were organized into *decuriae* for a *collegium* dedicated to the god Silvanus Aurelianus, as seen in a dedicatory inscription of 177 BCE (*CIL* VI, 631).
63. *CIL* IV, 2476 = The Ancient Graffiti Project, http://ancientgraffiti.org/Graffiti /graffito/AGP-EDR151725, 151725; *Die Inschriften von Smyrna* 409 = *Les gladiuteurs dans l'Orient grec* 241 = Packard Humanities Institute (hereafter PHI) 255633

= AGRW ID# 10509, Leiden, Rijksmuseum van Oudheden, inv. no. I.1901/7.10. Also note the epitaph (*CIL* VI, 10168) made by the gladiatorial *familia* of the Ludus Magnus in Rome for a *paegniarius* named Secundus, who was a kind of mock fighter who helped train the other gladiators using fake weapons.
64. *CIL* X, 1589 = CAPInv. 1099.
65. Fagan, "Training Gladiators," 122–44.
66. Fagan, "Training Gladiators," 125.
67. Plut. *Crass.* 8.2.
68. Appian, *Bella civilia* (hereafter App. *B Civ.*) 1.14.116–117.
69. Strauss, *Spartacus War*, 87.
70. Machado, "Community and Collective Action," 222.

Chapter 3. Freedom of Assembly during the Fall of the Republic

1. Cicero, *De domo sua* (hereafter Cic. *Dom.*) 54. Tribunes took office on December 10, and this event occurred on January 4, 58 BCE. Cicero refers to Clodius's closure of *tabernae*, which most modern scholars have simply translated as "shops"; however, combining literary and archaeological evidence, Claire Holleran and others have shown the overlap in the use of the term *"taberna"* to mean spaces for both retail and production. See Holleran, *Shopping in Ancient Rome*, 99–158. The best biographical analysis of Clodius is provided by Tatum, *Patrician Tribune*. For the violent discord in the late Republic, see Vanderbroeck, *Popular Leadership and Collective Behavior*. Note especially Russell, "Why Did Clodius Shut the Shops?" She sees the closure of the shops as symbolic rather than as a means to gather targeted supporters of shopkeepers (188).
2. Years after Clodius's death, Cicero continued to allude to the closing of the *tabernae* (shops and workshops) of Rome as a metonym for starting a popular revolution. In his *Lucullus*, written in 45 BCE, he characterizes as seditious the closing of the *tabernae* and the gathering of men from each quarter of the city of Rome to attend a *contio* (public assembly) (Cicero, *Academicae quaestiones* 2.144).
3. Plutarch, *Life of Lucullus* 34.1–5 (69–68 BCE). For doubts as to the validity of Plutarch's account of the mutiny, see Mulroy, "Early Career of P. Clodius Pulcher."
4. This happened with the aid of the Pontifex Maximus, Gaius Julius Caesar, and the vote of the rarely convened assembly called the Comitia Curiata.
5. Plutarch, *Life of Gaius Gracchus* 5.2; Velleius Paterculus 2.6.3.
6. Cicero, *Pro Sestio* (hereafter Cic. *Sest.*) 48: "*repugnabant boni, quod et ab industria plebem ad desidiam avocari putabant*" ("The good men were resisting, because they were thinking that it would divert the plebs from industry to idleness").
7. Cic. *Sest.* 34.
8. Asconius (hereafter Asc.) 7C, l.10–11. Asconius mentions this action in his commentary on Cicero's *In Pisonem* (hereafter Cic. *Pis.*) 7. In addition, see Asconius's remarks in his commentary on Cicero's *Pro Cornelio* speech (75C, l.17–19). See also Linderski, "Testimony of Asconius"; Minasola, *"Collegia"*; Cotter, "Collegia and Roman Law."

9. Arnaoutoglou, "Roman Law and *Collegia*," 29–44.
10. Flower, *Dancing Lares*, 248, argues that the injunction against the Compitalia must have just been temporary and that the conjoined ban on subversive *collegia* was largely moot, since such *collegia* had always been strictly controlled, alongside the right to assemble. As previously noted, the Laws of the Twelve Tables appear to have allowed the right to assemble, which would suggest that freedom of assembly was a regular right unless proven to be seditious or disruptive to laws, as in 186 BCE.
11. Asc. 7C.
12. Cic. *Pis.* 8; Asc. 7C. In his speech, Cicero is criticizing the new consul, Piso, who also took office on the Kalends of January with his co-consul, Gabinius, in 58 BCE.
13. Flambard, "Clodius."
14. Cic. *Dom.* 6.
15. See Lintott, *Violence in Republican Rome*, 83–84.
16. Sallust, *Bellum Catilinae* or *De Catilinae coniuratione* (hereafter Sal. *Cat.*) 30.
17. This is the famed line attributed by Tacitus to the British commander Calgacus (*Agricola* 30.5) describing how the Romans used war to create their empire, but one could say the same here of the Romans' use of proscriptions to suppress civil conflict.
18. App. *B Civ.* 1.100. The deference and required allegiance owed to a patron is generally referred to as *obsequium*. If an oath had been taken to provide certain services, called *operae*, the freedman might also owe these, along with certain inheritance rights. See Verboven, "Freedman Economy of Roman Italy," 95–96.
19. Santangelo, *Sulla, Elites and Empire*, 94.
20. Cicero, *Paradoxa stoicorum* (hereafter Cic. *Parad. Stoic.*) 6.46: "*cum servis, cum libertis, cum clientibus societates.*"
21. Plutarch notes (*Life of Sulla* 2.2) that, as a youth, Sulla hung around with actors and theater folks and, even later in life, loved the actor Metrobius. In a return to the days of his youth, the retired dictator surrounded himself with rather lower-class, infamous persons such as actors and harpists, who joined him in drinking and lounging on dining couches, until his death in 78 BCE. It was a common tactic in Roman literature and invective to disgrace statesmen through the company they kept; associating them with drinking and with theater troupes made them morally suspect.
22. Plut. *Vit. Sull.* 38.
23. Asconius, Commentary on Cicero's *Pro Milone* (hereafter Asc. *Mil.*), 45C.
24. Cic. *Pro Milone* (hereafter Cic. *Mil.*), 87: "*leges quae nos servis nostris addicerent.*"
25. Sal. *Cat.* 50.
26. Cicero, *In Catilinam* 1.8.
27. Cicero, *Post reditum ad populum* 13.
28. Quintus Cicero, *Commentariolum petitionis* 8.30: "*Deinde habeto rationem urbis totius, collegiorum omnium, pagorum, vicinitatum: ex iis principes ad amicitiam tuam si adiunxeris, per eos reliquam multitudinem facile tenebis*" ("Then, take account of the whole city—all the associations, the wards, the neighborhoods; if you add

the leading men among them to your supporters, you will easily control the rest through them").
29. Philo, *Legatio ad Gaium* (hereafter Ph. *Legat.*) 155–56.
30. López Barja de Quiroga, "On Freedom and Citizenship," 381. He estimates there were seventy-five thousand freedmen in the city of Rome out of a total population of about one million.
31. For a case study of the textile dealers in the *collegia centonariorum*, which reveals the broad range of economic levels possible within an association, see Liu, *Collegia Centonariorum*. On the composition of association membership, see 161–212.
32. *CIL* XIV, 2112 (130 CE). The idea that *collegia* were from the "upper echelons" and thus were "employers rather than employees" (echoed by some, such as Patterson, *Landscapes and Cities*, 255) must then be rejected, as many, like Kloppenborg, "Pauline Assemblies," 238, have stated.
33. Cuvigny, *Rome in Egypt's Eastern Desert*, 172.
34. *Die Demotischen Papyrus* II 30605.1.22–4, dated to 145 BCE. See Monson, "Ethics and Economics."
35. Van Nijf, *Civic World of Professional Associations*, 177. This view is then echoed by scholars like Rebillard, *Care of the Dead*, 39.
36. López Barja de Quiroga, "On Freedmen and Citizenship," 90. On freedmen using *collegia* to achieve social mobility, see also López Barja de Quiroga's earlier work, "Freedmen Social Mobility in Roman Italy," 345.
37. Veyne, "La 'plèbe moyenne,'" 1169–99, especially 1170–72, as noted by Kloppenborg, "Pauline Assemblies," 239.
38. Cassius Dio (hereafter Dio) 39.24.
39. Cic. *Sest.* 85. For enslaved persons occupying the Forum, Comitium, and Curia at night, see Cic. *Sest.* 75.
40. Although he may be wrong about the time, Asconius (48C) notes that it was during the *ludi Apollinares* in July of 57 BCE that a vaguely described mob of lower-class people burst into the theater, perhaps due to high grain prices. Cicero (*Att.* 4.1.6) later notes that, in September of 57, an angry mob first gathered in the theater before going to the Senate house.
41. Cic. *Sest.* 120–23, 106. Coleman, "Public Entertainments," 345–46; Davies, *Architecture and Politics*, 235. For the *contio*, see Mouritsen, *Plebs and Politics*, 38–62; and Vanderbroeck, *Popular Leadership and Collective Behavior*, 86–92.
42. *CIL* I² 2519. Jory, "Associations of Actors," 242–43, dates the inscription simply to the first century BCE.
43. Nicolet, "Temple des Nymphes," 29–51; Lott, *Neighborhoods of Augustan Rome*, 64.
44. Senatus Consultum of 56: Cicero, *Epistulae ad Quintum fratrem* (hereafter Cic. *QFr.*) 2.3.5; *lex Licinia* of 55: Cicero, *Pro Plancio* (hereafter Cic. *Planc.*) 36–48. For the threat of prosecution over disbanding, see Brennan, *Praetorship in the Roman Republic*, 423–24.
45. Lintott, "Electoral Bribery," 9.
46. Asc. 32C.
47. Julius Caesar, *Bellum Civile* 1.14.

48. Cic. *Att.* 7.14. Although the Latin reads "*scutorum*" rather than "gladiators," this is most likely a reference to Caesar's *familiae* of Capuan gladiators, given the location and the mention of shields.
49. Cic. *Att.* 7.14.
50. Suet. *Iul.* 42.1.
51. Jewell, "(Re)moving the Masses."
52. Suet. *Iul.* 42.1.
53. Suet. *Iul.* 42.3; Bond, *Trade and Taboo*, 43–45.
54. Suet. *Iul.* 41.3; Flower, *Dancing Lares*, 202.
55. *CIL* II, 5439 = *ILS* 6087 = *Fontes Iuris Romani Antejustiniani*, 2nd ed., 12 no. 21. ch. 106: "*ne quem in ea col(onia) coetum conventum coniu[rationem].*" See Liu, "Local Governments and *Collegia*," 283.
56. *CIL* I², 593 = Crawford, *Roman Statutes* I, 335–91, no. 24.
57. Josephus, *Antiquitates Judaicae* (hereafter Jos. *AJ*) 14.213–214. The debate over whether Jews and their synagogues and religious assemblies were viewed as *collegia* under Roman law has an extensive bibliography further explored in Chapter Five. Many decades ago, E. Mary Smallwood (*Jews under Roman Rule*, 133–34), argued that they were a special case among other *collegia*. See her groundbreaking work, along with that of other pivotal scholars, such as Rocca, "From Collegium to Ecclesia."
58. This phrase is most heavily tied to Richard Nixon's 1968 presidential campaign and his coded racial rhetoric of reviving criminal justice in America amid the civil rights movement.
59. App. *B Civ.* 2.113: "ἤ σοι δοκοῦσιν οἱ χειροτέχναι καὶ κάπηλοι καταγράφειν σου τὸ δικαστήριον ἀσήμως μᾶλλον ἢ οἱ Ῥωμαίων ἄριστοι." Plutarch says the rhetorical question asked if he thought it were "τοὺς ὑφάντας καὶ τοὺς καπήλους" ("the weavers and tavern keepers") (*Brut.* 10.3).
60. *CIL* VI, 2193 = *ILS* 4966.

Chapter 4. Anxiety and Associations in the Early Roman Empire

1. Tac. *Ann.* 14.17.
2. This intercity enmity is illustrated by a graffito from the largest brothel in Pompeii, called the Lupanare. Three to four different hands contributed to this impassioned message etched on the brothel wall: "'Good luck to the Puteolans; (good luck) to all Nucerians; [but] the cadaver hook for the Pompeians and Pithecusans" (*CIL* IV, 2183: "*Puteolanis feliciter | omnibus Nucherinis | felicia et uncu(m) · Pompeianis | Petecusanis*"). See Levin-Richardson, *Brothel of Pompeii*, 61–62. An *uncus* was not an "anchor," as Levin-Richardson translates it, but a type of hook used by executioners or by those clearing out dead or maimed bodies (for example, in the amphitheater), so as to drag rather than carry them for disposal. This was an infamous way to be treated after death, but also kept the worker from touching a dead body. See Suetonius, *Life of Tiberius* (hereafter Suet. *Tib.*) 61 for its use.
3. The ban may or may not have stayed in place for the whole ten years, but it ap-

pears that beast hunts and athletic competitions continued to be put on, while only the gladiatorial matches were halted.
4. Shaw, "Rural Markets in North Africa," 47.
5. Callistratus, *Digesta* 48.19.28.3.
6. *CIL* III, 7060 = *ILS* 7190. Cyzicus is near the Turkish town of Bandırma. The inscription is now at the British Museum (1876,1105.2). See Eckhardt, "Private Associations," 29. For these permissions, see Liu, "Roman Governments and *Collegia*," 294; and for her theory on the informality of many associations, see Liu, "Pompeii and *Collegia*," 56–57.
7. Liu, "Local Governments and *Collegia*," 294.
8. See Jaczynowska, "L'organisation intérieure,'" 95–119; Ladage, "*Collegia iuvenum*," 319–46.
9. Hemelrijk, *Hidden Lives, Public Personae*, 199–200.
10. Vesley, "Gladiatorial Training for Girls," 85–93.
11. Dio 52.26.1–2.
12. Kleijwegt, "*Iuvenes* and Roman Imperial Society," 79–102. Kleijwegt notes pantomimes at Lanuvium (*CIL* XIV, 2113) and Milan (*Inscriptions of Roman Tripolitania* 606, from Lepcis Magna) being made honorary members, largely due to emperors' affinity for pantomimes (90).
13. This is the proposition of Fagan, *Lure of the Arena*, 95–96, as well as of Moeller, "Riot of A. D. 59," 84–95.
14. *CIL* IV, 1293 = *ILS* 6443a (on the façade of the House of the Dioscuri): "*Campani victoria una / cum Nucerinis peristis.*"
15. Osanna, "Games, Banquets, Handouts."
16. Ausbüttel, *Untersuchungen zu den Vereinen*, 33; Liu, "Pompeii and *Collegia*."
17. *CIL* IV, 826. For more on this and other associations of fishermen in places like Rome, see Marzano, *Harvesting the Sea*, 39. For later legal definitions concerning membership numbers, see Marcellus, *Digesta* 50.16.85: "*Neratius Priscus tres facere existimat 'collegium,' et hoc magis sequendum est.*" Lucius Neratius Priscus, referred to here, was a jurist who served as suffect consul under Nerva in 97 CE and continued to be a prestigious legal analyst under Trajan.
18. Ausbüttel, *Untersuchungen zu den Vereinen*, 35–37.
19. The contrast was between the *utilitas civitas* and the *utilitas singulorum*. Gaudemet, "Utilitas publica," 465–99; Spagnolo and Sampson, "Principle and Pragmatism," 1–26.
20. Asc. 75C. Cicero, *De officiis* 3.47: "*in quibus publicae utilitatis species*" is the first to refer to the concept, but it becomes a hallmark of imperial-era legislation rather than late Republican law. See Verboven, "Associations, Roman"; and "Guilds and Organisation," 186–87. For the reorganized *fabri tignarii*, see Panciera, "Fasti Fabrum Tignariorum Urbis Romae."
21. The *curatores operum publicorum*. Suet. *Aug.* 37. For inscriptions noting *servi* of the public works, see *CIL* VI, 2336 and 2337. See Robinson, *Ancient Rome*, 46–47; Sudi, "Esclaves et les affranchis publics," 131–32. For the textile workers called the *centonarii* and the possible (?) timber merchants called the *dendrophori*, see Ver-

boven, "Guilds and Organisation," 177–78. As he notes, we are not at all completely sure the *dendrophori* were timber merchants only, but they were professional in nature and allowed to persist.
22. The barracks were called *excubitoria,* and the equestrian in charge was named the *praefectus vigilum.*
23. *CIL* VI, 2998–3091.
24. Suetonius, *Life of Claudius* (hereafter Suet. *Claud.*) 25.2, mentions cohorts of *vigiles* at Ostia-Portus that were about four hundred strong, who then acquired new barracks under Hadrian. Claudius also put *vigiles* at Puteoli, while Vespasian placed an urban cohort at Carthage. See Fuhrmann, *Policing the Roman Empire,* 157.
25. These were the *aquarii* in the *familiae aquariae.* See Frontinus, *De aquae ductu urbis Romae,* 116.
26. Dio 54.2.3–4. Individuals who did not belong to the imperial family could only display 120 gladiators at a time.
27. For the likely ban on private gladiatorial families under Augustus, see Kyle, *Sport and Spectacle,* 298.
28. Suet. *Aug.* 45. For the start of pantomime and the impact of Pylades, see Jory, "Pylades, Pantomime," 147–56.
29. These were the *lex Iulia de maritandis ordinibus* (18 BCE) and the *lex Papia Poppaea* (9 CE). See Paul. *Dig.* 23.2.44.
30. This was the *lex Aelia Sentia.* They were instead categorized as *peregrini dediticii.* See Gaius, *Institutiones* 1.1.13.
31. Suet. *Aug.* 43.3. We are told that the *princeps* only made an exception for a dwarf or little person named Lycius, who greatly amused him because of his small stature, weight, and voice.
32. Horsmann, *Die Wagenlenker der römischen Kaiserzeit.*
33. *Oxyrhynchus Papyri* (hereafter *P.Oxy.*) 27, 2476 = *Zehn agonistische Papyri* 3 (July 26, 288 CE). The papyrus cites Claudius's earlier confirmation of the special privileges given to the *technitai* of Dionysus under Augustus. See Kloppenborg, *Greco-Roman Associations,* 471–80 (no. 274); Fauconnier, "Organisation of Synods"; and *Athletes and Artists,* 95.
34. See Kloppenborg, *Christ's Associations,* 2–3.
35. Suet. *Tib.* 34.
36. Tac. *Ann.* 1.54. For the events of 14 CE, see Dio 56.47.2. Dio calls him an ὀρχηστής, which was the late Roman term in Greek for a pantomime dancer.
37. Tac. *Ann.* 1.77.
38. *ILS* 4966 (Rome, Augustan era).
39. Dio 57.14.10 calls them ὀρχησταί, originally a word for dancers that then comes to be used by Dio's time in the late second and early third century CE as a word for pantomimes in particular.
40. *Supplementum Epigraphicum Graecum* (hereafter *SEG*) 54:961. The dedication is for a five-year-old boy by the *grex Ionici pantomimi* (herd of Ionic pantomimes), which is simply the name used for the association. See Lazzarini, "Pantomimi a Petelia."

41. Tac. Ann. 2.85: "<quattuor milia> libertini generis ea superstitione infecta" ("<four thousand> of the freedman kind infected by those superstitions").
42. Suet. Tib. 36.
43. Jos. AJ 18.81–2.
44. Jos. AJ 18.65–80.
45. Dio 57.18.5. Smallwood, "Some Notes on the Jews."
46. CIL VI, 10109 = ILS 5217 = AGRW ID# 24913.
47. Groen-Vallinga, Work and Labour, 235–36.
48. Liu, Collegia Centonariorum, 179.
49. Veyne, Roman Empire, 190.
50. CIL VI, 33920. Collectives are given a masculine rather than feminine gender by default when spoken of in the plural, as in "Romani" (Romans), "socii" (associates), or "tabernarii" (tavern owners). If in Latin one were to speak of a collective of tradespeople, such as the textile dealers or vestiarii tenuiarii (cloth dealers or "tailors"), one would default to the masculine plural to describe the whole group, thus erasing any possible women embedded within. The feminine is only used in the plural when all members are women.
51. As Roman legal historian Thomas McGinn has stated about pimps called lenae: "Together with prostitutes, gladiators, trainers, beast-fighters and actors, they formed a category that stood at the core of disgrace, a category that was both legal and social in its implications" (McGinn, "Sex and the City," 383).
52. Cic. Planc. 12.30. See Knapp, Invisible Romans, 261. Note Jill Harries's telling remark that "Roman law, unlike some systems, did not blame the woman, provided that she was of respectable status" (Harries, Law and Crime, 88).
53. Suet. Nero 27. Here, Suetonius accuses Nero of having strong vices, exemplified by his eating dinner in entertainment spaces while being served by female musicians and sex workers.
54. Horace, Satirae 1.2.1–3: "Ambubaiarum collegia, pharmacopolae / mendici, mimae, balatrones, hoc genus omne / maestum ac sollicitum est cantoris morte Tigelli."
55. Traina, "Lycoris the Mime," 90.
56. CIL IX, 5368: "Allienae T(iti) f(iliae) / Berenice / C(aius) Vettius Polus / uxori / sanctissim(ae) et / C(aius) Vettius Polus / matri / pi(i)ssimae patr(onae) / col(legia) fabr(um) et cent(oniariorum) / l(ocus) d(atus) d(ecreto) d(ecurionum)."
57. Usually this woman was called a patrona collegii. The male version was a patronus collegii. See Hemelrijk, "Patronesses and 'Mothers.'"
58. The research and verbiage for this section on female patrons of collegia comes in large part from my own MA thesis: Bond, "Ob Merita," 30–31. For Eumachia's dedication of the building with her son, see CIL X, 810–11. For the statue of Eumachia, see CIL X, 813. For Claudia Iusta and Aemilia Synethia, see CIL X, 7 = L'Année Epigraphique (hereafter AE) 1985, 305; CIL V, 4388.
59. Philo, In Flaccum 1–21. For the dating of the treatise, see Gambetti, Alexandrian Riots, 250.
60. The word "ghetto" likely derives from the Italian verb "gettare" (to cast). The term was applied to a sector of Venice with a former copper foundry once used for

casting metal. Other European cities, such as Frankfurt, which constructed a *Judengasse* (Jew's lane) outside its city walls, had whole streets where Jews were confined to live and work, beginning in the mid-fifteenth century.

61. Philo, *In Flacc.* 8.
62. Marcianus, *Digesta* 47.22.1.pr.1.
63. Campbell, *Roman Army*, 137, notes that this anti-association policy for soldiers recorded by Marcian may go back to Augustus, but this is not certain. For examples of military *collegia* both before and after Caracalla, see *Roman Inscriptions of Britain* (hereafter *RIB*) I, 1268; *RIB* III, 3193; *ILS* 9100; *CIL* III, 3524; *CIL* VIII, 2554. Inscriptions demonstrate that associations for both active soldiers and for veterans were common.
64. Philo, *In Flacc.* 4, notes that Flaccus bans the "ἑταιρείας καὶ συνόδους," whom he accuses of holding these feasts under the pretext of sacrifice, when in reality, they are using sacrifice as a cover for their real objectives: getting drunk and hatching political plans.
65. Ph. *Legat.* 24.161.
66. Suetonius, *Life of Gaius Caligula* 56. Waiting until the end of the Palatine Games was no doubt a strategic move.
67. Jos. *AJ* 19.278.
68. Dio 60.6.6.
69. Dio 60.6.6. Specifically, the political clubs are called the ἑταιρεῖαι, a term that tended to be used for political factions and groups created for political purposes going back to classical Athens. This matches well with Philo's remarks on the ἑταιρεῖαι in Alexandria under Caligula.
70. Dio 60.6.7. Dio says this is because the clubs gathered there.
71. Acts 18:2; Oros. 7.6.15.
72. Suet. *Claud.* 25.4. For references to "Christ" commonly being misspelled with an "e," see Tertullian, *Apologeticus* (hereafter Tert. *Apol.*) 3; and Lactantius, *Divinae institutiones* 4.7.
73. His full name was Quintus Septimius Florens Tertullianus. He knew both Latin and Greek, and the bishop Eusebius (*Historia ecclesiastica* 2.2.4) would later explicitly note Tertullian's Roman legal knowledge.
74. The aforementioned *ius coeundi*, Tert. *Apol.* 39.1–2: "*Edam iam nunc ego ipse negotia Christianae factionis, ut, qui mala refutaverim, bona ostendam. Corpus sumus de conscientia religionis et disciplinae unitate et spei foedere*" ("I will now at once go on to explain the occupation of the Christian faction, thus, as I have refuted the evil charges against it, I will show the good things. We are a body with a common sense of religion, united discipline, and common hope").
75. Tert. *Apol.* 38.1–2: "*Proinde nec paulo lenius inter <il>licitas factiones sectam istam deputari oportebat, a qua nihil tale committitur, quale de illicitis factionibus timeri solet. Nisi fallor enim, prohibendarum factionum causa de providentia constat modestiae publicae, ne civitas in partes scinderetur, quae res facile comitia concilia curias contiones, spectacula etiam uemulis studiorum compulsationibus inquietaret, cum iam*

et in quaestu habere coepissent venalem et mercenariam homines violentiae suae operam."

76. Rebillard, *Care of the Dead*, 44, sees strong parallels between Tertullian's language and that of Suetonius (*Aug.* 32) in describing the laws that governed associations.

Chapter 5. Strikes, Riots, and Associations in the Roman Imperial Period

1. *Die Bremer Papyri* 63 = *Sammelbuch griechischer Urkunden aus Aegypten* I, 4515. Rowlandson, *Women and Society*, 94; Zeev, *Diaspora Judaism in Turmoil*, 169–71; Bagnall and Cribiore, *Women's Letters from Ancient Egypt*, 143–44. On Apollonius, see TM 19 at www.trismegistos.org/text/19. For the portion of the papyrus noting that these workers then took to the streets, see l.14–16 "περι-/ώδευσαν γὰρ οἱ ἡμῶν ὅλην / τὴν πόλιν [π]ροσπεύδοντεσ(*) / πλέον μισθόν" ("for our [workers] marched through the whole city for a higher wage"). See also Zimmermann, *Handwerkervereine im griechischen Osten*, 85.
2. O. Berlin P. 10633. See Cromwell, "First Recorded Strike"; Vernus, *Affaires et scandales sous les Ramsès*, 83–98; Edgerton, "Strikes in Ramses III's Twenty-Ninth Year," 137–45.
3. P.Turin Cat. (Turin Papyri) 1880: Amunnakht "The So-Called 'Strike Papyrus.'"
4. In Greek, such a strike would have normally been termed an ἀναχώρησις (*anachoresis*, a "withdrawal" or "secession"), a term that is also later used for Antony's flight into the desert and the growing phenomenon of anchorite monasticism. Compare with papyri such as P. Cairo Zen. I, 59133 (in 256 BCE, brick-workers swear to be present and not leave Philadelphia); Papiri della Società Italiana (hereafter PSI) V, 515 (251 BCE); and the Hibeh Papyri (P. Hib.) I, 93 (c. 250 BCE, in which a worker waives the right to *asylia*—that is, taking asylum in a temple). Each of these examples is noted by von Reden, *Money in Ptolemaic Egypt*, 147n83.
5. PSI V 502.21 (July 7, 257 BCE). Rigsby, *Asylia*, 542; Kruschwitz, "Arrogant Boss." In Greek, the concept is called ἀσυλία. For a Roman-era contract asking loan recipients not to engage in asylum, see Berliner griechische Urkunden (BGU) IV 1053 (April 2, 13 BCE); van Minnen, "Antichretic Loan."
6. Perry, "*Collegia* and Their Impact," 138. The vast number of association inscriptions from this time period is borne out by the compendia of associations begun in the late nineteenth century. As Perry notes, "The first monumental survey of *collegia* (Waltzing 1895–1900) compiled nearly 2,500 inscriptional references to these institutions, and this was supplemented a century later with a further ninety-one for Roman Italy alone (Mennella and Apicella 2000). As a result of Waltzing's labours, and of the subsequent investigations of twentieth-century scholars like Francesco Maria De Robertis (1910–2003), a portrait of a virtually unimpeded, unencumbered *fenomeno associativo* in the first two centuries AD emerged, and this remains the overall tenor of scholarship on the matter."
7. Under Nero in 58 CE, for instance, the *publicani* stood accused of excesses (Tac.

Ann. 13.50), and the emperor briefly considered abolishing indirect taxes and their collection; however, his financial advisors were able to persuade him that this would be the undoing of the empire's financial underpinnings. See Tan, *Power and Public Finance*, 40–67.

8. Josephus, *Bellum Judaicum* (hereafter Jos. *BJ*) 3.540. See Spielman, *Jews and Entertainment*, 75. Also note Jos. *BJ* 6.420.
9. For theories about the labor used to build the Colosseum, see Coleman, "Euergetism in its Place," 70.
10. On the reconstruction of *CIL* VI, 40454a, see Alföldy, "Eine Bauinschrift aus dem Colosseum"; Orlandi, *Epigrafia anfiteatrale*.
11. *AE* 1994, 297: *D(is) M(anibus) / P(ublius) Veracius Firmus / P(ublio) Veracio Proculo et / P(ublio) Veracio Marcello / fratribus pientis/simis coh(ortis) pip(erariorum) | (centuria) Firmi / heres fecit.* See AGRW ID# 24517.
12. McLaughlin, *Roman Empire*, 193–94.
13. Last and Harland, *Group Survival*, 9.
14. *CIL* VI, 940. This is a dedication by the *curator* of the *collegium subrutorum*, which was likely a group involved in removing and recycling materials from buildings in the city of Rome. See Peña, "Recycling in the Roman World," 33, who hypothesizes that the association may have been involved in dealing with the rubble left after the fire of Nero in 64 CE. For the letter of Vespasian (74 CE), see *AE* 1936, 128 – AGRW ID# 24691.
15. *AE* 1986, 333, Ch. 74: "*De coetu sodalicio collegio.*" González and Crawford, "Lex Irnitana," 172.
16. Plin. *HN* 18.90; see Scheidel, "Real Wages in Early Economies."
17. For the negative connotations of a private *coetus* versus a public *contio*, see Hiebel, *Rôles institutionnel*, 69–71.
18. The customs house for the fish toll has an inscription noting both fishermen and fish dealers: *Die Inschriften von Ephesos* (hereafter *IEph*) 20 = AGRW ID# 162 (54–59 CE). See Marzano, *Harvesting the Sea*, 2013; Harland, *Associations, Synagogues, and Congregations*, 3–4.
19. *IEph* 1168 = AGRW ID# 9030 (153/154 CE); *IEph* 596 = AGRW ID# 11100 (second century CE); *IEph* 553 = AGRW ID# 6589 (c. 350 CE); *IEph* 646 = AGRW ID# 8223 (100 CE); *IEph* 727 = AGRW ID# 1315 (c. 160s CE); *IEph* 728 = AGRW ID# 1313 (162/163 CE).
20. For the Book of Acts, we are here primarily concerned with Acts 19:23–40. Suggestions for the dating of Acts span from 60 to 150 CE, but strong arguments have been made for the first half of the second century CE as the time of its composition. See Nasrallah, "Acts of the Apostles."
21. For the souvenir economy at Ephesus and miniature shrines comparable to those made by Demetrius, see Popkin, *Souvenirs*, 25–28.
22. In Acts 19:35, he is referred to as a γραμματεύς—that is, a clerk or scribe; Acts 19:39 states: "ἐν τῇ ἐννόμῳ ἐκκλησίᾳ ἐπιλυθήσεται" ("in a lawful assembly, it will be settled").
23. For the silversmiths at Ephesus, see *SEG* XXXIV, 1094 = Iplikçioglu and Knibbe,

"Neue Inschriften aus Ephesos IX," 130–31 (inv. 4297) = PHI 249099 = AGRW ID# 9399. For the epitaph in Macedonia, see *SEG* II, 421 = AGRW ID# 2221 = CAPinv. 699; for the Hermeias epitaph, see *IEph* 2212 = AGRW ID# 1266.
24. *IEph* 215 = *SEG* IV, 512 = PHI 247938 = AGRW ID# 6299. See Buckler, "Labour Disputes."
25. In Jordan Rosenblum's estimate, the percentage of bread in the Palestinian diet was on the low side (at 50 percent), as might be expected in communities with a higher consumption of fresh fish and the ability to grow more fresh fruits, legumes, and vegetables. See Rosenblum, *Food and Identity*, 17. The oft-cited 70 to 75 percent is drawn from Foxhall and Forbes, "*Sitometreia*."
26. Broekaert and Zuiderhoek, "Industries and Services," 323.
27. Kruschwitz, "Strike, Legal Action, and Delusion."
28. Wendt, "*Iudaica Romana*."
29. Dio Chrysostomus, *Orationes* 34.21–23. Dio was himself from the Bithynian city of Prusa, but this speech addresses the civic assembly of Tarsus, capital of the province of Cilicia. We see many other trade groups at work in Tarsus. Under Caracalla, for instance, there is a dedication made by a συνέργιον of grain porters (*SEG* 27, 947 = AGRW ID# 13496 and CAPinv. 1012).
30. Pliny the Younger, *Epistulae* (hereafter Plin. *Ep.*) 10.33.
31. Petronius, *Satyrica* (hereafter Petron. *Sat.*) 78.7007: "*Itaque vigiles, qui custodiebant vicinam regionem, rati ardere Trimalchionis domum, effregerunt ianuam subito et cum aqua securibusque tumultuari suo iure coeperunt*" ("And so, the *vigiles*, who were guarding the neighboring area, thought that the house of Trimalchio was on fire; suddenly they broke down the door and they began to stir up confusion with their water and axes, in their official capacity"). Ancient fire scholar Virginia Closs rightly notes that we cannot securely date this text and thus cannot know whether this was an allusion to the large and destructive fire in Rome of 64 CE under Nero that began near the Circus Maximus. Closs, *While Rome Burned*, 108.
32. A member of the *vigiles* was called a νυκτοφύλαξ (night watchman) in Greek. For the *vigiles* in 31 CE, see Dio 58.9.6, 58.12.2. For Vespasian's brother using the *vigiles* for his own purposes in securing the city for his brother, see Jos. *BJ* 4.645. See particularly Fuhrmann, *Policing the Roman Empire*, 127.
33. Plin. *Ep.* 10.34.
34. Plin. *Ep.* 10.96.
35. Plin. *Ep.* 10.96.7: "*quod ipsum facere desisse post edictum meum, quo secundum mandata tua hetaerias esse vetueram.*" In Greek, these are the ἑταιρεῖαι.
36. For a counterargument, see Eckhardt, "Who Thought That Early Christians Formed Associations?"
37. Plin. *Ep.* 92–93. These are referred to as *eranoi* (10.92), which is yet another term for associations. The illicit assemblies that Trajan wishes to avoid in 10.93 are dubbed illicit *coetus*. See von Nijf, *Civic World of Professional Associations*, 21; Perry, "*Collegia* and Their Impact," 144.
38. Many other second-century associations were allowed to continue to exist in the area despite Trajanic bans. See Arnaoutoglou, "Roman Law and *Collegia*," 34–35.

39. Van Nijf, *Civic World of Professional Associations*, 180; de Ligt, "Governmental Attitudes," 245.
40. Minucius Felix, *Octavius* 8–9.
41. Plin. Ep. 10.96.8: "*ex duabus ancillis, quae ministrae dicebantur*" ("from two enslaved maidservants, who were called female deacons"). On suspicions regarding religious practices of enslaved persons, see Padilla Peralta, "Slave Religiosity."
42. See Rives, "Decree of Decius."
43. For example, in May 2023 in St. Louis, Missouri, the forty-two hundred heavy equipment operators in the Operating Engineers Union, Local 513, went on strike until an improved contract could be reached with the Associated General Contractors of Missouri. The stoppage was costly and had an impact on numerous building sites and local businesses in the area. Securing construction projects and ensuring their timely completion was a concern then, just as it is today.
44. *Inscriptiones graecae ad res romanas pertinentes* IV, 444 = *Mitteilungen des deutschen archäologischen Instituts. Athenische Abteilung* 24 (1899), 197.62; Buckler, "Labour Disputes," 34–35.
45. This is a mixed association of οἰκοδόμοι καὶ τεχνῖται (builders and craftspeople) whom we know are Christian because they swear to the Trinity. *Corpus Inscriptionum Graecarum* 3467 = CAPinv. 411. See Buckler, "'Labour Disputes," 36–41. As Garnsey, "Association of Builders," 85, notes, this was indeed a trade with a history of "conspicuous malpractice." Notably, Garnsey does not want to call this a trade union because these were "unlikely to have existed at this time and in this trade" (79).
46. Buckler, "Trade Union Pact." For arguments against using modern understandings when interpreting this inscription, see Di Branco, "Lavoro e conflittualità sociale." I do, however, agree that this is likely a type of Roman contract often used in construction work called a *stipulatio*. For the statistics on unions listed above, see The White House, "The State of Our Unions," September 5, 2022, https://www.whitehouse.gov/cea/written-materials/2022/09/05/the-state-of-our-unions/.
47. Grig, *Popular Culture*, 23–24.
48. Liv. 39.16.10. A prophecy of the mysterious Druids was also labeled a *superstitio* by Tacitus (*Historiae* 4.54.4).
49. Cicero, *Pro Flacco* 28.67: "*barbarae superstitioni*."
50. Ancient historian Mary T. Boatwright's remark that such associations "reenacted and reconfirmed the grateful acceptance of the emperor and Rome by staging the games" is here important to note. See Boatwright, *Hadrian and the Cities*, 95; and especially Gordillo Hervás, "Trajan and Hadrian's Reorganization."
51. *IG* XIV, 1054. This was to be a *curia* for the athletes in Rome. See Gordillo Hervás, "Trajan and Hadrian's Reorganization," 86–87.
52. P.Oxy. 27, 2476. The papyrus dates to July 26, 288 CE, but notes the earlier privileges granted to the athletes and *technitai* of Dionysus.
53. Seneca the Younger, *Apocolocyntosis*, 9.6; Petron. *Sat.* 45.13.
54. *CIL* III, 14165.8 = *ILS* 6987 = *AE* 1899, 161 = *AE* 1900, 201 = *AE* 1998, 876. This letter later turned up in Beirut, where it was excavated in 1899. For the overlap of

freedmen in Arles as both *navicularii* and *seviri augustales*, see Tran, "Social Organization of Commerce and Crafts"; Virlouvet, "Naviculaires d'Arles."
55. Schmidt, *Einfluss der Anachoresis*; Braunert, "ΙΔΙΑ"; Braunert, *Binnenwanderung*.
56. *CIL* VIII, 10570, 14454; Kehoe, *Law and Rural Economy*, 72–73.
57. Kehoe, *Economics of Agriculture*, 112–13.
58. *CIL* VIII, 14428; Kehoe, *Economics of Agriculture*, 113; Hauken, *Petition and Response*, vii, 31 and more generally 29–34.
59. As Noel Lenski has argued, they were certainly *not* workers "utterly lacking in agency or life options." Lenski, "Late Roman Colonate."
60. Augustine, *Epistulae*, 20*.9–21 (*Corpus Scriptorum Ecclesiasticorum Latinorum* [CSEL] 88.100–106). Lenski, "Peasant and Slave," 139; Lenski, "Late Roman Colonate."
61. Hauken, *Petition and Response*, 35–41; Kehoe, *Law and Rural Economy*, 84; Hekster, *Rome and Its Empire*, no. 17, 121–22.

Chapter 6. Castes, Law, and Compulsory Labor in Late Antiquity

1. *Prosopographia Imperii Romani*² F 140; Prosopography of the Later Roman Empire (hereafter PLRE) I, 3311.
2. Eutropius 9.14.
3. *Scriptores Historiae Augustae* (hereafter *SHA*), *Aurelian* (hereafter *Aur.*) 38.2.
4. *CIL* VI, 42–44 (115 CE, near San Clemente, in Rome). See Bond, "Currency and Control."
5. These were the *rationales*. *SHA, Aur.* 38.3: "*monetarii auctore Felicissimo, ultimo servorum, cui procurationem fisci mandaveram, rebelles spiritus extulerunt*" ("For under the leadership of Felicissimus, the lowest of slaves, to whom I had entrusted the care of the imperial fiscus, the mint workers have displayed the spirit of rebellion").
6. Kulikowski, *Triumph of Empire*, 174.
7. Propertius 2.33.43: "*Semper in absentes felicior aestus amantes*" ("Always passion [is] warmer towards absent lovers").
8. Dey, *Aurelian Wall*, 98.
9. Dey, *Aurelian Wall*, 42–3; Machado, *Urban Space and Aristocratic Power*, 88.
10. Aurelius Victor, *Caesares* 35.8; Eutr. 9.15.2.
11. *SHA, Probus,* 9.3–5, trans. David Magie.
12. *SHA, Probus,* 21.2–4, trans. Magie.
13. Phang, *Roman Military Service*, 202.
14. Phang, *Roman Military Service*, 202. For more on perceptions of "dirty work" in the Roman military philosophy, see Phang, "Soldiers' Slaves," 203–26.
15. There is continued disagreement over whether the events of the mid-third century should be termed a "crisis." See Witschel, who, in *Krise-Rezession-Stagnation?*, emphasizes a slow transition rather than a pan-imperial crisis. Also see Liebeschuetz, "Was There a Crisis of the Third Century?," 11–20. For contemporary literary perceptions of a "crisis" in the third century, see Alföldy, "Crisis of the Third Century," 89–111.

16. The modern titling of the period as the "Dominate" is meant to stand in contrast to the prior Principate, since Diocletian began to use the titles of *"dominus et deus"* on his coinage (as Aurelian and Carus had) and to approach rule like that of a Persian or Hellenistic king rather than as a *princeps* in the way that Augustus had fashioned his style of rule.
17. Lactantius, *De mortibus persecutorum* (hereafter Lac. *De mort. pers.*) 7.5: *"insatiabili avaritia."*
18. As observed by Kelly, *Ruling the Later Roman Empire*, 4. As Kelly notes, the term "corruption" is itself judgmental and oftentimes simply means an "abuse."
19. *Codex Theodosianus* (hereafter *CTh.*) 5.17.1 (a. 332).
20. Lenski, "Late Roman Colonate," 1.
21. Harries, *Law and Empire*, 5.
22. Kelly, "Emperors, Government, and Bureaucracy," 177.
23. MacMullen, *Corruption and the Decline of Rome*.
24. For critiques, see Kelly, "Emperors, Government, and Bureaucracy," 175–80; Harries, *Law and Empire*, 5; Lafferty, "Law," 164.
25. Segrè, "Studies in the Byzantine Economy," 101–27; Jones, "*Capitatio* and *Iugatio*," 88–94.
26. See, for example, *SEG* 7, 1055.
27. Lac. *De mort. pers.* 23; Aurelius Victor, *Caesares* 39.32. See especially Ziche, "Making Late Roman Taxpayers Pay," 127–36.
28. Ziche, "Making Late Roman Taxpayers Pay," 126.
29. Cameron, *Later Roman Empire*, 110. As Dominic Rathbone has persuasively argued, the antecedents of the late Roman colonate lay in part in Egyptian tax collectivities, rather than simply being an innovation of Diocletian's. See Rathbone, "Ancient Economy and Graeco-Roman Egypt," 163.
30. Part of the papyrological archive of the Fayum family of Aurelius Isidorus (hereafter P. Cair. Isid.), dating to the early fourth century (314 CE), is particularly illustrative of this. See, for instance, his petition in his position as a *tesserarius* of Karanis who oversaw the sending of supplies and the collection of taxes from the village, in which he complains about illegal exactions (P. Cair. Isid. 73).
31. Lac. *De mort. pers.* 23.2.
32. Harries's critique of the influential corruption model proposed by MacMullen is evident in her earlier review of his book *Corruption and the Decline of Rome* (1988). See Harries, "Ramsay MacMullen," 320–22. For the culture of knowledge organization and the archival "aesthetic" that developed in late antiquity, see Johnson, *Literary Territories*, 11–12.
33. Neither codex survives today, apart from a few pieces of parchment in the *Fragmenta Londiniensia Anteiustiniana*. The codices, which have been largely pieced together from later late antique legal works such as the *Justinianic Code*, were formed by a private initiative, but may have been influenced by Diocletian. See Corcoran, "*Gregorianus* and *Hermogenianus*," 285–304.
34. MacMullen, *Corruption and the Decline of Rome*, 170.
35. For the date and presentation of the map, see Talbert, *Rome's World*, 7.

36. P.Oxy. 1411.
37. Koenraad Verboven, "Bankers' Guilds and the Roman Monetary System," in *Detur Dignissimo: Studies in Honour of Johan Van Heesch*, ed. Fran Stroobants and Christian Lauwers (Brussels: Cercle d'études numismatiques—European Centre for Numismatic Studies, 2020), 417–36.
38. P.Oxy. 41, 2961–2967; P.Oxy. 20, 2271. Also note the papyri from the New York University Collection 65 (254 CE). The public bankers are specifically "δημόσιοι τραπεζῖται."
39. See *IEph* 454a II.1–2 = CAPinv. 1606 (150–250 CE) for the bankers' association of Ephesus referred to simply as τραπεζεῖται in the genitive. In Ephesus, they had three stalls in the latrines of the gymnasium of Vedius.
40. Lafaurie, "Réformes monétaires," 73–138; Harl, "Marks of Value," 263–70; *Coinage in the Roman Economy*, 149–50.
41. Lauffer, *Diokletians Preisedikt*, 93, Praef.10: see Graser, "Appendix," 305–421.
42. Groen-Vallinga and Tacoma, "Value of Labour," 123.
43. Corcoran, *Empire of the Tetrarchs*, 205–33.
44. Liu, *Collegia Centonariorum*, 118; James, "Fabricae," 257–331.
45. In Greek, they were called Φαβρικήσιοι.
46. *CTh.* 1.16.7 (331), specifically addressing *apparitores* of judges.
47. Julia Hillner, e-mail message to author, January 13, 2017. Those without status, such as *infames* and enslaved persons, had previously been the ones viewed as vulnerable to this type of corporal punishment. To have it inflicted on the *apparitores* to judges was a rather shocking development.
48. *CTh.* 9.21.1 (323/5).
49. Tertullian, *De fuga in persecutione* 13.5. See Purpura, "I curiosi," 165–275; and Fuhrmann, *Policing the Roman Empire*, 221, 152–55. The *curiosi* referred to by Tertullian are likely *frumentarii*, but this cannot be guaranteed.
50. *SHA, Hadrian* 11.4.
51. Aurelius Victor, *Caesares* 39.44: "Neque minore studio pacis officia vincta legibus aequissimis ac remoto pestilenti frumentariorum genere, quorum nunc agentes rerum simillimi sunt." Victor was a consular governor of Pannonia Secunda and later served in the prestigious post of urban prefect of Rome in 388/389.
52. *CTh.* 6.35.3. Kelly, "Bureaucracy and Government," 188. For the numerous collected laws pertaining to the *agentes de rebus*, see *CTh.* 6.27 and *Codex Justinianus* (hereafter *CJ*) 12.20.
53. For the *cursus publicus*, see Kolb, *Transport und Nachrichtentransfer*.
54. *CJ* 12.20.4.
55. *CTh.* 6.27.5 (386 CE).
56. Kelly, *Ruling the Later Roman Empire*, 206.
57. *CTh.* 10.20.3 = *CJ* 11.8.3 (365); *CTh.* 10.20.14 = *CJ* 11.8.11 (424), *CTh.* 10.20.17 = *CJ* 11.8.15 (427).
58. *CTh.* 14.4.2. For the *collegium suariorum* outside the law codes, see *CIL* VI, 1690, 1693. Book XIV of the *Theodosian Code* predominantly consists of laws concerning compulsory *collegia*.

59. Barnish, "Pigs, Plebeians and *Potentes*," 157–85.
60. *CTh.* 14.4.1.
61. See Jones, "Caste System." For a counter to this argument, see Skinner, "Political Mobility."
62. *CTh.* 6.29.1.
63. Libanius, *Orations* (hereafter Lib. *Or.*) 18.140: "ὥσθ' οἱ κωλυταὶ τῶν ἀδικημάτων αὐτοὶ τοὺς ἀδικοῦντας ἔσωζον κυσὶν ἐοικότες συμπράττουσι τοῖς λύκοις. διὰ ταῦτα ἴσον ἦν θησαυρῷ τε ἐντυχεῖν καὶ τούτων μετασχεῖν τῶν μετάλλων. ὁ γὰρ ἥκων Ἶρος ἐν βραχεῖ χρόνῳ Καλλίας" (trans. A.F. Norman).
64. In "Bishops and Clerics," 227–29, Raymond van Dam provided this estimate based on demographic estimates originally made by Bruce Frier for the early Principate. See Frier, "Demography," 811–16.
65. *CTh.* 6.27.23.
66. Lib. *Or.* 1.206–10.
67. Lib. *Or.* 1.226.
68. *CTh.* 9.45.3. This is an eastern law and may not have been promulgated in the western portion of the empire.
69. *CJ* 12.61.4: "*Curialibus et naviculariis omnibusque corporibus ita subveniri volumus, ut nihil apparitoribus universorum iudicum liceat, quod ad praedam provinciarum pertinet.*" In the later Roman Empire, "*iudex*" meant any imperial official with any power (for example, *CJ* 1.45.2 is a decree that refers to the provincial governor as a *iudex*). See Bond, *Trade and Taboo*, 54.
70. MacMullen, *Corruption and the Decline of Rome*, 122–48. Also note Kelly, *Ruling the Later Roman Empire*, 138–85.
71. Harries, "Constructing the Judge," 221.

Chapter 7. Athletic Factions, Associations, and Popular Rebellion in the Late Roman City

1. The circus as a political space with connecting palaces for imperial refuge is the argument of Heucke, *Circus und Hippodrom*.
2. Humphrey, *Roman Circuses*, 579, 134. On Thessaloniki's circus as built under Galerius, see Dodge, "Circuses in the Roman East," 133–46.
3. Horsmann, *Die Wagenlenker der römischen Kaiserzeit*; Bell, "Roman Chariot Racing," 495–96; Lee-Stecum, "Dangerous Reputations," 224.
4. Ulpian, *Digesta* (hereafter Ulp. *Dig.*) 3.2.4 pr. For the argument against charioteers incurring *infamia*, see Wacke, "*Gloria*"; Gamauf, "*Pro virtute certamen*"; Bell, "Horse Racing in Imperial Rome," 42.
5. *Canons from the Council of Arles* I.4–5; Munier, *Concilia Galliae*, a.314—a.506, 5: 4–5: "*De circissariis agitatoribus qui fideles sunt: placuit eos, quamdiu agitant, a communione separari; De theatricis: ipsos placuit, quamdiu agunt, a communione separari.*"
6. *CIL* VI, 10046 = Alonso-Alonso, *Médicos en las inscripciones latinas*, 238–39, no. 121.
7. See Tuck, "*Ludi* and *Factiones*," 541; Potter, "Entertainers in the Roman Empire," 317–19; MacLean, "People on the Margins," 583.

8. Potter and Mattingly, *Life, Death, and Entertainment*, 292.
9. Suetonius, *Life of Domitian*, 7.
10. Bell, "Roman Chariot Racing," 495.
11. Remijsen, *End of Greek Athletics*, 170; Cameron, *Circus Factions*, 218–19.
12. Theophylact Simocatta, *History* 8.7.10; Roueché, *Performers and Partisans*, 151.
13. PLRE I, Flavius Leontius 22.
14. Ammianus Marcellinus (hereafter Amm. Marc.) 15.7.2.
15. Washburn, *Banishment*, 36.
16. Washburn, *Banishment*, 36.
17. Amm. Marc. 28.1.27.
18. Amm. Marc. 28.4.25.
19. *CTh.* 9.16.4 (357).
20. Lee-Stecum, "Dangerous Reputations," 226.
21. *Collectio Avellana* 1.7 = *Corpus Scriptorum Ecclesiasticorum Latinorum* 35.1. See Bond, "Mortuary Workers," 138.
22. Trout, "Damasus," 298–315.
23. *CJ* 4.41.1.
24. Amm. Marc. 31.4.11. See Lenski, *Failure of Empire*, 326.
25. Zosimus, *History*, 4.20.6, trans. W. Green and T. Chaplin.
26. Lenski, *Failure of Empire*, 326.
27. *CTh.* 16.1.2 (380 CE).
28. *Papyrologica Lugduno-Batava* XXV, 62.
29. Theodoret, *Historia ecclesiastica* 5.17.
30. Sozomen 7.25.
31. Potter, "Anatomies of Violence," 61–72; Cameron, *Circus Factions*; Roueché, *Performers and Partisans*.
32. Potter, "Anatomies of Violence," 3.
33. Cameron, *Circus Factions*, 193–222; Remijsen, *End of Greek Athletics*, 230.
34. Roueché, *Performers and Partisans*, 130–31; van der Horst, "Jews and Blues in Late Antiquity," 53–58.
35. Fagan, *Lure of the Arena*, 122.
36. Roueché, *Performers and Partisans*, 58, 75–76.
37. Roueché, *Performers and Partisans*, 137–38.
38. Weiler, "Theodosius I. und die Olympischen Spiele," 53–75; Remijsen, *End of Greek Athletics*, 219.
39. Remijsen, "Surprisingly Long History," 129–42.
40. *CTh.* 4.6.3 (336 CE): "*humilis vel abiecta.*" See Grubbs, "Not the Marrying Kind," 241–57.
41. Marcian, *Novel* 4 (454); Grubbs, "Not the Marrying Kind," 253.
42. *CTh.* 14.3.21 (March 8, 403).
43. For the application of supply-chain management analysis, predominantly to Roman food provisions, see James, *Food Provisions for Ancient Rome*.
44. See Frova, "Il Circo di Milano," 423–31. For a digital reconstruction of the Milan circus in the southwestern part of the city center, see Guidi, Barsanti, Micoli, and

Malik, "Accurate Reconstruction of the Roman Circus in Milan." The circus existed until the Lombard period.

45. Socrates, *Historia ecclesiastica* (hereafter Soc. Schol. *Hist. eccl.*) 5.26.
46. Harris, Talbert, Gillies, Elliott, and Becker, "Frigidus."
47. *CTh.* 15.12.3 (June 6, 399).
48. MacMullen, "Epigraphic Habit in the Roman Empire"; Meyer, "Explaining the Epigraphic Habit," 74–96.
49. *CIL* VI, 41382.
50. Claudian, *De consulatu Stilichonis* 3.347–9. See Kinney, "First-Generation Diptychs," 149–66. Anicius Basilius was the last consul before Justinian absorbed the magistracy into his own duties and titles.
51. Cushing, "Economic Relationship," 239.
52. *CIL* VI, 33885 = *ILS* 7214 = AGRW ID# 30532.
53. Evers, *Worlds Apart Trading Together*, 18.
54. Plin. *HN* 8.4; Evers, *Worlds Apart Trading Together*, 45. On the prevalence of the *shreni* among Indian artisans and tradespeople, see Thapar, *Early India*, 248.
55. Evers, *Worlds Apart Trading Together*, 147.
56. Oros. 7.37.4.
57. Oros. 7.37.5.
58. Oros. 7.37.12–16. "*ut uilissimorum pecudum modo singulis aureis*" (7.37.16).
59. Kahlos, "Late Roman Ideas," 90–91; Augustine, *Epistulae* 199.12.
60. Zosimus, *History*, 5.41.4.
61. Procopius, *De bello Vandalico* (hereafter Procop. *Vand.*) 3.2.15–21.
62. Procop. *Vand.* 3.2.27: "τοῖς οἰκέταις ἐγκελεύσασθαι νύκτωρ ἀνοιγνύναι τὰς πύλας" ("she commanded that her household enslaved persons, they say, open the gates at night").
63. Stephanis, *Dionysiakoi Technitai*.
64. Sessa, *Daily Life in Late Antiquity*, 74.
65. Machado, "Statue Habit and Statue Culture."
66. Van Voorhis, *Sculptor's Workshop*.
67. PSI XII 1265 = AGRW ID# 31557. Kloppenborg, *Greco-Roman Associations*, 518–23, no. 284.
68. Banaji, "Mass Production," 5.
69. Klingshirn, *Caesarius of Arles*, 172.
70. Martroye, "Parabalani."
71. For sources on Hypatia, see Soc. Schol. *Hist. eccl.* 7.15.5–7; John of Nikiu, *Chronicle* 84.100–103; Rufinus, *Historia ecclesiastica* 11.23.
72. See Watts, *Hypatia*, 9.
73. *CTh.* 16.2.42 (416).
74. Holum, *Theodosian Empresses*, 166.
75. Jerome, *Epistulae* 108.14.
76. Palladius, *Historia Lausiaca* 7.3–5; Whiting, "Braided Networks," 75.
77. Palladius, *Historia Lausiaca* 7.4. See Bagnall and Rathbone, *Egypt from Alexander to the Copts*, 110, no. 4.2.a.

78. Dilley, "Dipinti in Late Antiquity," 116.
79. Maspero and Drioton, *Fouilles exécutées à Baouît,* no. 63; translation by Dilley, "Dipinti in Late Antiquity," 116.
80. Dilley, "Textual Aesthetics," 177.
81. Cassiodorus, *Variae* (hereafter Cassiod. *Var.*) 7.10.1; Bjornlie, *Politics and Tradition,* 171; Lim, "*Tribunus Voluptatum.*" Note that Lim places the position's *terminus post quem* at April 381 CE.
82. *CTh.* 15.7.13.
83. Salvian, *De gubernatione Dei* 6.12.
84. Dey, *Making of Medieval Rome,* 52. Dey calculates this number for 452 CE based on records for the pork dole.
85. For Rome, see especially Salzman, *Falls of Rome.*
86. Gregory of Tours, *Historia Francorum* 5, pref.
87. Cassiod. *Var.* 3.51.
88. Cassiod. *Var.* 1.20, 1.27 (c. 509 CE) mentions the petition of the Greens complaining about brothers and *illustres* named Theodorus and Inportunus.
89. Cassiod. *Var.* 1.20. See Lim, "Roman Pantomime Riot."
90. Cassiod. *Var.* 1.30–33.
91. See the *Antinoopolis Papyri* inv. 66 = TM 65096.
92. Humphrey, *Roman Circuses,* 539.
93. John Malalas, *Chronographia* (hereafter J. Mal.) 17.12.
94. Procopius, *Anecdota* (hereafter Procop. *Anec.*) 9.2–12. Her father's name was Acacius, and we are told that he had three daughters: Comito, Theodora, and Anastasia.
95. *CJ* 5.4.23; Procop. *Anec.* 9.47–54.
96. *Anthologia Planudea* 16.365, trans. W. R. Paton. See Cameron, *Circus Factions,* 273–74.
97. Alan Cameron (*Circus Factions,* 271–96), advanced the notion that it was rare for the circus factions to use their clout for political or economic ends. However, as Main, "Mob Violence," 20, argued: "Economic crises provide a case to observe the factions in their political capacity of voicing popular grievances." I support Main's argument that the factions could and did use their popularity and numbers for economic and political ends in the eastern Mediterranean from the fifth to the seventh centuries in important ways. Main's advisor, Geoffrey Greatrex, has frequently argued for the social and religious activism of the circus factions. See Greatrex, "Emperor, People and Urban Violence," 392.
98. John of Antioch, *Excerpta de insidiis,* fr. 41; J. Mal. 18.121. See particularly Whitby, "Factions, Bishops, Violence and Urban Decline," 444; Main, "Mob Violence," 19.
99. Kyle, *Sport and Spectacle,* 338; Milliman, "Decline and Fall of Spectacle," 199.
100. Ulp. *Dig.* 9.2.7.4. Nigel B. Crowther, "Slaves and Greek Athletics," *Quaderni Urbinati Di Cultura Classica* 40, no. 1 (1992): 35–42; Remijsen, *End of Greek Athletics,* 250, 341. Many of the earlier athletic associations seem to have been absorbed by circus factions around the fifth century CE.
101. Harper, *Slavery in the Late Roman World,* 278. Harper is here echoing similar

remarks made by Urbainczyk, *Slave Revolts in Antiquity*; Shaw, *Spartacus and the Slave Wars*; and Bradley, *Slavery and Rebellion*.

102. In 1985, James C. Scott (*Weapons of the Weak*) developed the concept, theory, and recognition of "everyday resistance" to oppression in rural Malaysia. This concept was then further developed in the field of resistance studies to include small, quotidian acts of resistance within slave systems. Keith Bradley ("Resisting Slavery at Rome") has of late developed this category more fully for the analysis of Roman slavery, focusing on the time from the late Republic to the Severans rather than late antiquity.

Conclusion

1. This can be deduced from the actions of Justin II (565–578 CE) in paying these loans off not long after his ascent. See Corippus, *In laudem Iustini* 2.361–4. For Ablabius's (PLRE IIIA, "Ablabius 1") likely membership in the factions due to his occupation, see Whitby, *Wars of Justinian I*, 298. For the "bankers' conspiracy," see J. Mal. 18.141 (493); Theophanes AM 6055 (AD 562/563).
2. These are the μεταξοπράται. See *Book of the Eparch* 6.16. Freshfield, *Roman Law*, 23.
3. Maniatis, "Guild System"; Vryonis, "Byzantine Δ."
4. Coscntino, "Structural Features," 66–67.
5. Gregory I, *Letters* 10.26.
6. Naismith, "Gilds, States and Societies."
7. Reyerson, *Women's Networks in Medieval France*, 73.
8. Eisenbichler, "Introduction," 1.
9. Epstein, "Craft Guilds." In the 1990s and early 2000s, Epstein fought the predominant view that late medieval and then early modern guilds stymied technological innovation and economic growth. He argued they actually improved the economy through the training of apprentices and the creation of product standards for quality control.
10. Ogilvie, *European Guilds*.
11. Moll-Murata, "Guilds and Apprenticeship," 225–57.
12. Wiessner, "Ex-Starbucks CEO Schultz"; Associated Press, "Heathrow Airport Workers End Strike"; Lucas, "Chipotle to Pay Ex-Employees."
13. Mayall, "Americans Love Unions."

BIBLIOGRAPHY

Alföldy, Géza. "The Crisis of the Third Century as Seen by Contemporaries." *Greek, Roman, and Byzantine Studies* 15 (1974): 89–111.

———. "Eine Bauinschrift aus dem Colosseum." *Zeitschrift für Papyrologie und Epigraphik* 109 (1995): 195–226.

Almagor, Eran. "Health as a Criterion in Ancient Ethnological Schemes." In *The Routledge Handbook of Identity and the Environment in the Classical and Medieval Worlds*, edited by Rebecca Futo Kennedy and Molly Jones-Lewis, 75–92. New York: Routledge, 2016.

Alonso-Alonso, María Ángeles. *Los médicos en las inscripciones Latinas de Italia (siglos II a.C.–III d.C.): Aspectos sociales y profesionales*. Santander: Universidad de Cantabria, 2018.

Amunnakht. "The So-Called 'Strike Papyrus' Written by Amunnakht." Translated by the Museo Egizio. Museo Egizio, cat. 1880.

Aneziri, Sophia. "Artists of Dionysus: The First Professional Associations in the Ancient Greek World." In *Skilled Labour and Professionalism in Ancient Greece and Rome*, edited by Edmund Stewart, Edward Harris, and David Lewis, 293–312. Cambridge: Cambridge University Press, 2020.

———. "World Travellers: The Associations of Artists of Dionysus." In *Wandering Poets in Ancient Greek Culture: Travel, Locality and Pan-Hellenism*, edited by Richard Hunter and Ian Rutherford, 217–36. Cambridge: Cambridge University Press, 2009.

Armstrong, Jeremy. *War and Society in Early Rome: From Warlords to Generals*. Cambridge: Cambridge University Press, 2016.

Arnaoutoglou, Ilias N. "Roman Law and *Collegia* in Asia Minor." *Revue international des droits de l'antiquité* 49 (2002): 27–44.

———. "Were There Craftsmen Associations in the Hellenistic World?" In *Statuts personnels et main-d'oeuvre en Méditerranée hellénistique*, edited by Stéphanie Maillot and Julien Zurbach, 263–84. Clermont-Ferrand: Presses universitaires Blaise-Pascal, 2021.

Ascough, Richard A., Philip A. Harland, and John S. Kloppenborg. Associations in the Greco-Roman World. http://www.philipharland.com/greco-roman-associations/.
Associated Press. "Heathrow Airport Workers End Strike, British Airways Says." *New York Times*, August 12, 2002.
Ausbüttel, Frank M. *Untersuchungen zu den Vereinen im Westen des römischen Reiches*. Frankfurter Althistorische Studien 11. Kallmünz: M. Lassleben, 1982.
Bagnall, Roger S., and Raffaella Cribiore. *Women's Letters from Ancient Egypt, 300 BC–AD 800*. Ann Arbor: University of Michigan Press, 2006.
Bagnall, Roger, and Dominic Rathbone. *Egypt from Alexander to the Early Christians: An Archaeological and Historical Guide*. Los Angeles: Getty, 2004.
Banaji, Jairus. "Mass Production, Monetary Economy and the Commercial Vitality of the Mediterranean." In *Exploring the Economy of Late Antiquity: Selected Essays*, 1–34. Cambridge: Cambridge University Press, 2016.
Barnish, S. J. B. "Pigs, Plebeians and *Potentes:* Rome's Economic Hinterland, c. 350–600 A.D." *Papers of the British School at Rome* 55 (1987): 157–85.
Beard, Mary, John North, and Simon Price. *Religions of Rome*. Vol. 1, *A History*. Cambridge: Cambridge University Press, 1998.
Beek, Aaron L. "The Pirate Connection: Roman Politics, Servile Wars, and the East." *Transactions of the American Philological Association* 146, no. 1 (2016): 99–116.
Bell, Sinclair W. "Horse Racing in Imperial Rome: Athletic Competition, Equine Performance, and Urban Spectacle." In *The Running Centaur: Horse-Racing in Global-Historical Perspective*, edited by Sinclair W. Bell, Christian Jaser, and Christian Mann, 28–77. London: Routledge, 2022.
———. "Roman Chariot Racing: Charioteers, Factions, Spectators." In *A Companion to Sport and Spectacle in Greek and Roman Antiquity*, edited by Donald G. Kyle and Paul Christesen, 492–504. Chichester: Wiley-Blackwell, 2014.
Benton, Jared T. *The Bread Makers: The Social and Professional Lives of Bakers in the Western Roman Empire*. London: Palgrave Macmillan, 2020.
Ben Zeev, Miriam Pucci. *Diaspora Judaism in Turmoil, 116/117 CE: Ancient Sources and Modern Insights*. Leuven: Peeters, 2005.
Bernard, Seth. *Building Mid-Republican Rome: Labor, Architecture, and the Urban Economy*. Oxford: Oxford University Press, 2018.
Bjornlie, M. Shane. *Politics and Tradition between Rome, Ravenna and Constantinople: A Study of Cassiodorus and the Variae 527–554*. Cambridge: Cambridge University Press, 2013.
Boatwright, Mary T. *Hadrian and the Cities of the Roman Empire*. Princeton: Princeton University Press, 2000.
Bodel, John. "Slave Labour and Roman Society." In *The Cambridge World History of Slavery*. Vol. 1, *The Ancient Mediterranean World*, edited by Keith Bradley and Paul Cartledge, 311–36. Cambridge: Cambridge University Press, 2011.
Bond, Sarah E. "The Corrupting Sea: Law, Violence, and Compulsory Professions in Late Antiquity." In *Anticorruption in History: From Antiquity to the Modern Era*, edited by Ronald Kroeze, André Vitória, and Guy Geltner, 49–64. Oxford: Oxford University Press, 2018.

———. "Currency and Control: Mint Workers in the Later Roman Empire." In *Work, Labour, and Professions in the Roman World,* edited by Koenraad Verboven and Christian Laes, 227–45. Leiden: Brill, 2017.

———. "Fasces, Fascism, and How the Alt-Right Continues to Appropriate Ancient Roman Symbols." Hyperallergic, September 13, 2018. https://hyperallergic.com/459504/fasces-fascism-and-how-the-alt-right-continues-to-appropriate-ancient-roman-symbols/.

———. "Mortuary Workers, the Church, and the Funeral Trade in Late Antiquity." *Journal of Late Antiquity* 6, no. 1 (Spring 2013): 135–51.

———. "*Ob Merita:* The Epigraphic Rise and Fall of the *patrona civitatis* in Roman North Africa." MA thesis, University of North Carolina, 2007.

———. *Trade and Taboo: Disreputable Professions in the Roman Mediterranean.* Ann Arbor: University of Michigan Press, 2016.

Bradley, Keith. "Resisting Slavery at Rome." In *The Cambridge World History of Slavery.* Vol. 1, *The Ancient Mediterranean World,* edited by Keith Bradley and Paul Cartledge, 362–84. Cambridge: Cambridge University Press, 2011.

———. *Slavery and Rebellion in the Roman World, 140 B.C.–70 B.C.* Bloomington: Indiana University Press; London: B. T. Batsford, 1989.

Branco, Marco Di. "Lavoro e conflittualità sociale in una città tardoantica. Una rilettura dell'epigrafe di Sardi CIG 3467 (Le Bas-Waddington 628 = Sardis VII, 1, n. 18)." *Antiquité Tardive* 8 (2000): 181–208.

Braunert, Horst. *Die Binnenwanderung: Studien zur Sozialgeschichte Ägyptens in der Ptolemäer und Kaiserzeit.* Bonn: Röhrscheid, 1964.

———. "ΙΔΙΑ: Studien zur Bevölkerungsgeschichte des ptolemäischen Ägypten." *Journal of Juristic Papyrology* 9–10 (1955–56): 211–328.

Brennan, T. Corey. *The Fasces: A History of Ancient Rome's Most Dangerous Political Symbol.* Oxford: Oxford University Press, 2023.

———. *The Praetorship in the Roman Republic.* Vol. 2, *122 to 49 BC.* Oxford: Oxford University Press, 2000.

Brentano, Lujo. *On the History and Development of Gilds and the Origin of Trade-Unions.* London: Trübner, 1870.

Brice, Lee L. "Second Chance for Valor: Restoration of Order after Mutinies and Indiscipline." In *Aspects of Ancient Institutions and Geography: Studies in Honor of Richard J. A. Talbert,* edited by Lee L. Brice and Daniëlle Slootjes, 103–21. Leiden: Brill, 2015.

Broekaert, Wim, and Arjan Zuiderhoek. "Industries and Services." In *The Cambridge Companion to Ancient Rome,* edited by Paul Erdkamp, 317–35. Cambridge: Cambridge University Press, 2013.

Buckler, William H. "Labour Disputes in the Province of Asia." In *Anatolian Studies Presented to Sir William Mitchell Ramsay,* edited by W. H. Buckler and W. M. Calder, 27–50. Manchester: Manchester University Press, 1923.

———. "A Trade Union Pact of the Fifth Century." In *Studies Presented to David Moore Robinson on His Seventieth Birthday,* edited by G. E. Mylonas, 980–84. St. Louis: Washington University in St. Louis, 1951.

Calhoun, George Miller. *Athenian Clubs in Politics and Litigation.* Bulletin of the University of Texas 262. Humanistic Series 14. Austin: University of Texas, 1913.

Cameron, Alan. *Circus Factions: Blues and Greens at Rome and Byzantium.* Oxford: Clarendon, 1976.

Cameron, Averil. *The Later Roman Empire, AD 284–430.* Cambridge, MA: Harvard University Press, 1993.

Campbell, Brian. *The Roman Army, 31 BC–AD 337: A Sourcebook.* New York: Routledge, 1994.

Capogrossi Colognesi, Luigi. "Curie, centurie e 'heredia.'" In *Studi in onore di Francesco Grelle,* edited by Marina Silvestrini, Tullio Spagnuolo Vigorita, and Giuliano Volpe, 41–49. Bari: Edipuglia, 2006.

———. *Law and Power in the Making of the Roman Commonwealth.* Cambridge: Cambridge University Press, 2014.

Carandini, Andrea. *Rome: Day One.* Princeton: Princeton University Press, 2011.

Cifani, Gabriele. *The Origins of the Roman Economy: From the Iron Age to the Early Republic in a Mediterranean Perspective.* Cambridge: Cambridge University Press, 2021.

Clinton, Catherine. *The Plantation Mistress: Woman's World in the Old South.* New York: Pantheon, 1982.

Closs, Virginia M. *While Rome Burned: Fire, Leadership, and Urban Disaster in the Roman Cultural Imagination.* Ann Arbor: University of Michigan Press, 2020.

Coleman, Kathleen. "Euergetism in Its Place: Where Was the Amphitheatre in Augustan Rome?" In *Bread and Circuses: Euergetism and Municipal Patronage in Roman Italy,* edited by Kathryn Lomas and Tim Cornell, 61–89. New York: Routledge, 2003.

———. "Public Entertainments." In *The Oxford Handbook of Social Relations in the Roman World,* edited by Michael Peachin, 335–57. Oxford: Oxford University Press, 2011.

Conte, Gian Biagio. *Latin Literature: A History.* Translated by Joseph B. Solodow. Baltimore: Johns Hopkins University Press, 1994.

Corcoran, Simon. *The Empire of the Tetrarchs: Imperial Pronouncements and Government, AD 284–324.* Rev. ed. Oxford: Clarendon, 2000.

———. "The *Gregorianus* and *Hermogenianus* Assembled and Shattered." *Mélanges de l'École française de Rome—Antiquité* 125, no. 2 (2013): 285–304.

Cordery, Simon. *British Friendly Societies 1750–1914.* Houndmills, Basingstoke, Hampshire: Palgrave MacMillan, 2003.

Cornell, T. J. *The Beginnings of Rome: Italy and Rome from the Bronze Age to the Punic Wars (c. 1000–264 BC).* New York: Routledge, 1995.

———. "The Conquest of Italy." In *The Cambridge Ancient History.* Vol. 7, pt. 2, *The Rise of Rome to 220 B.C.,* edited by Frank W. Walbank, A. E. Astin, M. W. Frederiksen, and Robert M. Ogilvie, 351–419. Cambridge: Cambridge University Press, 1990.

———. "The Tyranny of the Evidence: A Discussion of the Possible Uses of Literacy in Etruria and Latium in the Archaic Age." In *Literacy in the Roman World.* Journal of Roman Archaeology Supplementary Series 3, edited by Mary Beard, 7–34. Ann Arbor: Journal of Roman Archaeology, 1991.

Cosentino, Salvatore. "The Structural Features of Ravenna's Socioeconomic History

in Late Antiquity." In *Ravenna and the Traditions of Late Antique and Early Byzantine Craftsmanship: Labour, Culture, and the Economy*, edited by Salvatore Cosentino, 59–82. Boston: De Gruyter, 2020.
Cotter, Wendy. "The Collegia and Roman Law: State Restrictions on Private Associations: 64 BCE–200 CE." In *Voluntary Associations in the Graeco-Roman World*, edited by John S. Kloppenborg and Stephen G. Wilson, 74–89. New York: Routledge, 1996.
Cromwell, Jenny. "The First Recorded Strike in History." Papyrus Stories, March 15, 2022. https://papyrus-stories.com/2022/03/15/the-first-recorded-strike-in-history/.
Csapo, Eric, and William J. Slater. *The Context of Ancient Drama*. Ann Arbor: University of Michigan Press, 1994.
Cushing, Alex. "The Economic Relationship between Patron and Freedman in Italy in the Early Roman Empire." PhD diss., University of Toronto, 2020.
Cuvigny, Hélène. *Rome in Egypt's Eastern Desert*. Vol. 1. Institute for the Study of the Ancient World Monographs. New York: New York University Press, 2021.
Dai, Jianbing, Luqian Peng, and Xiaorong Chen. *The Cultural Exchange History of Ancient Currency between China and Other Countries*. Newcastle-upon-Tyne: Cambridge Scholars, 2022.
Dam, Raymond van. "Bishops and Clerics during the Fourth Century: Numbers and Their Implications." In *Episcopal Elections in Late Antiquity*, edited by Johan Leemans, Peter Van Nuffelen, Shawn W. J. Keough, and Carla Nicolaye, 217–42. Berlin: De Gruyter, 2011.
Daniels, Megan. "Annexing a Shared Past: Roman Appropriations of Hercules-Melqart in the Conquest of Hispania." In *Rome, Empire of Plunder: The Dynamics of Cultural Appropriation*, edited by Matthew P. Loar, Carolyn MacDonald, and Dan-el Padilla Peralta, 237–60. Cambridge: Cambridge University Press, 2018.
Davies, Penelope J. E. *Architecture and Politics in Republican Rome*. Cambridge: Cambridge University Press, 2017.
de Ligt, L. "Governmental Attitudes towards Markets and *Collegia*." In *Mercati permanenti e mercati periodici nel mondo Romano: Atti degli Incontri Caprese di Storia dell'Economica Antica, Capri, 13–15 Ottobre 1997*, edited by E. Lo Cascio, 237–52. Bari: Edipuglia, 2020.
Dey, Hendrik W. *The Aurelian Wall and the Refashioning of Imperial Rome, AD 271–855*. Cambridge: Cambridge University Press, 2011.
———. *The Making of Medieval Rome: A New Profile of the City, 400–1420*. New York: Cambridge University Press, 2021.
Dilley, Paul. "Dipinti in Late Antiquity and Shenoute's Monastic Federation: Text and Image in the Paintings of the Red Monastery." *Zeitschrift für Papyrologie und Epigraphik* 165 (2008): 111–28.
———. "Textual Aesthetics: Dipinti and the Early Byzantine Epigraphic Habit." In *The Red Monastery Church: Beauty and Asceticism in Upper Egypt*, edited by Elizabeth S. Bolman, 175–82. New Haven: Yale University Press, 2016.
Diosono, Francesca. "*Professiones Gentiliciae*. The *Collegia* of Rome between Paganism and Christianity." In *Pagans and Christians in Late Antique Rome: Conflict, Competition, and Coexistence in the Fourth Century*, edited by Michele Renee Salzman, Marianne Sághy, and Rita Lizzi Testa, 251–70. New York: Cambridge University Press, 2015.

Dodge, Hazel. "Circuses in the Roman East: A Reappraisal." In *Le cirque romain et son image: Actes du colloque tenu à l'institut Ausonius, Bordeaux, 2006*, edited by Jocelyne Nelis-Clément and Jean-Michel Roddaz, 133–46. Bordeaux: Ausonius, 2008.

Dowse, Andrew, and John Blackburn. "Improving Supply Chain Resilience through Preparedness." *Security Challenges* 16, no. 4 (2020): 82–98.

Drury, John. "'When the Mobs Are Looking for Witches to Burn, Nobody's Safe': Talking about the Reactionary Crowd." *Discourse and Society* 13, no. 1 (2002): 41–73.

Eckhardt, Benedikt. "Private Associations in Hellenistic and Roman Cities: Common Ground and Dividing Lines." In *Private Associations and Jewish Communities in the Hellenistic and Roman Cities*, edited by Benedikt Eckhardt, 13–36. Leiden: Brill, 2019.

———. "Who Thought That Early Christians Formed Associations?" *Mnemosyne* 71, no. 2 (2018): 298–314.

Edgerton, William F. "The Strikes in Ramses III's Twenty-Ninth Year." *Near Eastern Studies* 10, no. 3 (1951): 137–45.

Edmondson, Jonathan. "Slavery and the Roman Family." In *The Cambridge World History of Slavery*, edited by Keith Bradley and Paul Cartledge, 337–61. Cambridge: Cambridge University Press, 2011.

Edwards, Catharine. *The Politics of Immorality in Ancient Rome*. Cambridge: Cambridge University Press, 2002.

Eisenbichler, Konrad. "Introduction: A World of Confraternities." In *A Companion to Medieval and Early Modern Confraternities*, edited by Konrad Eisenbichler, 1–19. Leiden: Brill, 2019.

Engels, Friedrich, and Karl Marx. *The Communist Manifesto*. Edited and translated by L. M. Findlay. Peterborough: Broadview, 2004.

Epstein, Stephan R. "Craft Guilds, Apprenticeship and Technological Change in Pre-Modern Europe." *Journal of Economic History* 53 (1998): 684–713.

Evers, Kasper Grønlund. *Worlds Apart Trading Together: The Organisation of Long-Distance Trade between Rome and India in Antiquity*. Archaeopress Roman Archaeology 32. Oxford: Archaeopress, 2017.

Fagan, Garrett. *The Lure of the Arena: Social Psychology and the Crowd at the Roman Games*. Cambridge: Cambridge University Press, 2011.

———. "Training Gladiators: Life in the *ludus*." In *Aspects of Ancient Institutions and Geography: Studies in Honor of Richard J. A. Talbert*. Vol. 19, *Impact of Empire*, edited by Lee L. Brice and Daniëlle Slootjes, 122–44. Leiden: Brill, 2014.

Fauconnier, Bram. *Athletes and Artists in the Roman Empire: The History and Organisation of the Ecumenical Synods*. Cambridge: Cambridge University Press, 2023.

———. "The Organisation of Synods of Competitors in the Roman Empire." *Historia: Zeitschrift für Alte Geschichte* 66, no. 4 (2017): 442–67.

Finley, Moses I. *The Ancient Economy*. Berkeley: University of California Press, 1973.

Flambard, Jean-Marc. "Clodius, les collèges, la plebe et les esclaves. Recherches sur la politique populaire au milieu du 1er siècle." *Mélanges de l'École française de Rome, Antiquité* 89 (1977): 115–56.

Flower, Harriet. *The Dancing Lares and the Serpent in the Garden: Religion at the Roman Street Corner*. Princeton: Princeton University Press, 2017.

Fountoulakis, Andreas. "When Dionysus Goes to the East: On the Dissemination of Greek Drama beyond Athens." In *Theatre World: Critical Perspectives on Greek Tragedy and Comedy: Studies in Honor of Georgia Xanthakis-Karamanos*, edited by Andreas Fountoulakis, Andreas Markantonatos, and Georgios Vasilaros, 75–117. Berlin: De Gruyter, 2017.

Foxhall, Lin A., and Hamish Alexander Forbes. "*Sitometreia:* The Role of Grain as a Staple Food in Classical Antiquity." *Chiron* 12 (1982): 41–90.

Frank, Tenney. *An Economic History of Rome to the End of the Republic*. Baltimore: Johns Hopkins University Press, 1920.

Freshfield, Edwin Hanson. *Roman Law in the Later Roman Empire: Byzantine Guilds, Professional and Commercial; Ordinances of Leo VI, c. 895, from the Book of the Eparch, Rendered into English*. Cambridge: Cambridge University Press, 1938.

Frier, Bruce W. "Demography." In *The Cambridge Ancient History*. Vol. 11, *The High Empire, A.D. 70–192*, 2nd ed., edited by Alan K. Bowman, Peter Garnsey, and Dominic Rathbone, 787–816. Cambridge: Cambridge University Press, 2000.

Fröhlich, Pierre, and Patrice Hamon. *Groupes et associations dans les cités grecques (IIIe siècle av. J.-C.–IIe siècle ap. J.-C)*. Actes de la table ronde de Paris, INHA, 19–20 juin 2009. Hautes études du monde gréco-romain 49. Geneva: Librairie Droz, 2013.

Frolov, Roman M. "The 'Wrong' Meetings? Some Notes on the Linked Usage of the Terms *Coetus* and *Contiones* in the Roman Republic." In *Institutions and Ideology in Republican Rome*, edited by Henrietta van der Blom, Christa Gray, and Catherine Steel, 236–51. Cambridge University Press: Cambridge, 2017.

Frova, Antonio. "Il Circo di Milano e i circhi di età tetrarchica." In *Milano capitale dell'impero romano 286–402 d.c.*, edited by Maria Paola Lavizzari Pedrazzini and Maria Pia Rossignani, 423–31. Milan: Silvana Editoriale, 1990.

Fuhrmann, Christopher. *Policing the Roman Empire: Soldiers, Administration, and Public Order*. Oxford: Oxford University Press, 2012.

Futrell. Alison. *Blood in the Arena: The Spectacle of Roman Power*. Austin: University of Texas Press, 1997.

Gabba, Emilio. "The *Collegia* of Numa: Problems of Method and Political Ideas." *Journal of Roman Studies* 74 (1984): 81–86.

Gabrielsen, Vincent. "Naval and Grain Networks and Associations in Fourth-Century Athens." In *Communities and Networks in the Ancient Greek World*, edited by Claire Taylor and Kostas Vlassopoulos, 177–212. Oxford: Oxford University Press, 2015.

Gamauf, Richard. "*Pro virtute certamen:* Zur Bedeutung des Sports und von Wettkämpfen im klassischen römischen Recht." In *Sport und Recht in der Antike. Beiträge zum zweiten Wiener Kolloquium zur Antiken Rechtsgeschichte*, edited by Kaja Harter-Uibopuu and Fritz Mitthof, 275–308. Vienna: Holzhausen, 2014.

Gambetti, Sandra. *The Alexandrian Riots of 38 C.E. and the Persecution of the Jews: A Historical Reconstruction*. Supplements to the Journal for the Study of Judaism 135. Leiden: Brill, 2009.

Garnsey, Peter. "An Association of Builders in Late Antique Sardis." In *Cities, Peasants and Food in Classical Antiquity: Essays in Social and Economic History*, 77–90. Cambridge: Cambridge University Press, 1998.

Gaudemet, Jean. "Utilitas publica." *Revue historique de droit français et étranger* (4th ser.) 29 (1951): 465–99.

González, Julián, and Michael H. Crawford. "The Lex Irnitana: A New Copy of the Flavian Municipal Law." *Journal of Roman Studies* 76 (1986): 147–243.

Gordillo Hervás, Rocío. "Trajan and Hadrian's Reorganization of the Agonistic Associations in Rome." In *Empire and Religion: Religious Change in Greek Cities under Roman Rule*, edited by Elena Muñiz Grijalvo, Juan Manuel Cortés Copete, and Fernando Lozano Gómez, 84–97. Leiden: Brill, 2017.

Graser, Elsa Rose. "Appendix: The Edict of Diocletian in Maximum Prices." In *An Economic Survey of Ancient Rome*. Vol. 5, *Rome and Italy of the Empire*, edited by Tenney Frank, 305–421. Baltimore: Johns Hopkins University Press, 1940.

Gray, Colin S. "Appendix C: Conceptual 'Hueys' at Thermopylae? The Challenge of Strategic Anachronism." In *The Strategy Bridge: Theory for Practice*, 267–77. Oxford: Oxford University Press, 2010.

Greatrex, Geoffrey. "The Emperor, the People and Urban Violence in the Fifth and Sixth Centuries." In *Religious Violence in the Ancient World: From Classical Athens to Late Antiquity*, edited by Jitse H. F. Dijkstra and Christian R. Raschle, 389–405. Cambridge: Cambridge University Press, 2020.

Grig, Lucy, ed. *Popular Culture in the Ancient World*. New York: Cambridge University Press, 2016.

Groen-Vallinga, Miriam J. *Work and Labour in the Cities of Roman Italy*. Liverpool: Liverpool University Press, 2023.

Groen-Vallinga, Miriam J., and Laurens E. Tacoma. "The Value of Labour: Diocletian's Price Edict." In *Work, Labour, and Professions in the Roman World*, edited by Koenraad Verboven and Christian Laes, 104–32. Leiden: Brill, 2016.

Grubbs, Judith Evans. "Not the Marrying Kind: Exclusion, Gender, and Social Status in Late Roman Marriage Law." In *La construction sociale du sujet exclu, IVe–XIe siècle: Discours, lieux et individus*, edited by Sylvie Joye, Maria Cristina La Rocca, and Stéphane Gioanni, 241–57. Turnhout: Brepols, 2019.

Gruen, Erich S. "Poetry and Politics: The Beginnings of Latin Literature." In *Studies in Greek Culture and Roman Policy*, 79–123. Leiden: Brill, 1990.

Guidi, Gabriele, Sara Gonizzi Barsanti, Laura Loredana Micoli, and Umair Shafqat Malik. "Accurate Reconstruction of the Roman Circus in Milan by Georeferencing Heterogeneous Data Sources with GIS." *Geosciences* 7 (3), 91 (2017): 1–18.

Halbwachs, Maurice. *On Collective Memory*. Translated by Lewis A. Coser. Chicago: University of Chicago Press, 1992.

Halloran, Claire. *Shopping in Ancient Rome: The Retail Trade in the Late Republic and the Principate*. Oxford: Oxford University Press, 2012.

Harl, Kenneth W. *Coinage in the Roman Economy, 300 B.C. to A.D. 700*. Baltimore: Johns Hopkins University Press, 1996.

———. "Marks of Value on Tetrarchic Nummi and Diocletian's Monetary Policy." *Phoenix* 39, no. 3 (1985): 263–70.

Harland, Philip. *Associations, Synagogues, and Congregations: Claiming a Place in Ancient*

Mediterranean Society. Rev. online ed., 2013. https://philipharland.com/publications/Harland%202013%20Associations-Synagogues-Congregations.pdf.

Harper, Kyle. *Slavery in the Late Roman World, AD 275–425*. Cambridge: Cambridge University Press, 2011.

Harries, Jill. "Constructing the Judge: Judicial Accountability and the Culture of Criticism in Late Antiquity." In *Constructing Identities in Late Antiquity*, edited by Richard Miles, 214–33. New York: Routledge, 1999.

———. *Law and Crime in the Roman World*. Cambridge: Cambridge University Press, 2007.

———. *Law and Empire in Late Antiquity*. Cambridge: Cambridge University Press, 1999.

———. "Ramsay MacMullen. *Corruption and the Decline of Rome*." *International History Review* 11, no. 2 (May 1989): 320–22.

Harris, William V., Richard J. A. Talbert, Sean Gillies, Tom Elliott, and Jeffrey Becker. "Frigidus (River): A Pleiades Place Resource." Pleiades: A Gazetteer of Past Places. https://pleiades.stoa.org/places/403209.

Hartnett, Jeremy. *The Roman Street: Urban Life and Society in Pompeii, Herculaneum, and Rome*. New York: Cambridge University Press, 2017.

Hasluck, Frederick William. "Unpublished Inscriptions from the Cyzicus Neighbourhood." *Journal of Hellenic Studies* 24 (1904): 20–40.

Hauken, Tor. *Petition and Response. An Epigraphic Study of Petitions to Roman Emperors, 181–249*. Monographs from the Norwegian Institute at Athens 2. Bergen: Norwegian Institute at Athens, 1998.

Hekster, Olivier. *Rome and Its Empire, AD 193–284: Debates and Documents in Ancient History*. Edinburgh: Edinburgh University Press, 2008.

Hemelrijk, Emily. *Hidden Lives, Public Personae: Women and Civic Life in the Roman West*. New York: Oxford University Press, 2015.

———. "Patronesses and 'Mothers' of Roman *Collegia*." *Classical Antiquity* 27, no. 1 (2008): 115–62.

Heucke, Clemens. *Circus und Hippodrom als politischer Raum. Untersuchungen zum grossen Hippodrom von Konstantinopel und zu entsprechenden Anlagen in spätantiken Kaiserresidenzen*. Altertums wissenschaftliche Texte und Studien 28. Hildesheim: Olms—Weidmann, 1994.

Hiebel, Dominique. *Rôles institutionnel et politique de la contio sous la république romaine 287–49 av. J.-C.* Paris: De Boccard, 2009.

Holleran, Claire. *Shopping in Ancient Rome: The Retail Trade in the Late Republic and the Principate*. Oxford: Oxford University Press, 2012.

Holum, Kenneth G. *Theodosian Empresses: Women and Imperial Dominion in Late Antiquity*. Berkeley: University of California Press, 1982.

Hoogenboom, Marcel, Christopher Kissane, Maarten Prak et al. "Guilds in the Transition to Modernity: The Cases of Germany, United Kingdom, and the Netherlands." *Theory and Society* 47, no. 3 (June 2018): 255–91.

Horsmann, Gerhard. *Die Wagenlenker der römischen Kaiserzeit: Untersuchungen zu ihrer sozialen Stellung*. Forschungen zur antiken Sklaverei 29. Stuttgart: Franz Steiner, 1998.

Horst, Pieter W. van der. "Jews and Blues in Late Antiquity." In *Jews and Christians in Their Graeco-Roman Context: Selected Essays on Early Judaism, Samaritanism, Hellenism, and Christianity*, 53–58. Tübingen: Mohr Siebeck, 2006.

Humphrey, John H. *Roman Circuses: Arenas for Chariot Racing*. Berkeley: University of California Press, 1986.

Iplikçioglu, B., and D. Knibbe. "Neue Inschriften aus Ephesos IX." *Jahreshefte des Österreichischen Archäologischen Institutes in Wien* 55 (1984): 107–49.

Isayev, Elena. *Migration, Mobility, and Place in Ancient Italy*. Cambridge: Cambridge University Press, 2017.

Ismard, Paulin. *La cité des réseaux. Athènes et ses associations VI e–I er siècle av. J.-C.* Paris: Sorbonne, 2010.

Jaczynowska, Marie. "L'organisation intérieure des 'collegia iuvenum' au temp du Haut-Empire romain." In *Gesellschaft und Recht im griechisch-römischen Altertum: Eine Aufsatzsammlung, Teil 2*, edited by Mihail N. Andreev, Elemér Pólay, Johannes Irmscher, and Witold Warkallo, 95–119. Berlin: Akademie, 1969.

James, Paul. *Food Provisions for Ancient Rome: A Supply Chain Approach*. Studies in Roman Space and Urbanism. Abingdon: Routledge, 2020.

James, Simon. "The *Fabricae*: State Arms Factories of the Later Roman Empire." In *Military Equipment and the Identity of Roman Soldiers*. BAR International Series 394, edited by J. C. Coulston, 257–331. Oxford: BAR, 1988.

Jensen, Erik. *Barbarians in the Greek and Roman World*. Indianapolis: Hackett, 2018.

Jewell, Evan. "(Re)moving the Masses: Colonisation as Domestic Displacement in the Roman Republic." *Humanities* 8 (2), 66 (2019): 1–41.

Johnson, Scott F. *Literary Territories: Cartographical Thinking in Late Antiquity*. Oxford: Oxford University Press, 2016.

Jones, A. H. M. "*Capitatio* and *Iugatio*." *Journal of Roman Studies* 47 (1957): 88–94.

———. "The Caste System in the Later Roman Empire." *Eirene* 8 (1970): 79–96.

Jory, E. J. "Associations of Actors in Rome." *Hermes* 98, no. 2 (1970): 224–53.

———. "Pylades, Pantomime, and the Preservation of Tragedy." *Mediterranean Archaeology* 17 (2004): 147–56.

Kahlos, Maijastina. "Late Roman Ideas of Ethnicity and Enslavement." In *Slavery in the Late Antique World, 150–700 CE*, edited by Chris L. de Wet, Maijastina Kahlos, and Ville Vuolanto, 87–104. Cambridge: Cambridge University Press, 2022.

Kay, Philip. *Rome's Economic Revolution*. Oxford: Oxford University Press, 2014.

Kehoe, Dennis P. *The Economics of Agriculture on Roman Imperial Estates in North Africa*. Hypomnemata 89. Göttingen: Vandenhoeck und Ruprecht, 1988.

———. *Law and Rural Economy in the Roman Empire*. Ann Arbor: University of Michigan Press, 2007.

Kelly, Christopher. "Bureaucracy and Government." In *The Cambridge Companion to the Age of Constantine*, rev. ed., edited by Noel E. Lenski, 183–204. Cambridge: Cambridge University Press, 2012.

———. "Emperors, Government, and Bureaucracy." In *The Cambridge Ancient History*.

Vol. 13, *The Late Empire, AD 337–425*, edited by Averil Cameron and Peter Garnsey, 138–83. Cambridge: Cambridge University Press, 1998.

———. *Ruling the Later Roman Empire*. Cambridge, MA: Harvard University Press, 2006.

Kinney, Dale. "First-Generation Diptychs in the Discourse of Visual Culture." In *Spätantike und byzantinische Elfenbeinbildwerke im Diskurs*, edited by Arne Effenberger, Anthony Cutler, and Gudrun Bühl, 149–66. Wiesbaden: Reichert, 2008.

Kleijwegt, Marc. "*Iuvenes* and Roman Imperial Society." *Acta Classica* 37 (1994): 79–102.

Klingshirn, William E. *Caesarius of Arles: The Making of a Christian Community in Late Antique Gaul*. Cambridge: Cambridge University Press, 1994.

Kloppenborg, John S. *Christ's Associations: Connecting and Belonging in the Ancient City*. New Haven: Yale University Press, 2019.

———. "Collegia and Thiasoi: Issues in Function, Taxonomy and Membership." In *Voluntary Associations in the Graeco-Roman World*, edited by John S. Kloppenborg and Stephen G. Wilson, 16–30. London: Routledge, 1996.

———. *Greco-Roman Associations: Texts, Translations, and Commentary*. Vol. 3, *Ptolemaic and Early Roman Egypt*. Berlin: De Gruyter, 2020.

———. "Pauline Assemblies and Graeco-Roman Associations." In *Receptions of Paul in Early Christianity: The Person of Paul and His Writings through the Eyes of His Early Interpreters*, edited by Jens Schröter, Simon Butticaz, and Andreas Dettwiler, 215–48. Berlin: De Gruyter, 2018.

Knapp, Robert. *Invisible Romans*. Cambridge, MA: Harvard University Press, 2011.

Kolb, Anne. *Transport und Nachrichtentransfer im römischen Reich*. Berlin: Akademie, 2000.

Korner, Ralph J. *The Origin and Meaning of Ekklēsia in the Early Jesus Movement*. Leiden: Brill, 2017.

Kruschwitz, Peter. "An Arrogant Boss, an Overwhelmed Manager, a Botched Valuation, and the Exploitation of Workers." *The Petrified Muse*, March 16, 2018. https://thepetrifiedmuse.blog/2018/03/16/an-arrogant-boss-an-overwhelmed-manager-a-botched-valuation-and-the-exploitation-of-workers.

———. "Strike, Legal Action, and Delusion." *The Petrified Muse*, February 26, 2018. https://thepetrifiedmuse.blog/2018/02/26/strike-legal-action-and-delusion.

Kulikowski, Michael. *The Triumph of Empire: The Roman World from Hadrian to Constantine*. Cambridge, MA: Harvard University Press, 2016.

Kyle, Donald G. *Sport and Spectacle in the Ancient World*. 2nd ed. Chichester: Wiley-Blackwell, 2015.

Ladage, Dieter. "*Collegia iuvenum*: Ausbildung einer municipalen Elite?" *Chiron* 9 (1979): 319–46.

Lafaurie, Jean. "Réformes monétaires d'Aurélien et de Dioclétian." *Revue Numismatique* 6, no. 17 (1975): 73–138.

Lafferty, Sean. "The Law." In *A Companion to Ostrogothic Italy*, edited by Jonathan J. Arnold, M. Shane Bjornlie, and Kristina Sessa, 147–72. Leiden: Brill, 2016.

Last, Richard, and Philip Harland. *Group Survival in the Ancient Mediterranean: Rethink-*

ing Material Conditions in the Landscape of Jews and Christians. New York: Bloomsbury Academic, 2020.

Lauffer, Siegfried, ed. *Diokletians Preisedikt*. Texte und Kommentare 5. Berlin: De Gruyter, 1971.

Lazzarini, Maria Letizia. "Pantomimi a Petelia." *Archeologia Classica* 55 (2004): 363–72.

Lee-Stecum, Parshia. "Dangerous Reputations: Charioteers and Magic in Fourth-Century Rome." *Greece and Rome* 53, no. 2 (2006): 224–34.

Le Guen, Brigitte. *Les Associations de Technites dionysiaques à l'époque hellénistique*. Vol. 1, *Corpus documentaire*. Vol. 2, *Synthèse (Études d'Archéologie Classique XI–XII)*. Nancy: Association pour la Diffusion de la Recherche sur l'Antiquité; Paris: De Boccard, 2001.

Lenski, Noel. *Failure of Empire: Valens and the Roman State in the Fourth Century A.D.* Berkeley: University of California Press, 2014.

———. "Framing the Question: What Is a Slave Society?" In *What Is a Slave Society? The Practice of Slavery in Global Perspective*, edited by Noel Lenski and Catherine M. Cameron, 15–60. Cambridge: Cambridge University Press, 2018.

———. "The Late Roman Colonate: A New Status between Slave and Free." In *The Oxford Handbook of Greek and Roman Slaveries*, online ed., edited by Stephen Hodkinson, Marc Kleijwegt, and Kostas Vlassopoulos. Oxford: Oxford Academic, 2022. https://doi.org/10.1093/oxfordhb/9780199575251.013.24.

———. "Peasant and Slave in Late Antique North Africa, c. 100–600 CE." In *Late Antiquity in Contemporary Debate*, edited by Rita Lizzi Testa, 113–55. Newcastle upon Tyne: Cambridge Scholars, 2017.

Lenski, Noel, and Catherine M. Cameron. *What Is a Slave Society? The Practice of Slavery in Global Perspective*. Cambridge: Cambridge University Press, 2018.

Levin, Flora R. *Greek Reflections on the Nature of Music*. Cambridge: Cambridge University Press, 2009.

Levin-Richardson, Sarah. *The Brothel of Pompeii: Sex, Class, and Gender at the Margin of Roman Society*. Cambridge: Cambridge University Press, 2019.

Liebeschuetz, Wolf. "Was There a Crisis of the Third Century?" In *Crises and the Roman Empire: Proceedings of the Seventh Workshop of the International Network Impact of Empire (Nijmegen, June 20–24, 2006)*, edited by Olivier Hekster, Gerda de Kleijn, and Daniëlle Slootjes, 11–20. Leiden: Brill, 2007.

Lim, Richard. "The Roman Pantomime Riot of AD 509." In *Humana Sapit. Études d'Antiquité Tardive Offertes à Lellia Cracco Ruggini*, edited by Jean-Michel Carrié and Rita Lizzi Testa, 35–42. Turnhout: Brepols, 2002.

———. "The *Tribunus Voluptatum* in the Later Roman Empire." *Memoirs of the American Academy in Rome* 41 (1996): 163–73.

Linderski, Jerzy. "Notes on CIL I² 364." In *Roman Questions: Selected Papers*, 1:362–65. Stuttgart: Franz Steiner, 1995.

———. "The Testimony of Asconius Concerning the Legal Status of the *Collegia* during the Decline of the Roman Republic." *Eos* 100 (2013): 202–10 (fasciculus electronicus). Originally published in Polish, *Eos* 50 (1959–60): 133–41.

Lintott, Andrew. *The Constitution of the Roman Republic*. Oxford: Oxford University Press, 1999.

———. "Electoral Bribery in the Roman Republic." *Journal of Roman Studies* 80 (1990): 1–16.
———. *Violence in Republican Rome*. Oxford: Oxford University Press, 1999.
Liu, Jinyu. *Collegia Centonariorum: The Guilds of Textile Dealers in the Roman West*. Leiden: Brill, 2009.
———. "Local Governments and *Collegia*: A New Appraisal of the Evidence." In *A Tall Order: Writing the Social History of the Ancient World: Essays in Honor of William V. Harris*, edited by Jean-Jacques Aubert and Zsuzsanna Várhelyi, 285–315. Leipzig: B. G. Teubner, 2005.
———. "Pompeii and *Collegia*: A New Appraisal of the Evidence." *Ancient History Bulletin* 22 (2008): 53–69.
———. "Professional Associations." In *The Cambridge Companion to Ancient Rome*, edited by Paul Erdkamp, 352–68. Cambridge: Cambridge University Press, 2013.
López Barja de Quiroga, Pedro. "Freedmen Social Mobility in Roman Italy." *Historia: Zeitschrift für Alte Geschichte* 44, no. 3 (3rd Qtr., 1995): 326–48.
———. "On Freedom and Citizenship: Freedmen as Agents and Metaphors of Roman Political Culture." In *A Companion to the Political Culture of the Roman Republic*, edited by Valentina Arena, Jonathan Prag, and Andrew Stiles, 374–86. Malden: Wiley-Blackwell, 2022.
López-Ruiz, Carolina. *Phoenicians and the Making of the Mediterranean*. Cambridge, MA: Harvard University Press, 2021.
Lott, J. Bert. *The Neighborhoods of Augustan Rome*. Cambridge: Cambridge University Press, 2011.
Lucas, Amelia. "Chipotle to Pay Ex-Employees $240,000 after Closing Maine Location That Tried to Unionize." CNBC, March 27, 2023. https://www.cnbc.com/2023/03/27/chipotle-to-pay-ex-employees-closing-location-union.html.
Machado, Carlos. "Statue Habit and Statue Culture in Late Antique Rome." *Journal of Roman Archaeology* 34, no. 2 (2021): 632–66.
———. *Urban Space and Aristocratic Power in Late Antique Rome: AD 270–535*. Oxford: Oxford University Press, 2019.
Machado, Dominic M. "Community and Collective Action in the Roman Republican Army (218–44 BCE)." PhD diss., Brown University, 2017.
MacLean, Rose. "People on the Margins of Roman Spectacle." In *A Companion to Sport and Spectacle in Greek and Roman Antiquity*, edited by Paul Christesen and Donald G. Kyle, 578–89. Malden, MA: Wiley-Blackwell, 2014.
MacMullen, Ramsay. *Corruption and the Decline of Rome*. New Haven: Yale University Press, 1988.
———. "The Epigraphic Habit in the Roman Empire." *American Journal of Philology* 103, no. 3 (Autumn 1982): 233–46.
———. "A Note on Roman Strikes." *Classical Journal* 58, no. 6 (March 1963): 269–71.
———. *Roman Social Relations: 50 B.C. to A.D. 284*. New Haven: Yale University Press, 1974.
Main, Robert William. "Mob Violence: The Political Influence of the Circus Factions in the Eastern Empire from the Reign of Leo I to Heraclius (457–641)," MA thesis, University of Ottawa, 2013.

Maniatis, George C. "The Guild System in Byzantium and Medieval Western Europe: A Comparative Analysis of Organizational Structures, Regulatory Mechanisms and Behavioral Patterns." *Byzantion* 76 (2006): 463–570.
Mann, Christian, and Sebastian Scharff. "Horse Races and Chariot Races in Ancient Greece: Struggling for Eternal Glory." In *The Running Centaur: Horse-Racing in Global-Historical Perspective,* edited by Sinclair W. Bell, Christian Jaser, and Christian Mann, 8–27. London: Routledge, 2022.
Martin, Jochen. "Die Provokation in der Klassischen und Späten Republik." *Hermes* 98, no. 1 (1970): 72–96.
Martroye, François. "Les parabalani." *Bulletin de la Société National des Antiquaires de France* (1923): 275–81.
Marx, Karl. *Value, Price and Profit: Addressed to Working Men.* London: Twentieth Century, 1908.
Marzano, Annalisa. *Harvesting the Sea: The Exploitation of Maritime Resources in the Roman Mediterranean.* Oxford Studies in the Roman Economy. Oxford: Oxford University Press, 2013.
Maspero, Jean, and Étienne Drioton. *Fouilles exécutées à Baouît.* Mémoires publiés par les membres de l'institut français d'archéologie orientale du Caire 59, 2. Cairo: Institut français d'archéologie orientale, 1943.
Maurice, Lisa. *The Teacher in Ancient Rome: The Magister and His World.* Plymouth: Lexington, 2013.
Mayall, Joe. "Americans Love Unions. The Supreme Court's Conservatives Are Gutting Them." Balls and Strikes, May 22, 2023. https://ballsandstrikes.org/law-politics/americans-love-unions-the-supreme-courts-conservatives-are-gutting-them/.
McGinn, Thomas A. J. "Sex and the City." In *The Cambridge Companion to Ancient Rome,* edited by Paul Erdkamp, 369–86. Cambridge: Cambridge University Press, 2013.
McLaughlin, Raoul. *The Roman Empire and the Indian Ocean.* Barnsley: Pen and Sword Military, 2014.
Meunier, Nicolas L. J. "The Decemvirate and the Second Secession of the Plebs (451–449 BCE): A Historiographical *fabula.*" In *Myth and History in the Historiography of Early Rome,* edited by Tim Cornell, Nicolas Meunier, and Daniele Miano, 155–84. Leiden: Brill, 2023.
Meyer, Elizabeth A. "Explaining the Epigraphic Habit in the Roman Empire: The Evidence of Epitaphs." *Journal of Roman Studies* 80 (1990): 74–96.
Mignone, Lisa Marie. *The Republican Aventine and Rome's Social Order.* Ann Arbor: University of Michigan Press, 2016.
Milliman, Paul. "The Decline and Fall of Spectacle." In *The Oxford Handbook Sport and Spectacle in the Ancient World,* edited by Alison Futrell and Thomas E. Scanlon, 194–206. Oxford: Oxford University Press, 2021.
Minasola, Castrenze. "*Collegia,* legislazione associativa e lotta politica nella tarda repubblica romana." *Teoria e Storia del Diritto Privato* 11 (2018): 1–58.
Minnen, Peter van. "An Antichretic Loan from Early Roman Alexandria Revisited ('BGU' IV 1053)." *Zeitschrift Für Papyrologie Und Epigraphik* 199 (2016): 144–54.
Moeller, Walter O. "The Riot of A.D. 59 at Pompeii." *Historia: Zeitschrift für Alte Geschichte* 19, no. 1 (January 1970): 84–95.

Moll-Murata, Christine. "Guilds and Apprenticeship in China and Europe: The Jingdezhen and European Ceramics Industries." In *Technology, Skills and the Pre-Modern Economy in the East and the West*, edited by Jan Luiten van Zanden and Marten Prak, 225–57. Leiden: Brill, 2013.

Monson, Andrew. "The Ethics and Economics of Ptolemaic Religious Associations." *Ancient Society* 36 (2006): 221–38.

Morris, Richard B. "Criminal Conspiracy and Early Labor Combinations in New York." *Political Science Quarterly* 52, no. 1 (March 1937): 51–85.

Mouritsen, Henrik. *Plebs and Politics in the Late Roman Republic*. Cambridge: Cambridge University Press, 2001.

Mueller, Hans-Friedrich. "Nocturni coetus in 494 BC." In *Augusto augurio: Rerum humanarum et divinorum commentationes in honorem Jerzy Linderski*, edited by C. F. Konrad, 77–88. Stuttgart: Franz Steiner, 2004.

Mulroy, David. "The Early Career of P. Clodius Pulcher: A Re-Examination of the Charges of Mutiny and Sacrilege." *Transactions of the American Philological Association* 118 (1988): 155–78.

Munier, Charles. *Concilia Galliae, a. 314–a.506*. Corpus Christianorum Series Latina 148. Turnhout: Brepols, 1963.

Naismith, Rory. "Gilds, States and Societies in the Early Middle Ages." *Early Medieval Europe* 28 (2020): 627–62.

Nasrallah, Laura. "The Acts of the Apostles, Greek Cities, and Hadrian's Panhellenion." *Journal of Biblical Studies* 127, no. 3 (2008): 533–66.

Nicolet, Claude. "Le temple des Nymphes et les distributions frumentaires à Rome à l'époque républicaine d'après des découvertes récentes." *Comptes rendus des séances de l'Académie des Inscriptions et Belles-Lettres* 120, no. 1 (1976): 29–51.

———. *The World of the Citizen in Republican Rome*. London: Batsford Academic and Educational, 1980.

Nijf, Onno van. *The Civic World of Professional Associations in the Roman East*. Amsterdam: J. C. Gieben, 1997.

Nuffelen, Peter van. "Deux Fausses Lettres de Julien l'Apostat (La Lettre aux Juifs, Ep. 51 [Wright], et La Lettre à Arsacius, Ep. 84 [Bidez])." *Vigiliae Christianae* 56, no. 2 (May 2002): 131–50.

Ogilvie, Sheilagh. *The European Guilds: An Economic Analysis*. Princeton: Princeton University Press, 2019.

———. *Institutions and European Trade: Merchant Guilds, 1000–1800*. Cambridge Studies in Economic History, 2nd ser. Cambridge: Cambridge University Press, 2011.

Orlandi, Silvia. *Epigrafia anfiteatrale dell'occidente romano VI. Roma. Anfiteatri e strutture annesse con una nuova edizione e commento delle iscrizioni del Colosseo*. Vetera 15. Rome: Quasar, 2004.

Osanna, Massimo. "Games, Banquets, Handouts, and the Population of Pompeii." *Journal of Roman Archaeology* 31 (2018): 310–22.

Padilla Peralta, Dan-el. "Slave Religiosity in the Roman Middle Republic." *Classical Antiquity* 36, no. 2 (October 2017): 317–69.

Padilla Peralta, Dan-el, and Seth Bernard. "Middle Republican Connectivities." *Journal of Roman Studies* 112 (2022): 1–37.

Pailler, Jean-Marie. "Dionysos against Rome? The Bacchanalian Affair: A Matter of Power(s)." In *Dionysus and Politics: Constructing Authority in the Graeco-Roman World*, edited by Filip Doroszewski and Dariusz Karłowicz, 63–88. New York: Routledge, 2021.

Panciera, Silvio. "Fasti Fabrum Tignariorum Urbis Romae." *Zeitschrift für Papyrologie und Epigraphik* 43 (1981): 271–80.

Patterson, John R. *Landscapes and Cities: Rural Settlement and Civic Transformation in Early Imperial Italy*. Oxford: Oxford University Press, 2006.

Patterson, Orlando. *Slavery and Social Death: A Comparative Study*. Cambridge, MA: Harvard University Press, 1982.

Peña, J. Theodore. "Recycling in the Roman World: Concepts, Questions, Materials, and Organization." In *Recycling and Reuse in the Roman Economy*, edited by Chloë Duckworth and Andrew Wilson, 9–60. Oxford: Oxford University Press, 2020.

Perry, Jonathan S. "*Collegia* and Their Impact on the Constitutional Structure of the Roman State." In *The Oxford Handbook of Roman Law and Society*, edited by Paul J. du Plessis, Clifford Ando, and Kaius Tuori, 137–50. Oxford: Oxford University Press, 2016.

———. "Organized Societies: *Collegia*." In *The Oxford Handbook of Social Relations in the Roman World*, edited by Michael Peachin, 498–515. Oxford: Oxford University Press, 2011.

———. *The Roman Collegia: The Modern Evolution of an Ancient Concept*. Mnemosyne Supplements. Vol. 277, History and Archaeology of Classical Antiquity. Leiden: Brill, 2006.

Phan, Hoang Gia. *Bonds of Citizenship: Law and the Labors of Emancipation*. New York: New York University Press, 2013.

Phang, Sara Elise. *Roman Military Service: Ideologies of Discipline in the Late Republic and Early Principate*. Cambridge: Cambridge University Press, 2008.

———. "Soldiers' Slaves, 'Dirty Work,' and the Social Status of Roman Soldiers." In *A Tall Order. Writing the Social History of the Ancient World: Essays in Honor of William V. Harris*, edited by Jean-Jacques Aubert and Zsuzsanna Várhelyi, 203–26. Leipzig: B. G. Teubner, 2005.

Pope, Rachel. "Re-Approaching Celts: Origins, Society, and Social Change." *Journal of Archaeological Research* 30 (2022): 1–67.

Popkin, Maggie. *Souvenirs and the Experience of Empire in Ancient Rome*. Cambridge: Cambridge University Press, 2022.

Potter, David S. "Anatomies of Violence: Entertainment and Politics in the Eastern Roman Empire from Theodosius I to Heraclius." *Studia Patristica* 60 (2013): 61–72.

———. "Entertainers in the Roman Empire." In *Life, Death, and Entertainment in the Roman Empire*, 2nd ed., edited by David S. Potter and David J. Mattingly, 280–329. Ann Arbor: University of Michigan Press, 2010.

Potter, David S., and D. J. Mattingly, eds. *Life, Death, and Entertainment in the Roman Empire*. Ann Arbor: University of Michigan Press, 1999.

Purpura, Gianfranco. "I curiosi e la schola agentum in rebus." *Annali de Seminario Giuridico dell'Università di Palermo* 34 (1973): 165–275.

Ramgopal, Sailakshmi. "Connectivity and Disconnectivity in the Roman Empire." *Journal of Roman Studies* 112 (2022): 215–35.

Rathbone, Dominic. "The Ancient Economy and Graeco-Roman Egypt." In *The Ancient Economy*, edited by Walter Scheidel and Sitta von Redden, 155–72. New York: Routledge, 2002.

Rauh, Nicholas K. *The Sacred Bonds of Commerce: Religion, Economy, and Trade Society at Hellenistic Roman Delos, 166–87 B.C.* Amsterdam: J. C. Gieben, 1993.

Rawson, Elizabeth. "*Discrimina Ordinum:* The *Lex Julia Theatralis.*" *Papers of the British School at Rome* 55 (1987): 83–114.

Rebillard, Éric. *The Care of the Dead in Late Antiquity*. Translated by Elizabeth Trapnell Rawlings and Jeanine Routier-Pucci. Ithaca: Cornell University Press, 2009.

Reden, Sitta von. *Money in Ptolemaic Egypt: From the Macedonian Conquest to the End of the Third Century BC*. Cambridge: Cambridge University Press, 2007.

Rehm, Rush. "Festivals and Audiences in Athens and Rome." In *The Cambridge Companion to Greek and Roman Theatre*, edited by Marianne McDonald and J. Michael Walton, 184–201. Cambridge: Cambridge University Press, 2007.

Remijsen, Sofie. *The End of Greek Athletics in Late Antiquity*. Cambridge: Cambridge University Press, 2015.

———. "The Surprisingly Long History of the Olympics of Antioch (AD 212–520)." *Syria* [En ligne] 97 (2020): 129–42.

Reyerson, Kathryn L. *Women's Networks in Medieval France: Gender and Community in Montpellier, 1300–1350*. Cham: Springer International, 2016.

Richard, Jean-Claude. "Sur les prétendues corporations numaïques: à propos de Plutarque, *Núm.* 17, 3." *Klio* 60 (1978): 423–28.

Richardson, Peter. "Early Synagogues as Collegia in the Diaspora and Palestine." In *Voluntary Associations in the Graeco-Roman World*, edited by J. S. Kloppenborg and S. G. Wilson, 90–109. London: Routledge, 1996.

Riggsby, Andrew. *Roman Law and the Legal World of the Romans*. Cambridge: Cambridge University Press, 2010.

Rigsby, Kent J. *Asylia: Territorial Inviolability in the Hellenistic World*. Berkeley: University of California Press, 1996.

———. "On the Early Technitai of Dionysus." *Studi ellenistici* 31 (2017): 283–86.

Rives, James B. "The Decree of Decius and the Religion of Empire." *Journal of Roman Studies* 89 (1999): 135–54.

Robinson, O. F. *Ancient Rome: City Planning and Administration*. New York: Routledge, 1992.

Rocca, Samuele. "From Collegium to Ecclesia: The Changing Outer Framework of the Jewish Communities in Roman Italy." In *In the Crucible of Empire: The Impact of Roman Citizenship upon Greeks, Jews, and Christians*, edited by Katell Berthelot and Jonathan J. Price, 217–48. Leuven: Peeters, 2019.

Roselaar, Saskia T. *Italy's Economic Revolution: Integration and Economy in Republican Italy*. Oxford: Oxford University Press, 2019.

———. "Roman State Prisoners in Latin and Italian Cities." *Classical Quarterly* 62, no. 1 (2012): 189–200.

Rosenblum, Jordan. *Food and Identity in Early Rabbinic Judaism*. Cambridge: Cambridge University Press, 2010.
Rostovtzeff, Mikhail. *The Social and Economic History of the Roman Empire*. Oxford: Clarendon, 1926.
Roueché, Charlotte. *Performers and Partisans at Aphrodisias in the Roman and Late Roman Periods*. Journal of Roman Studies Monographs 6. London: Society for the Promotion of Roman Studies, 1993.
Rowlandson, Jane. *Women and Society in Greek and Roman Egypt: A Sourcebook*. Cambridge: Cambridge University Press, 1998.
Rule, John. *The Labouring Classes in Early Industrial England, 1750–1850*. London: Routledge, 1986.
Russell, Amy. "Why Did Clodius Shut the Shops? The Rhetoric of Mobilizing a Crowd in the Late Republic." *Historia: Zeitschrift für Alte Geschichte* 65, no. 2 (2016): 186–210.
Rutgers, Leonard Victor. "Roman Policy towards the Jews: Expulsions from the City of Rome during the First Century C.E." *Classical Antiquity* 13, no. 1 (April 1994): 56–74.
Rutter, N. K. "The Coinage of Italy." In *The Oxford Handbook of Greek and Roman Coinage*, edited by William E. Metcalf, 128–41. Oxford: Oxford University Press, 2012.
Salzman, Michele Renee. *The Falls of Rome: Crises, Resilience, and Resurgence in Late Antiquity*. New York: Cambridge University Press, 2021.
Samuel, Alan E. *Greek and Roman Chronology: Calendars and Years in Classical Antiquity*. Munich: Beck, 1972.
Sancinito, Jane. *The Reputation of the Roman Merchant*. Ann Arbor: University of Michigan Press, 2024.
Santangelo, Federico. *Sulla, the Elites and the Empire: A Study of Roman Policies in Italy and the Greek East*. Impact of Empire 8. Leiden: Brill, 2007.
Scheidel, Walter. "Real Wages in Early Economies: Evidence for Living Standards from 1800 BCE to 1300 CE." *Journal of the Economic and Social History of the Orient* 53, no. 3 (2010): 425–62.
———. "The Roman Slave Supply." In *The Cambridge World History of Slavery*. Vol. 1, *The Ancient Mediterranean World*, edited by Keith Bradley and Paul Cartledge, 287–310. Cambridge: Cambridge University Press, 2011.
Schmidt, Walter. ""Der Einfluss Der Anachoresis Im Rechtsleben Ägyptens Zur Ptolemäerzeit." PhD diss., Universität zu Köln, 1966.
Scott, James C. *Weapons of the Weak: Everyday Forms of Peasant Resistance*. New Haven: Yale University Press, 1985.
Segrè, Angelo. "Studies in the Byzantine Economy: *Iugatio* and *Capitatio*." *Traditio* 3 (1945): 101–27.
Serrati, John. "Garrisons and Grain: Sicily between the Punic Wars." In *Sicily from Aeneas to Augustus: New Approaches in Archaeology and History*, edited by Christopher Smith and John Serrati, 115–33. Edinburgh: University of Edinburgh Press, 2000.
———. "Neptune's Altars: The Treaties between Rome and Carthaga (509–226 B.C.)." *Classical Quarterly* 56, no. 1 (2006): 113–34.

Sessa, Kristina. *Daily Life in Late Antiquity.* Cambridge: Cambridge University Press, 2018.
Shaw, Brent D. "Rural Markets in North Africa and the Political Economy of the Roman Empire." *Antiquités africaines* 17 (1981): 37–83.
———. *Spartacus and the Slave Wars: A Brief History with Documents.* Boston: Bedford/St. Martin's, 2001.
Sheldon, Richard D. "The London Sailors' Strike of 1768." In *An Atlas of Industrial Protest in Britain, 1750–1990,* edited by Andrew Charlesworth, David Gilbert, and Adrian Randall, 12–17. London: MacMillan, 1996.
Skinner, Alexander. "Political Mobility in the Later Roman Empire." *Past and Present* 218 (2013): 17–53.
Skotheim, Mali. "Association and Archive: The Technitai of Dionysus as Keepers of Knowledge." Paper presented at the 150th Annual Meeting of the Society for Classical Studies, San Diego, CA, January 3–6, 2019.
Smallwood, E. Mary. *The Jews under Roman Rule: From Pompey to Diocletian.* Studies in Judaism in Late Antiquity 20. Leiden: Brill, 1976.
———. "Some Notes on the Jews under Tiberius." *Latomus* 15, no. 3 (1956): 314–29.
Spagnolo, Benjamin, and Joe Sampson. "Principle and Pragmatism." In *Principle and Pragmatism in Roman Law,* edited by Benjamin Spagnolo and Joe Sampson, 1–26. Oxford: Hart, 2020.
Spielman, Loren R. *Jews and Entertainment in the Ancient World.* Texts and Studies in Ancient Judaism 181. Tübingen: Mohr Siebeck, 2020.
Ste. Croix, G. E. M. de. *The Class Struggle in the Ancient Greek World: From the Archaic Age to the Arab Conquests.* Ithaca: Cornell University Press, 1981.
Stephanis, I. E. *Dionysiakoi Technitai: Symboles stên prosôpographia tou theatrou kai mousikês tôn archaiôn Hellênôn.* Heraklion: University of Crete, 1988.
Stewart, Roberta. *Plautus and Roman Slavery.* Malden: Wiley-Blackwell, 2012.
Strauss, Barry. *The Spartacus War.* New York: Simon and Schuster, 2009.
Sudi, Francoise. "Les esclaves et les affranchis publics dans l'occident romain (IIe siècle avant J.-C.–IIIe siècle après J.-C.)." PhD diss., Université Blaise Pascal-Clermont-Ferrand II, 2013.
Talbert, Richard J. A. *Rome's World: The Peutinger Map Reconsidered.* Cambridge: Cambridge University Press, 2010.
Tan, James. *Power and Public Finance at Rome, 264–49 BCE.* Oxford Studies in Early Empires. New York: Oxford University Press, 2017.
Tatum, W. Jeffrey. *The Patrician Tribune: Publius Clodius Pulcher.* Chapel Hill: University of North Carolina Press, 1999.
Taylor, Lily Ross. *Local Cults in Etruria.* Papers and Monographs of the American Academy in Rome 2. Rome: American Academy in Rome, 1923.
Terrenato, Nicola. *The Early Roman Expansion into Italy: Elite Negotiation and Family Agendas.* New York: Cambridge University Press, 2019.
Thapar, Romila. *Early India: From the Origins to AD 1300.* Berkeley: University of California Press, 2002.
Thaplyal, Kiran Kumar. *Guilds in Ancient India: A Study of Guild Organization in North-*

ern India and Western Deccan from circa 600 BC to circa 600 AD. New Delhi: New Age International, 1996.
Toner, Jerry P. *Leisure and Ancient Rome.* Cambridge: Polity, 1995.
Traina, Giusto. "Lycoris the Mime." Translated by Linda Lappin. In *Roman Women*, edited by Augusto Fraschetti, 82–99. Chicago: University of Chicago Press, 2001.
Tran, Nicolas. *Les Membres des Associations Romaines: Le Rang Social des Collegiati en Italie et en Gaules sous le Haut-Empire.* Rome: Écoles Française de Rome, 2006.
———. "The Social Organization of Commerce and Crafts in Ancient Arles: Heterogeneity, Hierarchy, and Patronage." In *Urban Craftsmen and Traders in the Roman World*, edited by Andrew Wilson and Miko Flohr, 254–77. Oxford Studies on the Roman Economy. Oxford: Oxford University Press, 2016.
Trout, Dennis E. "Damasus and the Invention of Early Christian Rome." In *The Cultural Turn in Late Ancient Studies: Gender, Asceticism, and Historiography*, edited by Dale B. Martin and Patricia Cox Miller, 298–315. Durham, NC: Duke University Press, 2005.
Trümper, Monika. "Das Sanktuarium des 'Établissement des Poseidoniastes de Bérytos' in Delos. Zur Baugeschichte eines griechischen Vereinsheiligtums." *Bulletin de Correspondance Hellénique* 126, no. 1 (2002): 265–330.
———. "Where the Non-Delians Met in Delos: The Meeting-Places of Foreign Associations and Ethnic Communities in Late Hellenistic Delos." In *Political Culture in the Greek City after the Classical Age*, edited by Onno van Nijf and Richard Alston, 49–100. Leuven: Peeters, 2011.
Tuck, Steven L. "*Ludi* and *Factiones* as Organizations of Performers." In *The Oxford Handbook of Sport and Spectacle in the Ancient World*, edited by Thomas F. Scanlon and Alison Futrell, 534–44. Oxford: Oxford University Press, 2021.
Ungern-Sternberg, Jürgen von. "The Formation of the 'Annalistic Tradition': The Example of the Decemvirate." In *Social Struggles in Archaic Rome: New Perspectives on the Conflict of the Orders*, 2nd ed., edited by Kurt A. Raaflaub, 75–97. Malden: Blackwell, 2005.
United States Bureau of Labor Statistics. "Work Stoppages." January 23, 2019. https://www.bls.gov/opub/hom/wsp/concepts.htm.
United States Department of Labor. "Union Basics: What Is a Union?" December 24, 2022. https://www.workcenter.gov/what-is-a-union.
Urbainczyk, Theresa. *Slave Revolts in Antiquity.* Berkeley: University of California Press, 2008.
Vanderbroeck, Paul J. J. *Popular Leadership and Collective Behavior in the Late Roman Republic (ca. 80–50 B.C.).* Amsterdam: J. C. Gieben, 1987.
Velden, Sjaak van der. "8.3. Strikes, Lockouts, and Informal Resistance." In *Handbook: The Global History of Work*, edited by Karin Hofmeester and Marcel van der Linden, 521–48. Berlin: De Gruyter Oldenbourg, 2018.
Venticinque, Philip F. *Honor among Thieves: Craftsmen, Merchants, and Associations in Roman and Late Roman Egypt.* New Texts from Ancient Cultures. Ann Arbor: University of Michigan Press, 2016.

Verboven, Koenraad. "Associations, Roman." *Oxford Classical Dictionary*, December 22, 2015. https://doi.org/10.1093/acrefore/9780199381135.013.1695.

———. "The Freedman Economy of Roman Italy." In *Free at Last! The Impact of Freed Slaves on the Roman Empire*, edited by Sinclair Bell and Teresa R. Ramsby, 88–109. London: Bristol Classical, 2012.

———. "Guilds and Gods: Religious Profiles of Occupational *collegia* and the Problem of the *dendrophori*." In *The Economy of Roman Religion*, edited by Andrew Wilson, Nick Ray, and Angela Trentacoste, 267–309. Oxford: Oxford University Press, 2023.

———. "Guilds and the Organisation of Urban Populations during the Principate." In *Work, Labour, and Professions in the Roman World*, edited by Koenraad Verboven and Christian Laes, 173–202. Leiden: Brill, 2017.

———. "The Structure of Mercantile Communities in the Roman World: How Open Were Roman Trade Networks?" In *Roman Port Societies: The Evidence of Inscriptions*, edited by Pascal Arnaud and Simon Keay, 326–66. Cambridge: Cambridge University Press, 2020.

Verboven, Koenraad et al. *Ghent Database of Roman Guilds*, Ghent University, April 2020. https://gdrg.ugent.be.

Vernus, Pascal. *Affaires et scandales sous les Ramsès: La crise des valeurs dans l'Égypte du Nouvel Empire*. Paris: Bibliothèque de l'Égypte Ancienne, 1993.

Vesley, Mark. "Gladiatorial Training for Girls in the *Collegia Iuvenum* of the Roman Empire." *Échos du monde classique: Classical views*, n.s. 17, 42, no. 1 (1998): 85–93.

Veyne, Paul. "La 'plèbe moyenne' sous le Haut-Empire romain." *Annales: Histoires, Sciences Sociales* 55, no. 6 (November–December 2000): 1169–99.

———. *The Roman Empire*. Translated by Arthur Goldhammer. Cambridge, MA: Harvard University Press, 1997.

Virlouvet, Catherine. "Les Naviculaires d'Arles. À propos de l'inscription provenant de Beyrouth." *Mélanges de l'École française de Rome-Antiquité* 116, no. 1 (2004): 327–70.

Voorhis, Julie Van. *The Sculptor's Workshop*. Aphrodisias 10. Wiesbaden: Reichert, 2018.

Vryonis, Speros. "Byzantine Δ and the Guilds in the Eleventh Century." *Dumbarton Oaks Papers* 17 (1963): 287–314.

Wachtel, Howard M. *Labor and the Economy*. London: Academic, 1984.

Wacke, Andreas. "*Gloria* und *virtus* als Ziel athletischer Wettkämpfe und die Unbescholtenheit der Athleten sowie die erlaubten Sportwetten nach römischen Rechtsquellen." In *Kultur(en). Formen des Alltäglichen in der Antike*. Festschrift für Ingomar Weiler zum 75, edited by Peter Mauritsch and Christoph Ulf, 193–236. Graz: Leykam Buchverlag, 2013.

Walker, Cheryl. "Hostages in Republican Rome." PhD diss., University of North Carolina–Chapel Hill, 1980.

Walker-Ramisch, Sandra. "Graeco-Roman Voluntary Associations and the Damascus Document: A Sociological Analysis." In *Voluntary Associations in the Graeco-Roman World*, edited by John S. Kloppenborg and Stephen G. Wilson, 128–45. London: Routledge, 1996.

Waltzing, Jean-Pierre. *Étude historique sur les corporations professionnelles chez les romains depuis les origines jusqu'à la chute de l'empire d'occident. Mémoire couronne par l'Academie Royale des Sciences, des Lettres et des Beaux-Arts de Belgique.* 4 vols. 1895–1900; repr., New York: Arno, 1979.

Washburn, Daniel. *Banishment in the Later Roman Empire, 284–476 CE.* New York: Routledge, 2012.

Watts, Edward J. *Hypatia: The Life and Legend of an Ancient Philosopher.* Oxford: Oxford University Press, 2017.

Weiler, Ingomar. "Theodosius I. und die Olympischen Spiele." *Nikephoros* 17 (2004): 53–75.

Welch, Katherine E. *The Roman Amphitheatre: From Its Origins to the Colosseum.* Cambridge: Cambridge University Press, 2007.

Wendt, Heidi. "*Iudaica Romana:* A Rereading of Evidence for Judean Expulsions from Rome." *Journal of Ancient Judaism* 6, no. 1 (2015): 97–126.

Whitby, Michael. "Factions, Bishops, Violence and Urban Decline." In *Die Stadt in der Spätantike—Niedergang oder Wandel? Akten des internationalen Kolloquiums in München am 30. und 31. Mai 2003. Historia Einzelschriften Bd. 190,* edited by Jens-Uwe Krause and Christian Witschel, 441–61. Stuttgart: Franz Steiner, 2006.

———. *The Wars of Justinian I.* Havertown, PA: Pen and Sword, 2021.

Whiting, Marlena. "Braided Networks: Pilgrimage and the Economics of Travel Infrastructure in the Late Antiquity Holy Land." In *Pilgrimage and Economy in the Ancient Mediterranean,* edited by Anna Collar and Troels Myrup Kristensen, 62–90. Leiden: Brill, 2020.

Wiessner, Daniel. "Ex-Starbucks CEO Schultz Illegally Threatened Union Supporter, NLRB Judge Rules." *Reuters,* October 9, 2023. https://www.reuters.com/legal/government/ex-starbucks-ceo-schultz-illegally-threatened-union-supporter-nlrb-judge-rules-2023-10-09/.

Witschel, Christian. *Krise-Rezession-Stagnation? Der Westen des römischen Reiches im 3. Jahrhundert n. Chr.* Frankfurt: Clauss, 1999.

Woolf, Greg. *Rome: An Empire's Story.* 2nd ed. Oxford: Oxford University Press, 2022.

Zanda, Emanuela. *Fighting Hydra-Like Luxury: Sumptuary Regulation in the Roman Republic.* London: Bristol Classical, 2011.

Ziche, Hartmut. "Making Late Roman Taxpayers Pay: Imperial Government Strategies and Practice." In *Violence in Late Antiquity: Perceptions and Practices,* edited by Harold A. Drake, 127–36. Aldershot: Ashgate, 2006.

Zimmermann, Carola. *Handwerkvereine im griechischen Osten des Imperium Romanum.* Mainz: Verlag des Römisch-Germanischen Zentralmuseums, 2002.

Zosimus. *The History of Count Zosimus, Sometime Advocate and Chancellor of the Roman Empire.* Translated from the original Greek, with the notes of the Oxford edition. London: W. Green and T. Chaplin, 1814.

INDEX

Page numbers in *italics* refer to illustrations and maps.

acting troupes. *See* entertainers; entertainment associations
Adrianople, Battle of, 161, 162
Aelius Marcianus (jurist), 106
agonistic associations, 98, 126–27
akhis (guilds), 185
Alans, 165
Alaric (general), 165, 168–69
American Federation of Labor (AFL), 191n25
American Guild of Variety Artists (AGVA), 48
Ammianus Marcellinus (historian), 158–59
amphitheaters. *See* theaters and amphitheaters
Anastasius (emperor), 177
Antoninus Pius (Titus Aelius Hadrianus Antoninus Pius) (emperor), 127, 197n24
Appian (historian), 68, 76, 86
Appius Claudius Sabinus (consul), 25
Arcadius (emperor), 152–53
argyropratai (silversmiths) association, 117–19, 181
Arianism, 162

Aristotle (philosopher), 18
Arnaoutoglou, Ilias N., 106
artisans. *See also* laborers; merchant associations; merchants: contempt for and biases against, 36–38; cooking as *ars* (skill), 57; growth of, 30; monastic economies, 173–75; occupational pride, 174; as political instruments, 77; Second Punic War and, 53; as soldiers, 37; *zographoi*, 174–75
Asconius (historian), 74, 94, 199n8
assassins, 181
assemblies. *See also* Christ-followers; collective action and bargaining; Jews: anti-assembly legislation, 3, 46, 58–59, 104–8, 118–19; attempts to control, 112; Centuriate Assembly, 30–31; drinking clubs and religious pretence, 106; legislation on places for, 99, 107; permission for, 86–87, 90–91, 200n10; right revoked for associations, 84–85; senators' concern over plebeian, 26; taverns and pubs, 99, 107, 116; theatrical spaces and entertainers, 49, 99

INDEX

associations. *See also* athlete associations; Bacchus, cult of; Christ-followers; Christianity; collective action and bargaining; *coloni*; colonies; *corporati* system; corruption; entertainment associations; *familiae*; fire brigades; gladiators; inscriptions; Jews; labor unions; law and legislation; merchant associations; organized labor; patronage; Pompeii; private associations; slavery; trade; *individual associations*: agonistic associations, 98, 126–27; *akhis*, 185; *Ambubaiae* (female musicians), 103; in Ancient Greece, 17–19; appeals to, during elections, 78; associative networks, 119; Athenian attitudes, 32; bans on, 15, 73–74, 84, 85–86, 88–89, 90, 94, 116, 126; bishops and monks and, 171–73; under Clodius's plebeian tribunate, 73, 74, 78, 80; *collegia teniorum* loophole, 109; *collegium poetarum*, 49; as *coniurationes* (conspiracies), 183; continuity over time, 48; *corpus/collegium cocorum*, 56; decline traced, 171; elite religious associations, 27–28; entrance fees, 79; fear of, 26–27, 88–89, 99, 109, 112–13, 123, 125; freedmen within, 78, 79–80; gendered participation, 27–28, 101–4; golden age, 130; historiography of, 11–13; illegal associations, 15, 116; legal security, 48; licenses for gathering, 90–91, 115; mediators in long-distance trade, 115; medieval and Byzantine overview, 181–85; membership demographics, 27–28, 78–79; membership rules for men and women, 78–79, 101–2, 121, 171, 172; *mercatorum collegium*, 25; neighborhoods and, 73, 74, 78; number of, 5; organization of, 4, 112; origin stories and myths, 14–19; plebeian integration, 41; political associations dissolved, 82; political clubs, 82, 106, 107; as political instruments, 81–82; in Pompeii, 89–93; as private militia and bodyguards, 172–73; public utility, 94, 126; purposes of, 4, 12–13, 16–19, 55–56, 70, 79; regulations on, 32, 86, 93–98, 109; restrictions on those associated with, 85; rise in, 17, 44, 57, 94–95, 115; risk mitigation, 48–49; in Roman Egypt, 105–6; seating patterns and associative identity, 163–64; Senate resented by, 73–74; social mobility through, 80; solidarity and redress, 103; state interest in, 73, 120–21, 127–28, 148–49, 150–51, 153; Sulla's political program and, 76; terms for, 10, 209n37; unofficial, 115; women's presence in, 101–4; youth associations, 90–91

Athenion (enslaved leader), 64
athlete associations, 126–27, 130, 164. *See also* charioteers; *corporati* system; entertainment associations; gladiatorial combat
Attila (king), 175–76
augurs, college of, 27
Augustus (emperor). *See* Octavian-Augustus (emperor)
Aulus Avilius Flaccus (prefect), 104–5, 106–7
Aulus Gellius (writer), 57
Aurelian (emperor), 134, 135–36
Aurelian Wall, 135–36
Aurelius Victor (historian), 142, 148
Ausonius (writer), 50

Bacchus, cult of, 3, 46, 58–59, 126
Bailey, Shackleton, 198n61
baker associations, 45, 120–21, 149–50, 151–52, 165. *See also* cook associations
Banaji, Jairus, 171

banker and moneychanger associations, 28, 143–44, 171, 181, 183
barbarians, 160–61, 162, 165, 167–68, 175–76
barge-owner and fishermen associations, 166
bath worker (*Zeuxippitai*) associations, 172–73
Beek, Aaron, 65
Belisarius (general), 176, 181
Bernard, Seth, 40
Boatwright, Mary T., 210n50
Bona Dea festival, 27
Bradley, Keith, 218n102
Brentano, Lujo, 12
builder associations, 125–26, 136, 146–47. See also *fabri* (construction worker) associations
bureaucrat associations, 147, 149
Burgundians, 176
Buthericus (commander), 162–63

Caesarius (bishop), 171
Caligula (emperor), 104, 107
Callistratus (jurist), 90
Cameron, Alan, 163, 179, 217n97
Campbell, Brian, 206n63
Cassiodorus (statesman), 175
Cassius Dio. *See* Dio (Cassius Dio)
castes, 139, 150. *See also* class struggle; patricians and elites; plebeians; social order conflicts
Catilinarian conspiracy, 77–78
"Catiline" (Lucius Sergius Catilina) (politician), 75, 77–78
Celts, 38–39, 195n45
Censorinus (writer), 191n32
Centuriate Assembly, 30–31
Charioteer Papyrus, 177
charioteers. *See also* circuses and hippodromes: agency of enslaved and manumitted persons, 179–80; *artes lubricae* (slippery arts), 175; connections to elites, 159, 176–78;

enslaved people as, 158; *factiones*, 97, 156, 157, 158, 160, 175, 176–78; *familiae quadrigariae*, 157, 160; killing of Buthericus, 162–63; magic and, 159; marriage restrictions on, 165; organization, 97, 157, 158–59; as personal militias and bodyguards, 160; as public figures, 158, 178–79; rebellion and collective action, 157; rioting, 158–59, 177, 178–79; social stigma, 157, 158; sociopolitical sway, 177
Chipotle, 186
Christ-followers: assemblies, 98–99, 107, 108–9, 117–18, 123–24, 126; associations, 101, 117–18; exclusion of entertainers, 157; Jews and, 107; persecution of, 123, 138; religious and economic dissent, 124, 126; riots and, 107, 117–19; suspicion of, 101, 108–9, 123–24, 126
Christianity, 161–62, 173–75, 183
Cicero (Marcus Tullius Cicero) (orator), 8, 41, 72–73, 77, 80–82, 103, 191n32
circuses and hippodromes. *See also* charioteers; entertainers; gladiatorial combat: agency of enslaved and manumitted persons, 179–80; collective action, 156, 179; factions, 97, 156–57, 163; *ludi circenses* (circus races), 157–58; as mediating spaces, 163, 165; seating, 97, 163–64; space for honor and status, 166
citrus-wood trader associations, 166–67
class struggle, 6, 28, 33. *See also* castes; commerce; First Secession of the Plebs; migration; rebellions and riots; slave revolts; Struggle of the Orders; trade
Claudian (poet), 166
Claudius (Tiberius Claudius Caesar Augustus Germanicus) (emperor), 107–8, 197n24
Claudius Julianus (prefect), 128

Cleon (enslaved leader), 62, 63
Clinton, Catherine, 55
Clodius (Publius Clodius Pulcher) (statesman), 15, 70–76, 77, 80–81, 82, 83
Clodius's plebeian tribunate: Cicero's exile, 80–82; Clodius's death, 83; *collegia* under, 73, 74, 78, 80; Compitalia games resumed, 74; courting current and former enslaved, 73, 75–76, 77; freedmen's suffrage, 77; grain, 82; methods, derivation of, 74–76; populist politics and tactics, 73, 75, 80; rivalry with Pompey, 80–81; Senate's dissolving political associations, 82; violence during, 73, 75, 81
Closs, Virginia, 209n31
coercitio, 29
Coleman, Kathleen, 114
collective action and bargaining. *See also* First Secession of the Plebs; rebellions and riots; secession; wage strikes; work stoppages: bakers, 151–52; bans on, in eighteenth century, 2–3, 189n4; business owners' strategies against workers, 112; charioteers, 157; circus factions, 156, 179; commercial regulation, 143; Egyptian wage strike, 1–2, 7; entertainment associations, 45–49, 100; leverage, 127–28, 129–30, 133; marginalized persons and, 10; over wages, 99, 110–12; physical removal and, 26–27, 29, 111–12, 128–29, 151–52; plebian collective bargaining, 22–23; revoking sanctuary, 152–53
collectives. *See* associations
collegia. *See* associations
coloni (tenant farmers), 128–30, 139–40, 142
colonies, 84–85
commerce. *See also* grain; merchant associations; trade: biases against, 36–38; covert activity among elites, 36–37, 38; Edict of Maximum Prices, 144–46, 145; mint workers, 132–34; monastic economies, 173–75; property valued over, 36; public utility, 130–31; regulation, 143; supply chains, 113, 127–28, 130–31, 146–47, 165; treaties, 35–36
Compitalia, 52, 74, 77
conspiracies, 183. *See also* Christ-followers; secession
Constantine (emperor), 147, 149, 164
Constantius II (emperor), 150–51
cook associations, 45, 56. *See also* baker associations
cooking as *ars*, 57
Cornell, T. J., 195n55
corporati system, 113, 133, 149–50, 165
corpus/collegium cocorum, 56
corpus fabricensium. *See* builder associations
corruption. *See also* mint workers: anti-corruption efforts, 138–39, 141–46, 147–48, 153–54; coinage, 143–44; *cursus publicus* and, 148–49; defined, 138–39, 212n18; in historiography of Roman Empire, 140–41; power abuses, 29–31, 33–34, 147, 212n18; protections for associations, 153; recordkeeping, 143; state trade associations, 146; surveillance and spying, 148, 150–51; tax collection, 141–42
Council of the Plebs, 26, 29
Crisis of the Third Century, 138, 211n15
curiosi (snoopers), 148, 150–51
cursus publicus (postal system), 148–49
Cybele, cult of, 58
Cyril of Alexandria (patriarch), 172

Damasus (bishop), 160
debt bondage, 25–26, 28, 40, 41, 159. *See also* Roman military; Struggle of the Orders
decemviri, 31, 32, 34

INDEX

De Robertis, Francesco Maria, 207n6
Dey, Hendrik, 136
Dilley, Paul, 174
Dio (Cassius Dio) (historian), 80, 101, 107
Dio Chrysostom (orator), 121
Diocletian (emperor), 138, 139–40, 141–42, 144–45, 146, 147
Diodorus Siculus (historian), 62, 64
Dionysius. See *technitai* of Dionysus
Dionysius of Halicarnassus (historian), 22–25, 26, 191n32
Dioscorus (patriarch), 173
Diosono, Francesca, 5
divination, 159
documentary culture, 141–43
Domitian (emperor), 92, 116, 158
drinking clubs, 106, 184
Drury, John, 8

Edict of Thessalonica (*Cunctos populos*), 161–62
Egyptian riots, 104–5, 119
Eisenbichler, Konrad, 184
elites. See patricians and elites
Engels, Friedrich, 7
enslaved persons. See also freedmen (*liberti*); manumission; Servile Wars; slave revolts; slavery; Spartacus: acting as alternative states, 64, 65; agency of, 179–80; *calones* (military enslaved persons), 133; courted by Clodius's plebeian tribunate, 73, 75–76, 77; as entertainers and athletes, 65, 66, 114, 157, 158; *familiae* used by emperors, 95; fears raised by, 54, 65, 69, 77, 210n41; as gladiators, 50–51; Jews, 78; legal status, 55, 197n24; as political tools, 76–77, 80; professional enslaved cooks, 57; sack of Rome aided by, 169; *servi publici* (state-owned enslaved persons), 53, 95; *Zeuxippitai* (bath workers), 172–73

entertainers. See also athlete associations; circuses and hippodromes; games; gladiators; sex workers; theaters and amphitheaters: *Ambubaiae*, 103; assemblies, 49; clubhouses, 49; forced labor, 114; growth of and liberties, 49; marriage restrictions on, 164–65, 178; pantomimes and mimes, 99–100, 102, 175, 176–77, 178; patronage of, 100, 130; proxy for imperial family, 175; rioting, 99–100, 177; socioeconomic impact, 175; as soldiers, 81; stigmas and biases toward, 85, 97, 157, 200n21

entertainment associations. See also charioteers; *corporati* system; games: *artes lubricae* (slippery arts), 175; collective bargaining, 45–49, 100; festival circuits, 98; freedmen in, 81; funding and oversight, 175; labor unions, analogous to, 46–47; means of protection, 97, 103, 196n3; merging of, 164, 170; mobilization, 46–47, 100; organization of, 81, 163; patronage of, 45; political stances taken by, 81; Romanization of, 57–58; seating patterns at spectacles, 163–64; women in, 102–3

Ephesus riots, 117–20
Epstein, Stephen R., 218n9
Eunus (enslaved leader), 62, 63
Eutyches (abbot), 173
Evers, Kasper Grønlund, 167
exile, 159. See also Cicero (Marcus Tullius Cicero)

fabri (construction worker) associations, 79, 136, 137, 210n45–n46
fabricenses (imperial factory workers), 146–47
factions and *factiones*. See charioteers; circuses and hippodromes; collective action and bargaining

Fagan, Garrett, 68, 163–64
familiae. *See also* gladiatorial troupes: bonds of, 44–45, 68–69; charioteers, 157, 160; *familia publica*, 53; gladiators, 50–51, 66–68, 80–81, 83; labor organization under slavery, 45–46, 48, 55, 95, 133; Servile Wars and, 44–45, 62, 64, 68
farmers, 128–30, 139–40, 142
Fauconnier, Bram, 98
Finley, Moses, 12
fire brigades, 94–95, 112–13, 122–23
First Punic War, 51–52
First Secession of the Plebs, 23–27, 28, 29. *See also* debt bondage
First Triumvirate, 82
flamines (priests of the Capitoline Triad), 27
Flavian (patriarch), 173
Flavius Leontius (prefect), 158–59
Flavius Stilicho (commander, regent), 165, 166, 167, 168
Flower, Harriet, 200n10
foederati, 162, 165
fossores (gravedigger) associations, 160
Frank, Tenney, 8, 9, 190n14
freedmen (*liberti*). *See also* associations; enslaved persons; manumission; slavery; Struggle of the Orders: agency, 179–80; in associations, 78, 79–80, 81; in colonies, 84; growth of, 41, 201n30; as instruments of political will, 73, 75–77; legal rights and limitations, 41; population of, 78; *vicomagistri* (freedman magistrates), 52; voting rights, 77; as watchmen, 95
funeral workers and stretcher-bearers (*parabolani*), 172–73
Futrell, Alison, 196n11

Gabba, Emilio, 15
Gaius (Caligula) (emperor), 104, 107
Gaius (legal expert), 32
Gaius Aquilius (consul), 65
Gaius Gracchus (politician and tribune), 73
Gaius Julius Caesar. *See* Julius Caesar
Gaius Manilius (tribune), 77
Gaius Marius (consul), 63
Gaius Plautius (consul), 37
games. *See also* charioteers; circuses and hippodromes; Compitalia; entertainers; gladiatorial combat: *artes lubricae* (slippery arts), 175; *Iuvenalia*, 91; *ludi Augustales*, 99; *ludi circenses* (circus races), 157–58; as moral danger zones, 85, 97; Olympic Games, 164; organized labor, 52; oversight, 175; pantomime riots and, 99; popularity, 175, 177; prohibitions on, 74; reorganization under Augustus, 96; restrictions on those associated with, 85; ritual games, 52
Gauls, 39
gender: gendered power in religion, 27–28; inscriptions and association membership, 101–2; Latin grammar and, 205n50; membership in associations, 78–79, 101–3, 121, 171, 172; status, reputation, and law, 54; women as patrons, 103–4; women's presence in associations, 101–4
Gibbon, Edward, 140
gladiatorial combat. *See also* games: demand for, 48, 50; emergence of, 46, 50; games waning, 170–71; grave of Saturninus, 67; schools and training camps, 65, 66–68, 69, 75, 96; types of, 50–51, 65, 67–68, 196n11
gladiatorial troupes. *See also familiae*; Servile Wars: as associations, 66–68; as instruments of political will, 75, 80–81, 82, 83–84
gladiators. *See also* entertainers; *familiae*: *auctorati* (high-status free gladiators), 97; enslaved people as, 50–51; female training in youth associations, 91;

Jews as, 114; manumission, 97; as personal militias and bodyguards, 160, 166; senators and equestrians as, 6; stigma and biases toward, 6, 85, 97
Gnaeus Flavius (scribe), 41
goldsmith associations, 4, 171
Goths, 160–61, 162, 167–68, 175–76
grain. *See also* baker associations: grain dole (*annona*), 80, 82, 84, 139, 149–50, 153, 165; grain merchant associations, 36, 209n29; market, 35–36; shipowner associations and, 127–28; shortages, 35–36, 82; Sicily and, 51–52, 64; strikes threatening supply, 127–28; taxes on, 51–52
gravedigger (*fossores*) associations, 160
Great Mother Cybele, 58
Greatrex, Geoffrey, 217n97
Gregory I (pope), 183
Gregory of Tours (historian), 176
Gruen, Erich, 57–58
guilds, 11, 12, 183–85, 191n22

Harland, Philip, 115
Harries, Jill, 140, 154, 205n52, 212n32
Heathrow Airport, 186
Hemelrijk, Emily, 103–4
Hercules, 30
Herod Agrippa (king), 105
Herodotus (historian), 37
hetaireia/hetairia. *See* political clubs
Hillner, Julia, 213n47
hippodromes. *See* circuses and hippodromes
histriones (theater actors), 49
Holleran, Claire, 199n1
Honorius (emperor), 152–53, 166, 169, 175
Horace (Quintus Horatius Flaccus) (poet), 103
Horsmann, Gerhard, 97
Huns, 160, 175
Hypatia (philosopher), 172

inscriptions. *See also* patronage; statues: commercial networks, 114; conspiracies and, 86; evidence of associations, 17, 42, 56, 92, 106, 117, 142, 160; formalization of associations through, 112, 198n62; function, 48, 56; golden age of associations, 115; group identity, 119; membership in associations, 67, 101–2; religious elements, 48; waning of, 166
insurrections. *See* rebellions and riots; slave revolts
intelligence agent (*agentes in rebus*) associations, 148–49, 150–51
Isayev, Elena, 38
Ismard, Paulin, 192n41
ivory worker associations, 166–67

Jerome (priest, translator), 173
Jewell, Evan, 84
Jews: associations, 85–86, 105, 106–7; bans on assemblies, 85–86, 107; enslaved by Pompey, 78; expulsion of, 101, 107–8; fears of seditious assemblies, 105, 106, 107–8; forced labor by, 114; in gladiatorial combat, 114; guilds and, 184; Jewish tax, 114; Judaism as superstition, 126; neighborhood alliances, 78; presenting as nonthreatening to public order, 105, 108; rebellions and riots, 105, 107, 114
Josephus (historian), 86, 101, 114
Julian (emperor), 151
Julius Caesar (Gaius Julius Caesar) (politician, dictator), 15, 22, 75, 83, 84, 85, 86
Justin I (emperor), 177–78
Justinian (emperor), 177, 178, 181–82

Kahlos, Maijastina, 168
Kehoe, Dennis, 129
Kelly, Christopher, 212n18
Kruschwitz, Peter, 120
Kulikowski, Michael, 134

laborers. *See also* artisans; collective action and bargaining; enslaved persons; farmers; freedmen (*liberti*); Roman military; slavery; *individual associations and trades*: oversight and organization, 86
labor organizations. *See* associations; charioteers; *familiae*; organized labor
labor unions, 9, 11–12, 19–20, 46–47, 48, 185–86. *See also* associations; collective action and bargaining; organized labor
Lactantius (writer), 142
land surveyor associations, 142
Last, Richard, 115
law and legislation. *See also* assemblies; associations; commerce; trade: *Book of the Eparch*, 182; *Codex Gregorianus*, 143; *Codex Hermogenianus*, 143; Edict of Maximum Prices, 144–46, *145*; entertainment and games, 175; honor and morality, 96–97, 103, 164; hostility to foreigners, 57; intent vs praxis, 19, 140, 150; *ius commercii*, 36; language of liability and obligation, 154; legislative transparency, 31–32, 34, 140; *lex Aquilia*, 54; *lex Clodia de collegiis*, 80; *lex Cornelia de sicariis et veneficis*, 197n24; *lex Hortensia*, 41; *lex Irnitana*, 116; *lex Julia de collegiis*, 86, 109; *lex Julia Municipalis*, 85; *lex Licinia de sodaliciis*, 82; *lex Poetelia Papiria*, 40; *lex Valeria*, 193n22; *senatus consulta*, 34; social upheaval controlled, 70; sources, 140; status, gender, and reputation, 54; suffrage, 77; *Theodosian Code*, 213n58; Twelve Tables, 31–32, 34, 200n10; in United States, 186
Lenski, Noel, 139, 161, 196n20, 211n59
Levin, Flora R., 196n8
Libanius (rhetorician), 150–51, 152
liberti (manumitted persons). *See* freedmen (*liberti*)

Licinius (emperor), 148
linen-worker associations, 121
Liu, Jinyu, 90
Livius Andronicus (poet and dramatist), 49–50, 52
Livy (historian): accusations against cult of Bacchus, 58; Battle of the Allia, 39; on conscription, 37; First Secession of the Plebs catalyst, 25–26; patrician exemplars in, 26; plebeian collective bargaining, 22–23; on slavery, 53; on theatrical performances, 49; on Verginia and Appius Claudius Crassus, 33–34
Lucius Aemilius Mamercinus (consul), 37
Lucius Annaeus Florus (historian), 16, 192n38
Lucius Caecilius Metellus (consul), 50
Lucius Calpurnius Piso (politician, historian), 15
Lucius Cornelius Lentulus (consul), 83–84
Lucius Cornelius Sulla. *See* Sulla
Lucius Icilius (tribune), 33–34
Lucius Sergius Catilina "Catiline" (politician), 75, 77–78
Lucius Verginius (centurion), 33–34

macellum (indoor food market), 56
Machado, Carlos, 171
Machado, Dominic, 70
MacMullen, Ramsay, 12, 141, 143, 190n14
Macrobius (writer), 57
magic, 159
Main, Robert William, 217n97
manumission, 53, 63–64, 75–76, 97. *See also* freedmen (*liberti*)
Marcian (emperor), 164–65
Marcus Agrippa (general and statesman), 95
Marcus Aurelius Probus (emperor), 137

Marcus Claudius Tacitus (emperor), 136
Marcus Livius Salinator (consul), 50
Marcus Terentius Varro (writer), 54, 191n32
Marcus Tullius Cicero. *See* Cicero (Marcus Tullius Cicero)
marriage, 96–97, 164–65, 178
Marx, Karl, 7, 190n12
Maurice, Lisa, 194n34
McGinn, Thomas, 205n51
McLaughlin, Raoul, 115
men. *See* gender
mercatorum collegium, 25
merchant associations, 59–61, 185. *See also* artisans; baker associations; banker and moneychanger associations; citrus-wood trader associations; goldsmith associations; grain merchant associations; guilds; shipowner associations; silversmith (*argyropratai*) associations
merchants, 25, 35–36, 39. *See also* artisans; tradespeople; treaties
Mignone, Lisa, 34
migration, 38–39, 42, 46, 56–57
militias and bodyguards. *See also* police and paramilitary groups: associations as, 160, 172–73; charioteers as, 160; entertainers as, 81; gladiators as, 160, 166; secession strategies and, 33–34, 35; troupes and armies akin to associations, 78
Milo (Titus Annius Milo) (tribune), 80–81, 82–83
mimes. *See* entertainers
mint workers, 132–35, 139, 147–48
Minucius Felix (writer), 124
mobility, 38
Mommsen, Theodor, 12
monastic economies, 173–75
moneylenders. *See also* banker and moneychanger associations
Morris, Richard B., 189n4
mutinies, 70, 72, 75, 137

Naismith, Rory, 183
neighborhoods, 52, 73, 74, 78
Nero (emperor), 5–6, 205n53, 207n7
Nestorius (patriarch), 172
Nicomedia, Pontus-Bithynia, 122
Nika riots, 178, 179
Numa Pompilius (king), 14, 22, 27–28

Octavian-Augustus (emperor). *See also* Principate: fear of dissent, 96; honor and morality, 96–97, 103; patronage and creation of associations, 94–95, 97–98; police force and paramilitary groups, 94–95; public welfare and utility rhetoric, 93; regulations and bans on associations, 86, 93–98, 109; ritual calendar and games reorganized, 96; use of enslaved *familiae*, 95
Odoacer (king), 176
Ogilvie, Sheilagh, 11, 184–85
Operation Engineers Union, Local 513, 210n43
optimates, 22, 77
Orestes (prefect), 172
organized labor, 14–19, 39–40, 44–45, 47–49, 52. *See also* associations; collective action and bargaining; labor unions
Orosius (historian), 167–68
Ostrogoths, 176

Pailler, Jean-Marie, 59
Palladius (bishop), 173–74
pantomime riots, 99–100
pantomimes. *See* entertainers
parabolani (funeral workers and stretcher-bearers), 172–73
Parasites of Apollo association, 100
patricians and elites. *See also* patronage: charioteers and, 159, 176–78; fear of associations, 3, 26–27, 32, 88–89, 109, 112–13, 116, 123, 125; fear of factions, 156–57; fear of political

patricians and elites (*continued*)
clubs, 123; fear of seditious assemblies, 3, 32, 96, 105, 106, 107–8, 116; fear of slavery system, 54, 65, 69, 77; fear of superstition and foreign cults, 58, 101, 124, 126, 197n36; migration suspect, 38–39, 42, 46; monopolization of power, 27–29, 30–34; plebeian dissatisfaction with, 25; plebeians distained by, 33–34; power abuses by, 29–31, 33–34; power reduced by plebeian secession, 26, 29, 34; priestly *collegia* dominated by, 27–28; senators and equestrians as gladiators, 6; trade and, 38; xenophobia of, 42, 46, 57, 70

patriotism and property, 31

patronage. *See also* Clodius; inscriptions; statues: associations and, 45, 60, 94–95, 97–98, 166, 172; *collegia* and, 103–4; diffusing threats, 94–95, 97–98; of entertainers, 100, 130; of merchant associations, 60; as sign of state control, 130–31; women as patrons, 103–4

Patterson, Orlando, 9–10

Paul the Evangelist, 117

pax deorum, 27

Perry, Jonathan S., 190n17, 207n6

Petronius (writer), 122

Phang, Sara Elise, 137

Philagrius (count), 152

Philo of Alexandria (writer), 78, 105, 106–7, 206n64

pilgrims, 117, 173–74, 175

Plebeian Assembly, 34, 41

plebeians. *See also* artisans; associations; First Secession of the Plebs; laborers; merchants; rebellions and riots; Roman military: power gains, 26, 29, 33–34, 40

Pliny the Elder (writer, statesman), 36, 41, 167

Pliny the Younger (writer, governor), 121–24

Plutarch (biographer), 14, 65, 68, 192n33, 200n21

poets, 49. *See also individual poets*

police and paramilitary groups, 94–95. *See also* militias and bodyguards; watchmen (*vigiles*)

political clubs: bans on, 82, 106, 107, 123; fear of, 123; *hetaireia/hetairia*, 18, 32, 120, 123; political clout, 18, 82; pretense for feasting and intrigue, 106, 206n64, 206n69

Polybius (historian), 35, 51, 53

Pompeii: about, 92, *92*; associations, 89–93; riot, 88–90, *89*, *91*

Pompey (general and statesman), 80, 82, 83

pontifex maximus, 27

populares (popular assemblies), 22

postal system. *See cursus publicus*

Potter, David, 163

Praetorian Guard, 94

Principate, 94. *See also* Octavian-Augustus (emperor)

prisoners of war, 53–54

private associations: *coetus*, 32; fears of sedition and secrecy, 29, 32, 65, 116; during First Secession of the Plebs, 26–27, 29; protection and political representation through, 29

Procopius (historian), 169, 178

Propertius (poet), 135

property, 31, 36, 37

proscriptions, 76

provocatio ad populum (right to appeal to the people), 29

Publius Clodius Pulcher. *See* Clodius

Publius Servilius Priscus (consul), 25–26

Pyrrhic War, 49

Quintus Tullius Cicero (statesman), 78, 200n28

Radagaisus (king), 167–68
Ramses III (pharaoh), 1–2, 111
Rathbone, Dominic, 212n29
rebellions and riots. *See also* collective action and bargaining; First Secession of the Plebs; mutinies; secession; slave revolts; Struggle of the Orders: and arrest of Philoromus, 158–59; Catilinarian conspiracy, 77–78; charioteers, 158–59, 177, 178–79; Christ-followers and Christians, 107, 117–19; closing of shops, 199n1–n2; Egyptian riots, 104–5, 119; by entertainers, 99–100, 177; Ephesus riots, 117–20; Jewish riots, 105, 107, 110, 114; Nika riots, 178, 179; Pompeii riots, 88–90, 89, 91; social upheaval controlled, 70; by war hostages and enslaved retinues, 53–54; youth associations, 90, 91
Rebillard, Eric, 109
Reden, Sitta von, 111
regina sacrorum (queen of sacrifices), 27
religion. *See also* Bacchus, cult of; Christ-followers; Christianity; Cybele, cult of; Jews; merchant associations; *technitai* of Dionysus; Vesta, college of: drinking clubs, 106; foreign cults, 57, 58, 65, 70, 101; gendered power in, 27–28; power of, in Early Republic, 27–28; superstitions feared, 101, 124, 126; xenophobia and, 70
Remijsen, Sofie, 164
rex sacrorum (king of sacrifices), 27
riots. *See* rebellions and riots
ritual calendar, 25, 52, 96. *See also* games
Roman military. *See also* Adrianople, Battle of; First Punic War; First Secession of the Plebs; militias and bodyguards; police and paramilitary groups; rebellions and riots; Second Punic War; Servile Wars; slave revolts; Volscians, war against: anti-association policy, 106, 206n63; artisans as soldiers, 37; *calones* (state-owned military enslaved persons), 133; conscription, 37; debt from service, 21–22, 23, 28–29; Goths in, 161, 168–69, 175–76; levy as catalyst to First Secession of the Plebs, 23–26, 193n2; mutinies, 70, 72, 137; supply chains relied upon, 146–47; troupes and armies akin to associations, 78; used as construction workers, 136, 137
Roman Republic map of the city of Rome, 24
Romulus Augustulus (emperor), 176
Rosenblum, Jordan, 209n25
Rostovtzeff, Mikhail Ivanovich, 8
Roueché, Charlotte, 163

sacks of Rome, 168–69, 176
sailor associations, 172
salt, 39
Salvius-Tryphon (enslaved leader), 64
sanctuary and asylum, 111–12, 152–53
Santangelo, Federico, 76
schools, 194n34. *See also* gladiatorial combat
Schultz, Howard, 186
Scott, James C., 218n102
Screen Actors Guild and American Federation of Television and Radio Artists (SAG-AFTRA), 185–86
scribes, actors, and poets associations, 57
Scythians, 161
secession, 26–27, 29, 33–35, 41, 42. *See also* Catilinarian conspiracy; collective action and bargaining; First Secession of the Plebs; rebellions and riots; Servile Wars; slave revolts; troops and armies
Second Punic War, 35, 52–54

Second Triumvirate, 93
Septimius Severus (emperor), 127
servi publici (state-owned enslaved persons), 53, 95
Servian Walls, 39–40
Servile Wars, 61–62; *familiae* and, 44–45, 62, 64, 68; First Servile War, 62–63, 64; polis and state structures replicated in, 64, 65, 68; ramifications and reverberations, 63, 69–70, 74–75; Second Servile War, 63–65; Third Servile War (Spartacan War), 65, 68–69, 74–75
Servius Tullius (king), 16
sex workers, 55, 85, 103, 164–65, 178, 202n2, 205n51. *See also* entertainers
Sextus Pomponius (jurist), 31
Shaw, Brent, 88–89, 192n36
shipowner (*navicularii*) associations, 127–28
silversmith (*argyroprutai*) associations, 117–19, 181
sit-ins, 34
Skotheim, Mali, 48
slave revolts. *See also* rebellions and riots; Servile Wars: agency of enslaved and manumitted persons, 179–80; Battle of Adrianople, 161, 162; near Enna, 62; inspired by Servile Wars, 63; sack of Rome aided by enslaved people, 169; in wake of Second Punic War, 53–54
slavery. *See also* barbarians; enslaved persons; freedmen (*liberti*); gladiatorial combat; Jews; manumission; Servile Wars; Spartacus: *familiae* and labor organization, 45–46, 48, 55, 95, 133; fears raised by system, 54, 65, 69, 77; Goths and, 161; increase in, 45; labor issues and organization, 40, 42–43; *lex Aquilia* governing, 54; *mangones* (slave traders), 167; merchant associations and, 60–61; reliance on enslaved labor, 39–40, 45–46, 53, 61, 95, 133, 134; in Second Punic War, 53; slave trade, 167, 168
Smallwood, Mary, 101, 202n57
social order conflicts, 6, 28, 33. *See also* First Secession of the Plebs; rebellions and riots; slave revolts; Struggle of the Orders
soldiers. *See* militias and bodyguards; Roman military
Sozomen (historian), 163
Spartacus (enslaved leader), 44–45, 65–66, 68–69. *See also* Servile Wars
Starbucks, 186
statues, 104, 119, 121, 171, 178. *See also* inscriptions; patronage
Ste. Croix, G. E. M. de, 28
Stewart, Roberta, 62
Strauss, Barry, 68
strikes, historiography of, 7–10, 12, 190n14, 190n17. *See also* assemblies; associations; collective action and bargaining; rebellions and riots; secession; Servile Wars; slave revolts; wage strikes; work stoppages
Struggle of the Orders, 22, 35; end of, 41, 42; goals of, 28–29, 40, 41, 195n55; manumitted persons and, 41; Marxist analysis of, 7, 190n12; plebeian political clout, 33–34; power abuses by patricians, 29–31; wealth determining meaning for plebeians, 28–29. *See also* debt bondage; First Secession of the Plebs; secession
Suetonius (biographer), 6, 84, 97, 101, 103, 107, 205n53
suffrage, 77, 97
Sulla (Lucius Cornelius Sulla) (general and statesman), 76–77, 200n21
supply chains. *See* commerce
systemic inequality, 30–31

Tacitus (historian), 5–6, 99, 101
Tarratius Bassus (prefect), 159
taverns and pubs, 99, 107, 116

taxes, 51–52, 59, 113–14, 141–42, 193n2, 207n7
technitai of Dionysus, 47, 48–49, 57–58, 127, 170
Temple of Mercury, 25
Tertullian (writer), 108, 148
Tervingi, 161
Tetrarchy (Rule of Four), 138, 141–42, 143, 144–45, 148
theaters and amphitheaters, 91, 99, 163–64, 170, 201n40. *See also* circuses and hippodromes; entertainers; games; ritual calendar
theatrical performances. *See also* entertainers; entertainment associations: as moral danger zones, 85, 97; origins in Rome, 49, 52; pantomimes, 96, 99–100; use of theater for political ends, 81; violence during Clodian years, 81; youth associations and, 91
Themistocles (general, statesman), 18
Theodora (empress), 178
Theodoret (historian), 163
Theodoric (king), 176
Theodosius I (emperor), 161–63, 165
Theodosius II (emperor), 172
Third Servile War. *See* Servile Wars; Spartacus
Tiberius Claudius Caesar Augustus Germanicus (Claudius) (emperor), 107–8
Tiberius Gracchus (tribune), 63
Tiberius Julius Caesar (emperor), 98–99, 100, 101, 103
Titus Annius Milo. *See* Milo (Titus Annius Milo) (tribune)
Titus Flavius Vespasianus (emperor), 114
trade. *See also* commerce; grain; merchant associations: autonomy of associations, 171; with barbarians, 160, 162; *collegia* as mediators, 115; commemorative gifts and, 166–67;
commercial networks, 59–60, 114–15; cultural mixing, 39; economic networks, 35–36, 38, 173–75; luxury market, 166–67, 168; middling class and, 171–72; ransom market, 168; sack of Rome and, 168–69; senators barred from maritime, 38; slave trade, 60–61, 167, 168; state warehouses, 115; trade associations, 141, 146, 149–50, 151, 153, 166–67; treaties, 35–36
tradespeople, 29–30, 35–38, 39. *See also* artisans; commerce; laborers; merchants; trade
Trajan (Marcus Ulpius Traianus) (emperor), 122–24
treaties, 35–36
tribunate, 26, 34. *See also* Clodius's plebeian tribunate
tribune of the plebs, office of, 29
troops and armies. *See* gladiatorial troupes; militias and bodyguards; Roman military
Twelve Tables, Laws of the, 31–32, 34

union busting, 186
unions. *See* labor unions
Ursinus (episcopal candidate), 160

Valens (emperor), 161
Valerius Maximus (writer), 50
van der Velden, Sjaak, 190n14
van Nijf, Onno, 79
Vandals, 176
Verboven, Koenraad, 144
Verginia (plebeian daughter of Lucius Verginius), 33–34
Vesley, Mark, 91
Vespasian (Titus Flavius Vespasianus) (emperor), 95, 110, 113–14, 115
Vesta, college of, 27–28, 32
Veyne, Paul, 80, 102
Volscians, war against, 23, 25–26. *See also* First Secession of the Plebs

Wachtel, Howard M., 191n25
wage strikes, 1–3, 7, 99, 110–11. *See also* collective action and bargaining; secession; work stoppages
Waltzing, Jean-Pierre, 12, 207n6
Washburn, Daniel, 159
watchmen (*vigiles*), 94–95, 122, 204n24, 209n31. *See also* police and paramilitary groups
Witschel, Christian, 211n15
women. *See* gender
work stoppages, 21–22, 125, 210n43. *See also* collective action and bargaining; secession; strikes; wage strikes
workers. *See* laborers
Writers Guild of America (WGA), 185–86

youth associations, 90–91

Zeno (emperor), 176
Zeuxippitai (bath workers) association, 172–73
zographoi (painters), 174–75
Zosimus (historian), 161, 169